The
Romance
of Ballooning

The Romance of Ballooning

The Story of the Early Aeronauts

A Studio Book · The Viking Press · New York

CONTENTS

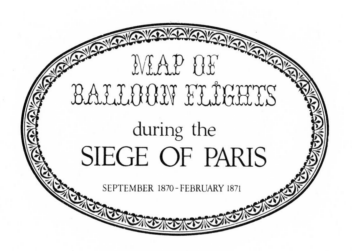

MAP OF
BALLOON FLIGHTS
during the
SIEGE OF PARIS
SEPTEMBER 1870 - FEBRUARY 1871

NEDERLAND

NORTH SEA
ORD

Düsseldorf

Köln

Bruges Gand

Louvain 30

Aachen

Liège

59

Anvers 28

Wetzlar 39

Koblenz

Bruxelles

BELGIQUE

Lille 57

Namur

Charleroi 61

Meuse

Valenciennes

Dinant 12

Jules-Favre 11

8

Cambrai 7

Avesnes

Moselle

Péronne

Rocroy 14

Mézières

Luxembourg

DEUTSCHLAND

Karlsruhe

5

Réthel

Montdidier

41

Stuttgart

60 40

Metz 18

27

Reims 15 52

Verdun 17

43

PARIS

Marne

Châlons-sur-Marne

13 9

Strasbourg

Nancy

Melun 25

26

Bar-le-Duc

16

Provins 10

Arcis-sur-Aube

19

Epinal

Fontainebleau

Colmar

Chaumont

Schaffhausen

Auxerre

Belfort

Basel

Zürich

Clamecy 53

Dijon

Besançon

SUISSE

Beaune 42

Saône

Nevers

Mâcon

Genève

Clermont

Lyon

Rhône

Grenoble

NORGE SVERIGE

Christiania 29

Stockholm

BALLOONS

1	Le Neptune	33	Bataille-de-Paris
2	Ville-de-Florence	34	Le Volta
3	Les Etats-Unis	35	Le Franklin
4	Le Céleste	36	Armée-de-Bretagne
5	Armand-Barbès	37	Denis-Papin
6	George-Sand	38	Général-Renault
7	Washington	39	Ville-de-Paris
8	Louis-Blanc	40	Parmentier
9	Général-Cavaignac	41	Guttemberg
10	Jean-Bart	42	Davy
11	Jules-Favre	43	Général-Chanzy
12	Lafayette	44	Lavoisier
13	Victor-Hugo	45	La Délivrance
14	République-Universelle	46	Rouget-de-l'Isle
15	Garibaldi	47	Merlin-de-Douai
16	Montgolfier	48	Tourville
17	Le Vauban	49	Le Bayard
18	La Bretagne	50	Armée-de-la-Loire
19	Colonel-Charras	51	Newton
20	Le Fulton	52	Duquesne
21	Ferdinand-Flocon	53	Gambetta
22	Le Galilée	54	Képler
23	Ville-de-Châteaudun	55	Le Monge
24	La Gironde	56	Général-Faidherbe
25	Niepce	57	Vaucanson
26	Daguerre	58	Steenackers
27	Général-Uhrich	59	La-Porte-de-Paris
28	Archimède	60	Général-Bourbaki
29	Ville-d'Orléans	61	Général-Daumesnil
30	Egalité	62	Torricelli
31	Le Jacquard	63	Richard-Wallace
32	Jules-Favre	64	Général-Cambronne

PREFACE

Some 200 years ago, one of man's oldest dreams came true—he soared into the skies. The Montgolfier brothers pointed the way with their fire balloons, making all else possible. From this time forward, man was able to travel the heavens, and compete with the birds and with the clouds. It is difficult to imagine today the enthusiasm of those who hailed the miracle come true, the incredulity of the unbelievers. Imagination caught fire, everything seemed possible, even the wildest dreams, so rapidly did the invention achieve its present, perfected form. In these great events, France took an early lead, Frenchmen were the first to fly, and, typically, French charlatans provoked the greatest excesses on the part of the public. England, America and Italy did not lag far behind, and the movement spread rapidly. Thanks to these early pioneers, ballooning ceased to be quite so dangerous, quite so much a matter of blind chance. Experience showed how risks could be foreseen, and reduced to a minimum. Still, however, aeronauts were frustrated in their attempts to control the course of their balloons. All dreamed of the day when their airy machines would change into practical methods of travel from point to point. When, however, the aeroplane and the controllable airship arrived, the balloon was freed from its utilitarian aspirations, its place taken by the noisy heavier-than-air monsters. Thus, the free balloon seemed to have finished its career— it had been, in changing circumstances, the attraction of fêtes and the skies' decoration at times of national rejoicing; the observation post of the soldier, and the laboratory of the scientist; and reached its finest hour as the link between besieged Paris and unoccupied France.

But becoming purposeless did not cause the balloon to disappear. Heedless of the noisy machines which supplanted it, it continued to ride on the winds. Man continued to enjoy the unique sensations brought of silence and of calm. Borne up in his wicker basket, man shed his burden of gravity, and while the flight lasted, was transformed from a terrestrial creature into a poet who surveyed all creation from the heavens.

In this book, we have given pride of place to the actors and witnesses who actually made the history of ballooning. These are no dry impersonal accounts, but the colourful, real-life, breathless descriptions of the new enthusiasm that seized the world. And the reader too, so immediate is the writing and illustration, will be borne along on the wings of the winds.

J. JOBÉ

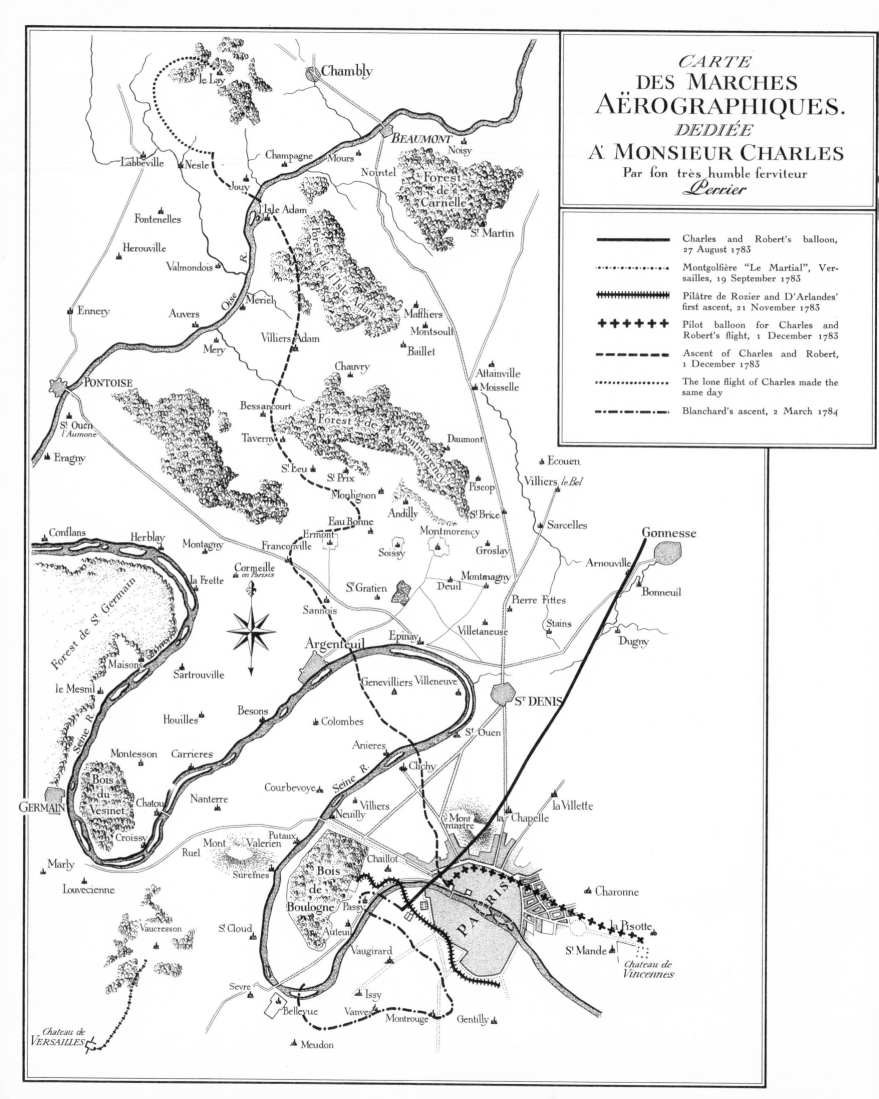

CARTE
DES MARCHES
AËROGRAPHIQUES.
DEDIÉE
A' MONSIEUR CHARLES
Par fon très humble ferviteur
Perrier

Charles and Robert's balloon,
27 August 1783

Montgolfière "Le Martial", Versailles, 19 September 1783

Pilâtre de Rozier and D'Arlandes'
first ascent, 21 November 1783

Pilot balloon for Charles and
Robert's flight, 1 December 1783

Ascent of Charles and Robert,
1 December 1783

The lone flight of Charles made the
same day

Blanchard's ascent, 2 March 1784

THE ASTONISHING YEAR

5 June 1783	The first ballooning experiments of the brothers Joseph and Etienne de Montgolfier took place at Annonay, near Lyons. Their balloon was filled with hot air, and was unmanned.
27 August 1783	At Paris, Jacques Charles and the Robert brothers sent up the "Globe", a balloon filled with hydrogen.
12 September 1783	The first ascent of a captive montgolfière-type balloon in Paris. Rain stopped the experiment.
19 September 1783	Etienne de Montgolfier's experiment in Paris before Louis XVI. A cock, a duck and a sheep were sent up on board the "Martial" balloon.
15 October 1783	Pilâtre de Rozier ascended 5o ft above the ground in a captive balloon.
19 October 1783	Pilâtre de Rozier repeated his experiment of 15 October, and reached a height of 34o ft.
21 November 1783	Pilâtre de Rozier and the Marquis D'Arlandes became the first men to make an aerial journey, ascending in a montgolfière-type balloon and flying over Paris.
25 November 1783	The first ballooning experiments to take place in England were held by Francesco Zambeccari.
1 December 1783	Charles and Nicolas Robert ascended from the Tuileries gardens in Paris and made a journey of 22 miles.

E. MONGOLFIER.

The brothers Etienne (1745-1799) and Joseph Montgolfier (1740-1810), were directors of Annonay papermill, not far from Lyons. In the spring of 1783 they made the first practical balloon trials, constructing a type of linen globe which rose when heated air was imprisoned inside it. This was known as a montgolfière.

JOURNAL DE PARIS.

Dimanche 27 Juillet 1783, de la Lune le 29

The Montgolfier brothers' first experiment, Annonay, 5 June 1783

Discoveries made several years ago in the field of inflammable air or gas have made possible an extraordinary experiment carried out by M. Montgolfier on 5 June 1783 at Annonay in the Vivarais counties. He had fashioned a sphere 35 feet in diameter made from linen mounted on a wooden or iron wire frame and coated with sized paper; into this he introduced inflammable gas, obtained by the burning of damp straw. The sphere, thus filled with gas, rose, as soon as it was released, until it was lost from sight to a height which was estimated by some to be 500 fathoms and by others to be 1,000. The sphere came down to earth 10 minutes later, doubtless owing to the loss of the gas it con-

tained. According to M. Montgolfier's calculations, the weight of the volume of air the sphere displaced was 2,156 pounds, but since the gas only weighed 1,078 pounds and the sphere 500, this left an excess of 578 pounds to provide the force with which the sphere was inclined to rise.

M. Montgolfier was already known for his manufacture of the most beautiful papers ever produced in France. The experiment which we report above heralds a curiosity and intelligence of another kind; details of this experiment were sent to the Académie Royale des Sciences on 2 July by the Minister of Finance, with the official report to verify the facts.

Narrative of Joseph Montgolfier
(Statement read to Lyons Academy)

"The thought occurred to one of my brothers and myself of enclosing a fluid specifically lighter than air in a light container in order to profit from the upsetting of the equilibrium between these two fluids to raise into the air masses proportionate in weight to that of the ascending vessel. Of all the fluids impermeable through glass, we know of none lighter than inflammable gas purified by lime and caustic alkalis. We therefore made haste to fill large paper and silken fabric bags with this gas, closing them as completely as possible. These balloons rose effectively, as we had expected, with a disturbance of the equilibrium proportionate to the difference in weight of the two fluids; but this force was shortlived, for the gas was escaping imperceptibly, either through the paper or through small openings which had somehow escaped our notice. This gas was replaced by atmospheric air and this drawback would have necessitated the use of envelopes which were more substantial and less porous. However, conceiving that such envelopes would be very heavy, we rejected this method and returned to our original ideas."

LETTER FROM ETIENNE MONTGOLFIER TO FAUJAS DE SAINT-FOND

"The aerostatic machine which was tested in the presence of gentlemen from the States of Vivarais on Thursday, 5 June 1783, was made of linen backed with paper and sewn on to a network of string attached to the strips of linen. It was roughly spherical in shape, with a circumference of 110 feet, and had a wooden frame 16 feet square holding it rigid at the base. It had a capacity of about 22,000 cubic feet; consequently, supposing the mean weight of air to be 1/800th that of water, it displaced 1,980 pounds of air.

"The weight of the gas was approximately half that of air, since it weighed 990 pounds and the machine with the frame weighed 500 pounds. This left, therefore, 490 pounds to upset the equilibrium, which corresponded with the results of the experiment. The various parts of the machine were attached to each other by buttons; although two men sufficed to assemble it and fill it with gas, it needed eight men to hold it down, and this they did until the signal was given for letting it go: it rose rapidly, but slowed down as it neared the top of its ascent until it reached a height of 1000 fathoms (6,000 feet). A scarcely perceptible ground wind carried it 1200 fathoms (7,200 feet) from the point of departure. It stayed in the air for ten minutes; the loss of air though the button-holes, the holes made by stitching, and through other flaws in the machine prevented it from staying up any longer. At the time of the experiment there was a southerly wind and it was raining. The machine came down to earth so gently that it did no harm either to the vineyard plants or their props upon which it came to rest."

The first balloon flight took place on 5 June 1783 at Annonay, witnessed by the States of Vivarais. When the local peasants saw the balloon floating in the sky, they believed that the moon had fallen from the heavens to herald the Last Judgement.

EXTRACT FROM THE REPORT MADE BY THE ACADÉMIE DES SCIENCES

"MM. de Montgolfier, having proved to themselves by a very simple experiment that a temperature of 70 degrees on the thermometer (70 degrees Réaumur = 87.5 degrees Centigrade) sufficed, according to their report, to rarify the air in a closed container by one half, soon conceived the hope of achieving their aims by this method. Now, everything points to the belief that their ideas on this subject have their origins further back than August of last year, 1782; but the interesting experiment provoked by these ideas was not attempted until November of that same year. The elder M. de Montgolfier carried it out for the first time at Avignon; there he saw, with no small pleasure—as one can well imagine—simply a small hollow parallelepiped made out of taffeta with a volume of approximately 40 cubic feet which, when the interior had been heated by the burning of paper, rose rapidly to the ceiling. On his return to Annonay, a short while later, uppermost in his mind was the need to repeat this experiment in the open, accompanied by his brother. They saw the parallelepiped rise to a height of 70 feet.

"Spurred on by such successful tests, they had a much larger machine made which had a volume in the region of 650 cubic feet, this machine was equally successful, for by reason of its excess of lightness, it rose with such force that it broke the ropes holding it down and came to earth on the neighbouring hillsides, after having achieved a height of 100 to 150 fathoms (600 to 900 feet) ... MM. de Montgolfier resolved to test this machine on a large scale. They tried to send it up on 3 April, but a boisterous wind prevented them from so doing... On the 25 April, as the weather was more auspicious, they tried once more to get it off the ground; however, the people who helped them, astonished by the vigour with which it pulled on the ropes, abruptly let go and the machine rose so rapidly that it escaped them and came down a ¼ of a league away (¾ mile) having risen to a height of more than 200 fathoms (1,200 feet) and having stayed in the air for longer than 10 minutes. At last, on the 5 June they carried out this experiment in the presence of gentlemen from the various States of Vivarais and of all the town of Annonay."

On 27 August 1783, the physician Jacques Charles, accompanied by Jean and Nicolas Robert, mechanics, "repeated the Annonay experiment" from the Champ-de-Mars, Paris. Their balloon caused a general panic, following which, Lenoir, the Lieutenant of Police, published an "Avertissement" to allay the fears of the population.

The Robert brothers' experiment:
Journal de Paris, 28 August 1783

Before today we were only familiar with inflammable air in Volta's pistols, in india-rubber bottles and in soap bubbles; it was reasonable to suspect that the presence of a large amount of such a rarified substance could have nothing but dangerous results. It seemed wise not to gather an audience before a few tests had been effected; these were carried out and fears were allayed.

This particular operation took place yesterday at exactly five o'clock. A lighted powder match gave the signal and two cannons were discharged to announce the start of the experiment to the public; these shots were also intended to alert observers placed at various posts. As soon as the signal had been given the sphere rose and within a few minutes disappeared. This instant was recorded by two further cannons being discharged. The cloud masking the sphere dispersed and it was seen once more. The apparent smallness of the sphere led to the assumption that it had attained a considerable height, and the unfortunate contingency of bad weather no doubt impeded the onlookers from making a true assessment of its height. The repeated applause gave proof once more of the public's interest. We should be grateful if any person finding the machine would inform the office of this newspaper, stating as far as possible, the condition in which it is found. The glory attaching to this discovery belongs solely to M.M. de Montgolfier.

De Paris, le 27 Août 1783.

AVERTISSEMENT
AU PEUPLE,

Sur l'Enlevement des Ballons ou Globes en l'air; celui dont il est question, a été enlevé à Paris, ledit jour 27 Août 1783, à cinq heures du soir, au Champ de Mars.

ON a fait une découverte dont le Gouvernement juge convenable de donner connoissance, afin de prévenir les terreurs qu'elle pourroit occasionner parmi le Peuple. En calculant la différence de pesanteur entre l'air appellé *inflammable*, & l'air de notre atmosphère, on a trouvé qu'un Ballon rempli de cet air inflammable, devoit s'élever de lui-même vers le Ciel, pour ne s'arrêter qu'au moment où les deux airs seroient en équilibre; ce qui ne peut être qu'à une très-grande hauteur. La premiere Expérience a été faite à Annonay en Vivarais, par les Sieurs MONTGOLFIER, Inventeurs: un Globe de toile & de papier, de cent cinq pieds de circonférence, rempli d'air inflammable, s'est élevé de lui-même à une hauteur qu'on n'a pu calculer. La même Expérience vient d'être renouvellée à Paris (le 27 Août, à cinq heures précises du soir) en présence d'un nombre infini de Personnes: Un Globe de taffetas, enduit de gomme élastique, de trente-six pieds de tour, s'est élevé du Champ de Mars jusques dans les nues, où on l'a perdu de vue: il a été dirigé par le vent vers le nord-est, & on ne peut prévoir à quelle distance il sera transporté (*). On se propose de répéter cette Expérience, avec des Globes beaucoup plus gros. Chacun de ceux qui découvriront dans le Ciel de pareils Globes, qui présentent l'aspect de la Lune obscurcie, doit donc être prévenu que, loin d'être un Phénomene effrayant, ce n'est qu'une Machine toujours composée de taffetas, ou de toile légere revêtue de papier, qui ne peut causer aucun mal, & dont il est à présumer qu'on fera quelques jours des applications utiles aux besoins de la Société.

La *Sphère Aérostatique*, ou Globe volant, d'environ douze pieds de diametre, pesant vingt-cinq à trente livres, abandonné aux vents dans le Champ de Mars, le 27 Août 1783, à cinq heures du soir, par un temps pluvieux. Il est construit de taffetas gommé, bien clos à sa surface, de maniere que l'air extérieur n'y peut pénétrer. Il est rempli d'air inflammable, vapeur provenante d'une dissolution de limaille de fer avec l'huile vitriolique. En s'élevant, il a décrit une courbe parabolique dirigée du sud au nord, & s'est élevé très-promptement dans les airs à perte de vue; & il a tombé à Gonnesses, le même jour, à six heures.

(*) On a sçu depuis qu'il est tombé trois-quarts-d'heure après à Gonnesses, à quatre lieues de Paris.

Lu & approuvé, ce 3 Septembre 1783. DE SAUVIGNY.
Vu l'Approbation, permis d'impr., le 3 Sept. 1783. LE NOIR.

Consternation in Gonesse: the Robert brothers' balloon lands

(Mercure de France no 37 - 13 September 1783)

At a quarter to six the same day, two carters, working near Gonesse, were startled by the apparition of the flying machine over the village. Thunderstruck by this unaccustomed phenomenon, the carters stopped work, and releasing their horses, started to run. Although they were naturally courageous, they were overwhelmed by fear, and refused to look behind them. By now, the machine had landed, but after it had hit the ground, it continued to twist and turn, bouncing and bounding in all directions. The carters remembered the threats of a neighbouring shepherd, and thinking that it was one of his tricks, they continued to make off with all possible speed. But in vain: a sudden gust of wind sent the monster rolling in their direction, and it rapidly overhauled them. It became necessary to turn and fight. Still it chased after them, and there was no time to lose, so they gathered up some stones and hurled them at the monster in a frenzy of fear. The creature, shaking and bounding, dodged the first blows. Finally, however, it received a mortal wound, and collapsed with a long sigh. Then a shout of victory arose; and a new valour reanimated the victors. The bravest of the two, like another Don Quixote, approached the dying beast, and with a trembling hand plunged his knife into its breast. The knife slid in easily, and in allowing the foul air to escape, sufficiently chastised the foolhardy peasant. Still the globe retained enough air to inspire fear. The machine was fastened to the tail of a horse, and dragged through the mud to Gonesse in a very dishevelled condition. The engineer to whom the balloon belonged arrived to reclaim it on the morrow, and with some pain, gave a small recompense to the carters, who might well have received a much larger reward if only they had taken the trouble to take a few lessons in physics...

The balloon came down at Gonesse, 10 miles north of Paris. The frightened villagers took it for a monster, and called in the local curé to exorcise it before they attacked and destroyed it.

Excerpt from a report submitted to the Académie des Sciences
23 December 1783

Since the machine and all the apparatus were ready, on Friday, 12 September, it was tested in our presence; and despite the efforts of the men who were employed in holding it down, it opened out in a manner which surprised all who looked on, and lifted up a weight of about 400 lbs; but as the wind which came up and the rain which fell abundantly throughout the rest of the day completely destroyed the machine because of the effect of the dampness on the paper and linen from which it was made, another one had to be built. This unfortunate occurrence was all the more disagreeable given the fact that the King, who had commanded that the experiment should be carried out in his presence at Versailles, had fixed the date for the following Friday.

Nevertheless, M. de Montgolfier was in no way discouraged by this accident, but had built a spheroid out of linen and calico, which measured 41 feet in diameter by 57 feet in height.

They put it to the test on Thursday. We then observed it float steadily in the air in a most majestic fashion for five or six minutes. Reassured by this single experiment of its efficacy, we had no doubts about its success.

Friday, 19 September 1783

Apparatus similar to that of which we have given you a general idea was set up in the centre of the large courtyard of Versailles, called the Courtyard of the Ministers, with the aerostatic machine laid out on the platform. When all was ready and properly arranged, it was tested, at a given signal, in the presence of the King, Queen and all the court with as successful a result as we had forecast the day before. On this occasion, in less than 10 minutes, and by burning only 80 pounds of straw and 7 or 8 of wool, we saw the machine swell in a way which stupefied all those present, lift off and rise eventually to a height of more than 240 fathoms despite the fact that it was loaded with 200 pounds of extraneous weight. Having covered an appreciable distance it came down 1,700 fathoms from the point of departure after staying in the air for 10 minutes. One should note the fact that the machine came down so gently that it did no more than bend the branches of the trees upon which it came to rest and that the animals which were suspended from the machine came to no harm whatsoever.

The height which we state that the balloon reached was merely estimated. M. le Gentil and M. Jeaurat, who observed the experiment independently, have since fixed the height—one at 280 fathoms above the second storey of the Observatory, the other at 293 above ground level; but it is certain that the machine would have stayed much longer in the air and travelled much further had it not been for the tear of the previous day, which was of no small dimensions; indeed, as the rent opened up again, a part of the heated gases was let out from the inside of the machine, and these gases, together with those which escaped during two or three lurches which the machine underwent, detracted greatly from the force keeping the machine airborne.

Never before has an experiment been carried out with more brilliance and splendour, never before have there been such eminent spectators, nor in such great numbers for a like event. It must yet be said that the King, before the experiment, condescended to visit the location of the aerostatic machine, and that he took the trouble of passing under the platform where the brazier was sited that he might see the preparations and that M. de Montgolfier might explain to him the method to be used to fill out this great mass, so shapeless at the moment, and so make it lift off and rise into the air; the Queen and the Royal Family followed His Majesty's example.

Dodie'. a M. M. de Montgolfier.

Friday, 19 September 1783

Etienne de Montgolfier tried (left) an experiment on 12 September at Réveillon's, another paper merchant, before delegates from the Academy of Sciences. Rain halted the proceedings.

Versailles, 21 November 1783. For the first time, King Louis XVI showed an interest in ballooning. Pilâtre de Rozier demonstrated before the King his experiment with the "Martial" balloon, which was remarkable for carrying the first three aerial passengers in history — a cock, a duck, and a sheep. The scene at the start is shown in the engraving on the right. The trial proved that it was "possible to breath at a great height above the ground". The cock broke its neck on landing, but the flying sheep lived out an honoured life in Marie-Antoinette's private zoo.

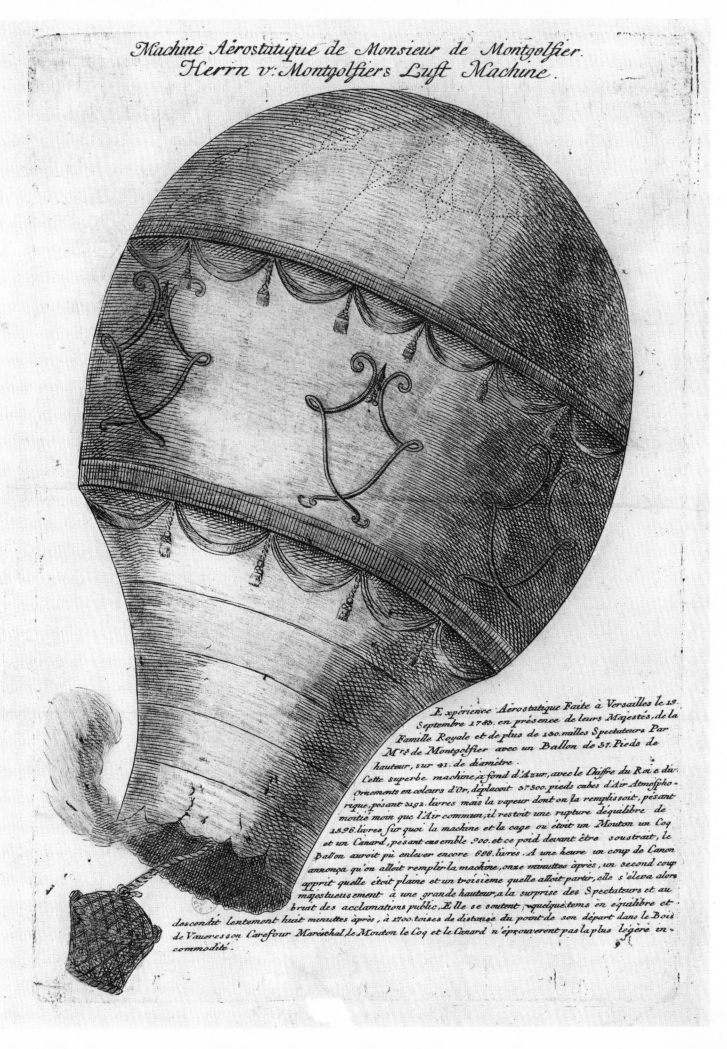

Machine Aérostatique de Monsieur de Montgolfier.
Herrn v: Montgolfiers Luft Machine.

Expérience Aérostatique Faite à Versailles le 19.
Septembre 1783. en présence de leurs Majestés, de la
Famille Royale et de plus de 130. milles Spectateurs Par
M.rs de Montgolfier avec un Ballon de 57. Pieds de
hauteur, sur 41. de diamètre.
Cette superbe machine à fond d'Azur, avec le Chiffre du Roi e div.
Ornements en coleurs d'Or, deplaçoit 37300. pieds cubes d'Air Atmospho-
rique, pesant 2192. livres mais la vapeur dont on la remplissoit, pesant
moitie moin que l'Air commun; il restoit une rupture d'équalibre de
1596. livres sur quoi la machine et la cage ou étoit un Mouton un Coq
et un Canard, pesant ensemble 900. et ce poid devant être soustrait, le
Ballon auroit pu enlever encore 696. livres. A une heure un coup de Canon
annonça qu'on alloit remplir la machine, onze minuttes après, un second coup
apprit qu'elle étoit plaine et un troisième quelle alloit partir, elle s'éleva alors
majestueusement à une grande hauteur, a la surprise des Spectateurs et au
bruit des acclamations public, Elle se soutent quelque tems en équalibre et
descendit lentement huit minuttes après, à 1700. toises de distance du pont de son départ dans le Bois
de Vaueresson Carefour Mariéchal, le Mouton le Coq et le Canard n'éprouverent pas la plus légère in-
commodité.

F. PILATRE DE ROZIER
Premier Navigateur Aérien
Et Pensionnaire du Roi

M.r LE MAR.is D'ARLANDE,
Premier Navigateur Aérien.

The first aeronauts : Jean-François Pilâtre de Rozier (1756-1785) was a professor of physics and chemistry at Reims. He was to be the first victim of ballooning. The Marquis François d'Arlandes was an Infantry major.

THE CONQUEST OF THE SKIES:

Journal de Paris, 22 November 1783

Official report drawn up at the Château de la Muette after the experiment with the aerostatic machine of M. Montgolfier.

On this day, 21 November 1783, at the Château de la Muette, an experiment with the aerostatic machine of M. Montgolfier was carried out.

The sky was, in several places, obscured by cloud, in others clear, a north-westerly wind prevailed.

At eight minutes past noon, a mortar was fired — a signal to begin the filling of the machine. Within eight minutes, despite the wind, it was filled out evenly and ready to take off, with the Marquis D'Arlandes and M. Pilâtre de Rozier on the observation deck.

Their first intention was to send the machine into the air, but to restrain at the same time with ropes in order to test it, study the precise weights it was capable of carrying and ensure that everything was as it should be for the important experiment that was about to be carried out.

But the wind caught the machine which, far from rising vertically, drifted in the direction of one of the pathways of the garden, and the ropes which were holding it down, working too violently, caused several rents to appear — one more than six feet in length. When the machine had been brought back to the platform it was repaired in less than two hours.

It left, refilled, at six minutes to two, carrying the same gentlemen as before. It was seen to rise in a most majestic fashion and when it reached about 250 feet above the ground, the intrepid travellers, taking off their hats, bowed to the spectators. At that moment one experienced a feeling of fear mingled with admiration.

Soon the aerial navigators were lost from view, but the machine, floating on the horizon and displaying a most beautiful shape, climbed to at least 3,000 feet at which height it was still visible; it crossed the Seine below the gate of la Conference and, passing between the Military Academy and the Hôtel des Invalides, it was borne to a position where it could be seen by all Paris.

When the travellers were satisfied with this experiment, not wishing to make a longer journey, they agreed to descend; but realising that the wind was bearing them down upon the houses of the Rue de Seve, in the Faubourg Saint-Germain, they retained their calm and, increasing the production of gas, rose once more and continued on their way through the sky until they had passed over the outskirts of Paris.

They made a gentle descent into a field beyond the new boulevard, opposite the Croulebarbe mill, without suffering the slightest discomfort, with two-thirds of their supplies still intact; so they could, if they had wanted to, have journeyed three times as far. Their voyage had taken them 20 to 25 minutes over a distance of 4-5000 fathoms.

The machine measured 70 feet in height and 46 in diameter; its volume was 60,000 cubic feet and on this occasion it carried between 1,600 and 1,700 lbs in weight.

Written at the Château de la Muette at five o'clock in the afternoon. Signed, the Duke of Polignac, the Duke of Guines, the Comte de Polastron, the Comte de Vaudreil, d'Hunaud, Benjamin Franklin, Faujas de Saint-Fond, Delisle and Lercy from the Académie des Sciences.

Pilâtre de Rozier and the Marquis D'Arlandes were the first men to go up in a balloon. Their montgolfière type balloon was constructed in M. Réveillon's garden, but was then taken to the château de la Muette, as the Dauphin and his suite had expressed a desire to watch the ascent. This took place at 1.45 pm on 21 November 1783. After an abortive attempt, the aeronauts rose to a height of 3,000 ft, and flew over Paris, landing some 5 miles from the launching site. A brazier hung underneath the envelope kept the air hot, and enabled the flight to be prolonged at will.

The first London trials, 25 November 1783

Count Francesco Zambeccari (1762-1812), of Italian birth, was known for his rashness and his intelligence. He was an officer in the Spanish Navy, he fought against the Turks, was captured and spent three years in the slave-barracks at Constantinople. In 1783, he became interested in the Montgolfiers' experiments, and made several dangerous ascents from Bologna in the north of Italy.

THE PHILOSOPHER'S VIEW: FREDERIC-MELCHIOR GRIMM

Never has a soap bubble held the attention of a group of children in the way that the air-balloon has been, for a month now, holding the attention of the town and the court. Among all our circles of friends, at all our meals, in the ante-chambers of our lovely women, as in the academic schools, all one hears is talk of experiments, atmospheric air, inflammable gas, flying cars, journeys in the sky. One would make a much more amusing book than that of Cyrano de Bergerac if one were to collect together all the plans, all the dreams, all the follies which are indebted to the new discovery.

So, all it needs to make the most marvellous invention work is a puff of smoke, and who would doubt this? There is every reason to believe that this secret had long ago been guessed. Who has not heard tell of the smoke of pride, of glory, of opinion? It is with smoke that one lifts a man above himself, that one creates heroes, poets, great men of every kind. In matters physical just as in matters moral, everything comes from smoke and everything must return to smoke; of all the laws of nature, this one is the most invariable, the most universal, but we shall speak of that some other time...

The air-balloon, built by MM. Robert lifted off majestically from the Champ de Mars on 27 August, at exactly five o'clock in view of all Paris. The date of the experiment had been announced a few days previously; never before had a royal review drawn a larger crowd made up of people from all walks of life. The sphere was about 12 feet across. We were not agreed on the height to which it rose as the bad weather made it difficult to judge. But its apparent smallness led one to believe that it was at no mean distance from the ground. Within a few minutes it had completely disappeared. Our admiration was such that we would have wished it to reach the furthest point in the universe; this was not to be; instead of dumbfounding distant shores with its august presence, it modestly cut short its journey at Gonesse, a village four leagues from Paris, where it terrified the peasants who saw it come to earth in the field where they were working.

It will come as no surprise to learn that three days later, Paris was inundated with etchings depicting both the arrival and the departure of the sphere.

Many who pride themselves on remaining unmoved in the midst of public fervour, have not missed the opportunity of repeating the question, "But what use do these experiments serve? Tell me, what is the point of this discovery which is causing so much disturbance?" The venerable Franklin replies to them with his usual lack of verbiage—"Well! what is the point of the child who has just been born?" Indeed, this child could die while still in the cradle, could develop into no more than an idiot, but he could equally become the pride of his country, the shining light of his century, the benefactor of humanity...

Zambeccari's letter of 28 November 1783

"The news of the extraordinary experiments being carried out in Paris with the flying sphere of M. Montgolfier prompted me to set about building one myself, and this I accomplished without difficulty. On the first of this month I succeeded in sending up a sphere, five feet in diameter, from the roof of a certain Biaginni, a trader in artificial flowers who made a financial contribution to the experiment. Although this sphere was sent into the air with no witnesses to the event, and from a purely private location, some amazed person spotted it in the sky and by the next day the news had run through London. Spurred on by this interest I then built another sphere 10 feet in diameter, in order to satisfy the curiosity of the public. I took great pains in the accomplishment of this task, and this unusual display took place at the Artillery Ground on 25 November, attended by a dense crowd. The satisfaction gained on my part from this experiment was multiple... I first studied the fortifications which enable one to resist a powerful enemy and then applied them to aerial spheres; at the moment I am in the process of making one which has the diameter of 30 feet. I hope that it will be of assistance to me in carrying out what I am sure will be some extremely productive experiments; I would like to be able to navigate it horizontally and steer it in any direction I wish. For me, the most intense pleasure is in the thought that this news will bring you some measure of consolation and should alleviate the disappointments of the past."

Zambeccari was the first to conduct a ballooning experiment in England. On 25 November 1783, he launched a small unmanned hot-air balloon from the London Artillery ground.

THE AIR BALLOON.

23

An entrance ticket for the famous ascension that took place on 1 December 1783 from the Tuileries gardens in Paris. More than 800,000 spectators came to marvel at Charles and Robert's flight.

Charles and Robert's flight:

Journal de Paris, 2 December 1783

The departure of the balloon built by MM. Charles and Robert took place yesterday in the Tuileries gardens at 1.40 pm; the occasion of this experiment had drawn a prodigious gathering of spectators. It had been rumoured that MM. Charles and Robert would not leave a sinking ship; for this reason the emotion was much more intense when the machine was seen to set off smoothly into the sky carrying with it M. Charles and M. Robert junior in the car, that car which became for them a car of victory; and it may well be that never before has a victor received more rapturous acclaim. However, first the on-lookers had to be reassured as to the safety of the voyagers. Indeed, at the time of departure the assembly was hushed, for they were torn between feelings of wonder, surprise and fear; but soon the applause spread throughout the company, which was now of one mind in its wish for the safe return of our new Argonauts. As the machine drew away, in addition to the applause, hats were now raised and even the Swiss mercenaries took part in the general celebration by throwing their sabres into the air. Never has science produced such a majestic and imposing display, and the nation should rightly be proud of a discovery which, only six months ago, we would have discounted and banished into the realm of historic untruth if anyone, even Archimedes himself, were to tell us of it. M. de la Lande, from the Académie des Sciences, fired with enthusiasm by this marvellous experiment and convinced of its inevitable success, asked, as a favour, that he might be allowed to climb into the machine to observe the experiments which had been planned, but it was only fair that precedence should be given to MM. Charles and Robert.

Lack of time prevents us from entering into details of the preliminaries to this experiment. M. Meunier, lieutenant in the Royal Corps of Engineers, has been asked by several members of the Académie Royale des Sciences with whom he is corresponding to draw up the plan

THE RESULT OF A YEAR'S EXPERIENCE:

Extract from the Report made to the Académie des Sciences 23 December 1783

It will no doubt be asked whether MM. de Montgolfiers' method or that of M. Charles and M. Robert is superior in keeping balloons airborne; but reckless would be he who made a decision on this question at a time when the discovery is still so novel and not even one thousandth part of the research which could be undertaken to perfect the machine has in fact been started. MM. de Montgolfier can already see many ways of simplifying the workings, some of which they have already indicated; on the other hand, who knows what discoveries can yet be made with the aim of obtaining inflammable air in much larger quantities, or by much simpler means than have heretofore been found? Who knows but that a fluid lighter still than this inflammable air might not be found? For a long time spirits of wine was thought to be the lightest of all liquids, but then ether, which is even lighter, was discovered. The study of gases is still too new to allow us to make pronouncements on these various topics. All we can say is that the simplicity of MM. Montgolfier's method, and the ease and speed with which it can be applied, seem to give it a great advantage in its use in civilian life; but that that method using inflammable air has the advantage of lessening considerably the volume of the balloon while still carrying the same weight and needing no provisions or attention from those who are carried in the machine, and, consequently, this method seems the more suitable for many uses in Physics. In fact, leaving all others aside, M. Charles has shown how, with a balloon, one can rise up into the clouds for the purpose of observation, and everything points to the possibility of making a great number of such observations, putting us in the way of explaining many meteorological phenomena which, until now, have remained mysteries.

Let us, therefore, until further research has been carried out, defer a decision on this question of the superiority that should be allowed either to M. Montgolfier's method of sending up balloons or to that of inflammable gas.

The next day, the aeronauts made a triumphal entry into Paris. Their balloon was carried in the procession in a cart, and taken to the workshop of the Robert brothers in the place des Victoires. Their flight clearly demonstrated the superiority of the gas balloon over the montgolfière type—less risk of fire, a smaller volume envelope needed for the same lift, and no need to re-heat air during the flight.

DELIRIOUS ENTHUSIASM

19 January 1784	An ascent from Lyons of the giant montgolfière balloon called "La Flesselles", which was constructed by Joseph Montgolfier. The balloon rose to a height of 3280 ft carrying 7 people.
25 February 1784	Paul Andreani made the first free ascent in Italy. He took off from Milan in a balloon made for him by the brothers Agostino and Carlo Gerli.
25 April 1784	Guyton de Morveau and the Abbé Bertrand made an attempt to control the flight of their balloon by using a rudder and fixing oars to the car. This unsuccessful device was tried out at Dijon.
4 June 1784	Elisabeth Tible, the first female aeronaut, flew over Lyons singing operatic arias. Her montgolfière balloon was called "La Gustave" in honour of the King of Sweden, who was watching the ascent.
14 June 1784	The ascent of the "Suffren" from Nantes carrying Coustard de Massi and R.P. Mouchet.
23 June 1784	King Louis XVI and King Gustave III of Sweden watched the ascent of a balloon, the "Marie-Antoinette", carrying Pilâtre de Rozier. The flight took place at Versailles.
24 June 1784	Edward Warren, a boy of 13, became the first to fly in a balloon in the United States. The lifting power of the balloon was too small to carry its constructor, P. Carnes. Baltimore was the scene of the ascent.
11 July 1784	The Abbé Miollan and Janinet made a disastrous attempt at an ascent from the Luxembourg gardens in Paris. The angry spectators set fire to their balloon.
14 September 1784	Vincent Lunardi made the first free flight in England.
19 September 1784	The ascent of the Robert brothers and Colin-Hullin from the Tuileries gardens.
7 January 1785	Jean-Pierre Blanchard and Dr Jeffries made the first Channel crossing from Dover to Calais.
5 May 1785	James Sadler, the first English aeronaut, made an ascent from Moulsey Hurst. He was accompanied by William Windham, M.P.
15 June 1785	Pilâtre de Rozier attempted to cross the Channel in the oposite direction. He was killed when his balloon exploded and became the first victim of ballooning.
29 June 1785	Vincent Lunardi flew over London with George Higgin and a Mrs Sage. After a short stop, he flew on alone, and set a new record by flying a total of 162 miles in 4 hours.
26 August 1785	Blanchard and the Chevalier de l'Epinard made an ascent from Lille. They landed at Servon, after dropping a dog by parachute, and made a journey of 157 miles in 7 hours.
20 November 1785	The first ascent in Belgium was made from Ghent by Blanchard.

Joseph Montgolfier, Pilâtre de Rozier—seated on the edge of the car—and five passengers made the first ascent in the provinces from Lyons on board the "La Flesselles" balloon.

BALLOON MANIA

Mercure de France, No 3, 17 February, 1784

Balloon mania, or if you prefer it, the taste for aerostatic machines, has made great progress in foreign countries, but above all, in our own provinces.

There is no small physician, chemist, or apothecary who does not wish to obtain the glory of being the first to dazzle his fellow-citizens. Most of them achieve nothing, and are rewarded by satirical songs and verses. In some cases, as in Bordeaux, their lack of success might have had a graver consequence, for now the people are starting to believe that they are gathering together only to be cheated, and this they will not brook lightly.

So, it was fashioned from ordinary linen, an open-weave fabric, such as is used in the packing of comparatively worthless merchandise. Two double thicknesses of this linen sewn and stitched together with four sheets of paper lining them formed the substance of the envelope; the whole was stitched and reinforced with pink tape sewn in diamond shapes over the exterior...

The top of the machine was lined on the outside with white calico placed in the shape of a canopy; and we are informed that more than three hundred ells of the material was needed for the fabrication, although when the sphere was filled, this part seemed small in proportion to the rest of the surface, rather as the Polar ice cap to the remainder of the earth's surface. The sleeve was made out of wool cloth called Cadis, less prone to catching fire than linen. To this was fastened a wicker base 22 feet in diameter on the outside and 17 feet on the inside, the brazier or grill being, according to orders, hung a little above the base within reach of the passengers and directly in the centre. A mesh or

---

On 19 January 1784, the "La Flesselles" rose before an audience of 60,000 persons to the sound of a military fanfare. Enthusiasm reached great heights—the men cheered loudly, while the women were crying with emotion. On their return the aeronauts were carried in triumph to the Opera.

The flight of the " La Flesselles "

described by Faujas de Saint-Fond
Lyons, 19 January 1784

network of rope was destined to encompass the upper hemisphere and maintain the equilibrium of the base.

When the envelope had been completed as far as was possible, the next day, 16 January, was chosen for the great experiment, but during the night it rained and snowed, in the morning it froze and nobody had put the envelope under cover.

The envelope was wet and covered in globules of ice, so at the beginning of the experiment, when the top of the machine is too near the heat, it was necessary to use a fiercer fire than was suitable in order to inflate the balloon; consequently when the top part began to swell out, the combination of the damp and the over-hot fire caused several rents to appear in the envelope; it would have been quite possible for fire to have caught hold, especially when the machine suddenly subsided on to the brazier. The flames were soon extinguished with the use of pumps, but the general panic and the disappointment of the passengers who were dressed in garments befitting the occasion and were ready to leave, would be impossible to describe. It is

with no little regret that we have to say that many of the onlookers rumoured, unjustly, that the Physicists were to blame, although in fact this disaster was caused solely by the inordinate impatience of the public...

However, since there was a slight improvement in the weather on the Sunday evening, the decision was taken that to satisfy public demand the departure would take place the next day, 19 January, and so our Physicists made themselves ready. But what could we expect from an envelope made from coarse, weak linen and paper, which had been exposed to rain and frost for days at a time and which, on top of this, had undergone several tests? MM. de Montgolfier and Pilâtre made no secret of the fact that they were most dubious about the probable results...

At a quarter to twelve everything was ready and the observation deck was equipped with ballast and provisions. The signal for lighting the fire was given by the firing of a mortar. The sad event of Saturday, 17 January led them to keep the fire at a modest level and to fill this splendid sphere very gradually; at a quarter to one it provided us with a perfect view of its glorious shape with the observation deck beneath; it was a really magnificent and imposing sight. Everything pointed to a veritable success; the weather was fine, the wind was coming from east-south-east and would carry the machine over the Rhône and towards the Saint-Clair district and la Croix Rousse...

A mortar was fired to announce the departure and the ropes were cut; it was one o'clock in the afternoon: at that precise moment, when the machine had already risen three or four feet above the platform, a young man by the name of Fontaine, one of the most enthusiastic helpers in the fabrication of the machine, with great spirit, foolishly caught hold of the observation deck and threw himself in, despite the efforts of the six illustrious travellers to make him do otherwise. This incident caused the machine to decrease its speed, and since the two ropes were still being held fast by those in the enclosure who had forgotten to loose them, the sphere came down again with a definite list to westward; in this position it dragged itself along away from the balcony for several fathoms, very close to the ground and brushing the spectators. Panic spread among the onlookers, one of the ropes became entangled in the western pole, the observation deck caught on the side of the enclosure and knocked part of it over; the moment was near when the sphere would either explode or continue on its way at this precarious angle till it must inevitably become enmeshed in the trees. At last the ropes were cut, but this violent tug in a direction opposed to the centre of gravity caused a fissure to develop in the upper half of the sphere which later in the day was not far from costing these famous and celebrated travellers their lives.

Nevertheless, they encouraged the fire and the sphere redressed itself perfectly, steadied itself and began to rise most majestically; it started to travel under the influence of a light easterly wind which did not take it far from a point above the ground from which it had risen, but it seemed to be drifting towards the Rhône and to be going to cross the bank of the Saint-Clair district: M. Pilâtre, who had pointed out the grave danger which might be incurred by leaving in such a frail machine, as indeed had M. Montgolfier, when he saw the slow rate of their ascent and the river ahead, declared "Gentlemen, we are going to go down into the Rhône". So they fed the fires once more, throwing bottles of spirits of wine on to the flames; at once the sphere rose with great speed, and since the wind was now coming from the west they were fortunately rescued from their hapless fate; they came back over the platform travelling east-south-east having risen to a height of more than 500 fathoms.

The spectators' mixed feelings of fear and joy were translated into cries and applause; from all sides were heard the good wishes of the company for the successful progress of such a fine invention for the sake of the intrepid voyagers, who were so obviously putting their lives at risk. These gentlemen, waving their handkerchiefs to reassure the disturbed assembly of their safety, at first replied by shouting, then by talking through a speaking-trumpet; soon they could no longer be heard. For their part, after subjection to the excessive and riotous noise of the cheering multitudes, they experienced a fantastic sensation on entering the complete silence of the celestial regions.

For a third time the direction of the wind changed and was now south-south-west carrying them over the new buildings of the Loge de la Bienfaisance. At the moment of their changing course, the flag of *la Renommé* came away and drifted to the ground; until then the line they had followed as far as the Loge had been exactly described by various pieces of timber which had fallen from the machine. When they arrived at a point directly above the Loge, they maintained their position for some four minutes; the sphere at this great height presented the most beautiful sight; its shape, illuminated by the sun's rays was marvellous; it seemed to be fixed in the sky like a new star.

It was at this time that we thought we could see it nearing the ground, travelling along the line it had followed. Indeed, soon we could discern the travellers and they seemed, alas, to be descending rapidly; they spoke through their speaking-trumpets, but could not be understood. At first general opinion had it that they were coming down of their own volition to sail into the wind at a lower level and thus to escape their stationary plight. But the experts, who could see only too well that the gentlemen were feeding the flames but were having no effect on the speed of their descent, were struck with terror and made all speed to arrive at the spot where it seemed the machine would land...

The first news we had was most terrifying; those who, nearing the site of the fallen sphere, had perceived naught but flames and a vast heap of canvas, catching no glimpse of any of the gentlemen, declared the unhappy passengers to be either burned or suffocated; others averred that they had been crushed in their fall; but the fortunate and intrepid travellers, when they had withdrawn from the fire and had extricated themselves from the wreckage, made haste to seize the speaking-trumpet, shouting that they had sustained no injury; this news was passed from mouth to mouth and soon the crowd was reassured; then perturbation gave place to joy and a great horde ran eagerly to meet the returned voyagers.

The Marquis d'Anglefort had acquired a broken tooth, Prince Charles a bruised leg. However, we observed how, even in time of stress, these bold travellers remained calm and clear-headed; for their only worries were the extinguishing of the fire to prevent the envelope from catching alight—as it was in danger of so doing—and the necessity of reassuring the first on the scene by stating that they had come to no harm.

THE FIRST ITALIAN ASCENT

Milan, 25 February 1784

The repeat performance of the experiment was planned for 25 February; there was no doubt as to its successful outcome. Towards noon the fire was lit under the machine; we, the brothers Agostino and Giuseppe, climbed into the car with M. Don Paolo and found that the machine was already beginning to lift itself slightly off the ground. Encouraged by this observation, we enjoined some men to help to lift the car. Knowing that with this assistance the car would rise more easily, we retained the services of our helpers until we had risen over the platform. Then the ropes holding the machine down were cut, and, freed, the vessel began to rise slowly, still keeping close to the platform. Then it seemed as though the machine would descend; some men ran up carrying stakes and gave it a light push upwards while we encouraged the fire, and the machine began to rise and move most majestically in a southerly direction; climbing still higher, it veered in a northerly direction and on its descent resumed a southerly course. Once we were settled in our course, the machine fulfilled our expectations at last by climbing to a height of 600 Milanese brasses—equivalent to 1,100 French feet.

As we rose we waved happily to the spectators below us—they were more than 2,000 strong. Instead of showing anxiety their joy and pleasure was so evident that our hearts were warmed. Carried away

Paolo Andreani, a wealthy gentleman from Milan, entrusted the construction of a montgol-fière type balloon to the well-known architects Agostino and Carlo Gerli. The balloon was taken to Moncucco, the seat of the Andreani family, and flew for the first time for twenty minutes on 25 February 1784. This was the first free ascension outside France.

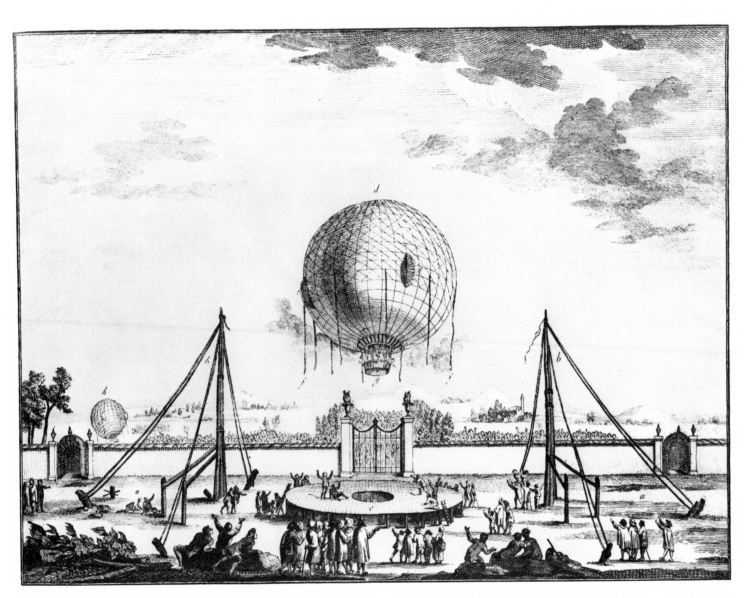

with delight and drunk, as it were, on this delectable sensation, we were so imprudent as to burn all the combustibles we had with us while we were still climbing, keeping none in reserve for the descent. This was a serious mistake which could have had fatal results, for, at the time when we should have been able to direct the descending balloon in one direction rather then in another, we found that we were obliged to come down with no means of control, to see the imminent danger and even perhaps our deaths, without being able to intervene in the course of events in any way whatsoever. But who could not find it in his heart to forgive us this serious act of negligence?

The great pleasure we obtained in seeing the ground below us; the inebriating impression we had of dominating a vast continent from our height; seeing so many things under a new guise, in an unusual form; all this entranced us. No one could ever put into words the sheer bliss of a voyage in the sky.

Seeing that we had no more fuel, we talked to the perturbed and stupefied onlookers, who had not taken their eyes off us, through the speaking-trumpet, asking that some men should run to the spot where it seemed the machine would come down. Scarcely had we finished speaking than we saw a large number of

the crowd running towards the balloon; from our height they could have been taken for ants. The inhabitants of Monza, only about three miles away, had vaguely caught our voices; they would have fully understood our words had we thought to detach the syllables carefully, one from another. So, we began to go down, slowly; soon we were 100 Milanese brasses from the ground. At this moment we increased speed, one of us shouted, "Hurry up!" Coming down, hitting a tree, seeing the car gently lean over, one of us falling, our jumping clear from the car—all this happened very quickly. Truly, scarcely had the car bumped against the tree than the balloon, somewhat lightened, rose a little once more and then plunged into the field below, and we chose this moment to leap out of the car.

From this incident we learned that if one hits a high obstacle when coming down one runs no risk of injury. If one has the wherewithal to feed the fire, one can easily avoid descending in an inconvenient spot and can, in fact, choose the place where one would wish to land.

Having lost some considerable weight by our departure, the machine began to rise vigorously; the helpers who had loosed the cut ropes which hung down from the balloon took hold of them again. As for us, seeing the machine take once more to the air, we decided to take advantage of its lift to guide it back to the point of departure about a quarter of a mile away from our present position. We began to implement our plan at once, taking hold of the ropes and thereby guiding the machine over the trees, over two of the garden walls and above a road lined with hornbeams.

The spectators greeted us with rapture and more than one shed tears of relief. As for us, the two brothers Agostino and Carlo Giuseppe, our satisfaction could not have been more complete. We had proved that our labours had not been in vain, that the mockery of those who had criticized our project as being insane and the hope of success as being rash, had been given the lie by the results; we had not deceived the generosity of the illustrious person who had financed our venture, nor had we disappointed him in his hopes. The honour of sharing eternally in the glory of being the first in Italy to attempt and succeed in voyaging through the unlimited pastures of celestial space is assuredly his.

Journal de Paris, 1 April 1784

EXTRACT FROM A LETTER WRITTEN BY THE BROTHERS GERLI IN MILAN TO M. PILATRE DE ROZIER.

15 March 1784

Count Andreani had asked us to build an aerostatic machine and we thought it best to model it on the most recent machine tested by MM. Montgolfier. Thanks to the Count's generosity, and the energy we brought to the completion of the construction, after only six weeks the public witnessed our first tests.

On 25 February, in comparatively settled weather we sent the machine up, without using ropes, to a height of 1,200 feet; it had a diameter of 66 feet and could carry Count Andreani, my brother and myself quite easily. When we had used all our fuel, we came down very slowly a quarter of a mile from the town. The most interesting aspect of the proceedings is that, scarcely had we left the car than the machine started to rise once more with the result that, by using the ropes, we were able to guide it back to the starting point, passing it over the houses, gardens and trees. It was in such good condition by the time we arrived that we used it for the experiment carried out on 13 March, details of which we shall be only too pleased to send you by the first messenger.

Since we are the first foreigners after Prince Charles to dare to attempt a voyage in the sky, we hope, sir, that you will find it in your heart to give all possible publicity to our experiment, so that our anteriority in Italy might be assured. We would be eternally indebted to you, and remain your humble servants,

CARLO and AGOSTINO GERLI

The Gerli brothers, who had taken part in the experiment made by Paolo Andreani, drew the first technical designs for balloons.

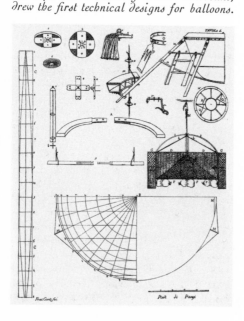

THE DIJON ACADEMY'S REPORT OF ITS EXPERIMENTS:

In March 1784, an optician named Adorne made an ascent at Strasbourg which nearly caused a disaster. His montgolfière balloon crushed itself on the roofs of the town, luckily without loss of life.

An unfortunate experience:

Extract from the Memoirs of the Baroness of Oberkirch

On my arrival at Strasbourg I found the town in uproar because of the unhappy issue of the testing of a new balloon built by a M. Adorne, an optician in the town. The inventor was apparently in the car with one of his relatives, the aerostatic machine rose for a few seconds and then fell on to a roof where it caught fire. These latter-day Icaruses were both injured. The disaster caused great consternation notably among the upper classes and the commercial world. It makes one's blood run cold to think that these unhappy men could have fallen on to the spire of the cathedral, and what a terrible death would have awaited them there!

Journal de Paris, 2 May 1784

"We, the undersigned, members of the commission for sending up the balloon *The Académie de Dijon*, have drawn up, as here follows, a preliminary short official report before leaving the site of our arrival.

"The very strong, swirling wind that had come up a few moments before we left had already pushed us back down to earth from the height of the length of our ropes and had given us cause to fear that all our gear might be smashed or that we might be thrown down upon the roofs of the town, and, since we were at the foot of the highest steeple, we decided to throw out at a steady rate as much ballast as was required to conquer the force which was opposing us. This course of action more or less exhausted our supplies which we had estimated at 75 or 80 pounds. Scarcely had we risen above the height of the roofs of the church than our speed of ascent rose so rapidly that we could only see the steeple when the balloon pitched, and then it was a long way below us.

The shape of the balloon gave proof of a vigorous expansion of the contents caused by the heat of the sun and the lessening in the density of the surrounding air; consequently, we opened both valves, but the fluid did not escape in a sufficiently large quantity and a split seven or eight inches long developed in the lower portion of the balloon, close to the appendix, an event which comforted rather than troubled us.

"There then came a period of such absolute calm that we thought that we had stopped making any progress, but we soon saw that in fact we were already quite a distance from the town.

"At five minutes past five we passed over a village which we did not recognize and where we dropped a note tied to a ball filled with bran and with a streamer attached. On this we wrote that we felt perfectly fit, that the barometer reading was 20 inches and 9 lines, that the thermometer was at 1½ degrees below zero and the hygrometer at 59 degrees on M. de Retz' scale and 24½ on M. Copineau's scale.

"We dropped two further notes written in pencil, as the extreme cold prevented us from holding a pen: at eleven minutes past five it was 3 degrees below zero, that is to say that the temperature had dropped by 14½ degrees since our departure.

"We counted the time it took for one of the notes to touch the ground on a watch with a second hand. It must have been held up by the loose ribbon because, although it fell virtually in a direct line to the ground, we counted 57 seconds before it arrived.

"The piercing cold bit at our ears and this was the only disconfiture we experienced, and one for which we have been amply recompensed by the similar experience described by M. Charles. We have only one detail to add to his picture which is that the cold seemed diminished rather than increased when we saw a sea of clouds flowing beneath us and cutting us off from the earth; at this moment we repeated with one accord the motto on the crest of our aerostat: *Surgit nunc gallus ad aethera.* (Now climbs the cock to the heavens.)

"The sun began to set, having given us a sight of a wonderful parhelion. We saw that the lower part of the balloon was flattening out and that it was therefore time to choose our landing site: with the aid of the compass we calculated that we were not far from Auxonne and we thought that we could make out the town, by its size, at 25 degrees to our right. We were not mistaken. We determined to use all our means of controlling the balloon in order to sail in that direction but our equipment had been severely damaged by the gusts of wind at the time of our departure. The rudder was dislocated, one of the oars had been broken at its loom and had

come away at the moment when we wanted to use it in order to sail to some distance from Dijon. The equatorial oar on the same side had become caught up in one of the four thick ropes paid out when we left, and we had not been able to lift up the ropes and disengage it. So all that we had left were the other two oars which, being on the same side, were of absolutely no use to us for the greater part of the journey when there was no breeze, and even when we were carried along continually turning with no perceptible wind. But having fallen into a current which was taking us eastwards we were able to move the oars with no difficulty for eight or nine minutes and to some effect, for they were steering us so well towards our south-easterly destination, that we already felt that this power should be controlled so that we might make a diversion when the time came, especially since we had no means of returning eastwards.

"We hoped, therefore, to be able to go down near to the dark expanse that we thought to be Auxonne, but we were losing a great deal of gas through the hole in the balloon. We came to a wood-covered area; we felt the balloon descend. We kept the little ballast that was left, which consisted of no more than movable planks which served as benches for us, in case we should have to slow down our fall. We threw one plank over and landed gently into a copse which we have since learned is called 'Le Chaignet' and is the property of the Comtesse Ferdinande de Brun, and is in la Marche district. Scarcely had our gondola touched the tips of the branches than it lifted off again quite violently; we held on to the branches in an attempt to anchor the balloon and so to prevent it from being thrown recurrently against the trees which were scattered about us. We tried to go down by pulling on the limbs and trunks of the copse as one does in travelling across the water on a chain-ferry, but it was impossible. We heard voices and shouted for help in reaching the ground. The voices belonged to the inhabitants of Magny-les-Auxonne; one of them replied that he would willingly come to our aid if we had no intention of doing him any harm; we gave him our word. Our reiterated requests and his example made up the minds of his companions and we finally touched the ground at 6.25 pm; amongst the country-folk who came up we noticed two men and three women who knelt down in front of our balloon.

"Almost as soon as we had tied our aerostat down, left someone on guard and sent off a messenger to give news of us in Dijon, we found several people on the road to Magny who had seen our arrival from Auxonne and were coming to meet us. They were perfectly willing to sign this report which was drawn up in the vicarage of Athé, the village next to Magny, on 25 April 1784. Signed—Morveau and Bertrand, commissioners.

"Signed— subsequently—Bidal, Vicar of Athé; Buvée, civil and criminal Lieutenant of the bailiwick of Auxonne; Chevalier de Suremain, officer in the Artillery; Deneux, officer in the Artillery; Roussot, advocate at Parliament; de Belgrand, Doctor of surgery; Radepont, the younger, goldsmith; Cornu, contractor; Lagrange, Bellident, Terrier, Lanaud, Rude, Bourotte, Roussel, Frantin, Demartinecourt, and Matthey."

EXTRACT FROM A LETTER WRITTEN AT DIJON AND DATED 27 APRIL

Journal de Paris, 2 May 1784

On 25 April the Académie de Dijon's aerostatic machine lifted off from the garden of the lands of the Abbey of St Bénigne. When everything was prepared for the departure, we tested the weight the sphere could lift. We found that its specific lightness was 550 pounds. The voyagers climbed into the car with their meteorological instruments, victuals and sand to provide ballast.

At twelve minutes to four the cannon and drums gave the signal for the departure. The balloon was held down by six ropes until it had risen above the towers of St Bénigne, since the wind seemed to be carrying it towards them. The church of St Bénigne is at the east end of the garden; the wind was westerly and was blowing fiercely against the body of the church. It rebounded very violently and formed whirlpools in the garden which prevented the balloon from rising to any height. However, by throwing out a great quantity of ballast the voyagers enabled the balloon to extract itself from the force that was holding it down and so to rise.

The voyagers disappeared two or three times behind the clouds and came down owing to lack of ballast at twenty-five minutes past six at Magny-les-Auxonne, having covered a distance of six leagues and reaching a height of 2,000 fathoms.

MM. de Morveau and Bertrand sent word to Dijon of their arrival and their impending return. As soon as the news arrived a vast crowd poured on to the road to Auxonne and we can say without exaggeration that three quarters of the town had come out to participate in the triumph.

On 26 April, at a quarter to nine in the evening the travellers arrived. Before them went a very large cavalcade including the town trumpeters, and they themselves rode in an open carriage. The town was lit up; there was tumultuous applause, shouts of joy and warm embraces from their fellow-citizens, overjoyed to see them back.

M. Fleurant's account of his journey in an aerostatic sphere, taken up by himself and Mme Tible from Lyons on 4 June 1784, in the presence of the King of Sweden.

"We continued to rise, reaching so great a height that the houses of Lyons seemed to us like a shapeless mass of pebbles; we threw out the second flag which stayed in the air for seven minutes. Quite suddenly, bitter cold took hold of my companion and myself, and this was followed by such a humming in our ears that we feared that we might no longer be able to hear each other... these two sensations passed quickly and gave way to a feeling of well-being and sweet content which, in my opinion, could never be repeated in any other situation. Mme Tible gave voice to these feelings by singing the air from "La Belle Arsène": "I am victorious, I am Queen"; to which I replied with the song of Zémire and Azor: "What, travelling in the clouds"... The descent was smooth, but at the moment when the balloon touched the ground, it burst open at the

Gustave III of Sweden witnessed at Lyons the ascent on 4 June 1784 of the montgolfière balloon named "La Gustave" in his honour. It carried the painter Fleurant and the singer Elisabeth Tible, who is seen right, dressed as Minerva and holding a picture of the King.

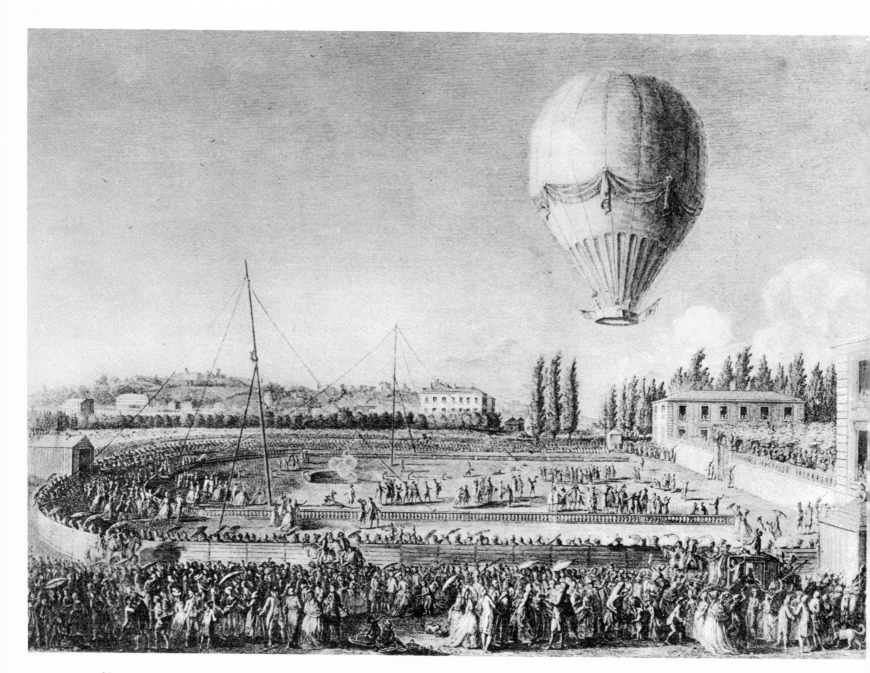

top and the canvas fell upon us: I cut my way out with a knife; I rushed to the aid of my fearless companion who was already out of danger. I embraced her with joy. In climbing out of the observation car she had slightly sprained her left ankle, and this marred my pleasure a little. People were running up from all directions. I heard someone say that one of our voyagers was crying for help; I replied that he must be mistaken, for there were only two of us in the party, Mme Tible and myself.

A moment later, on looking at the canvas, I saw that there was indeed someone trying to lift it up and we helped him to extricate himself. The gentleman was quite presentable and, coming round from his state of shock, he told us how, seeing that we were coming down to the ground, he had been running as fast as he was able in order to meet us, when the balloon had landed on top of him. The fire in the brazier had scorched a part of his clothing, but his body was unharmed.

The ascent of the "Marie-Antoinette" before the Kings of France and Sweden Versailles, 23 June 1784

The first test of the Montgolfière, the construction of which was commissioned by the King, and which was sent up in the presence of their Majesties, of the Royal Family, the Comte d'Haga, by M. Pilâtre de Rozier, Pensioner of the King, Administrator of the Department of Physics, Chemistry, Natural History to the brother of the King, Secretary to the Queen's Cabinet, member of several Academies in France and elsewhere; Head of the first Government-authorized museum, under the protection of the King and Queen, etc. on 23 June 1784.

A second salvo of three loud mortars announced the departure. The twelve Grenadiers sent up the Montgolfière; the drums beat the general salute; the musicians played the overture to "The Deserter" and the air rang with renewed praises, transports of joy, cries of "Long live the King! ... the Queen! ... the Comte d'Haga!", etc.: in short, all one could hear from a distance was a confused roar. The Montgolfière rose very slowly, describing a diagonal and showing to the crowd a pleasing, and at the same time, a marvellous sight. Like a vessel that has descended from the slipway into the water, this astonishing machine floated proudly in the air, which seemed to be snatching the Montgolfière out of human hands. For a

moment the irregular movements of the machine struck fear into the hearts of some of the spectators who, worried lest the fall of the balloon endanger their lives, strode hastily away. When I had lit the furnace, I waved to the onlookers who responded in a most flattering way: the Swiss grenadiers, moved by a feeling rooted in respect, involuntarily took hold of their sabres to return my salute. I had time to remark a mixture of interest, anxiety and joy on some of the faces. As we rose, I perceived that a current of air, coming from above, was causing the Montgolfière to list to one side; wanting to avoid a fire at all costs, I asked M. Proust to walk around the platform for 8 or 10 minutes of an arc, to restore the balance, then, increasing the heat, we rose. Since the size of the objects beneath us was diminishing perceptibly, we were in a position to calculate our height with some degree of accuracy. At that time the Montgolfière could be seen from the capital and the surrounding area. The height to which we had climbed was so great that the majority of onlookers though that we were motionless above their heads. The earth disappeared from view as we rose into the clouds; we seemed to be surrounded by a dense fog and then a clearer patch brought with it some light. Some more clouds, or rather, conglomera-

tions of snow, were rapidly gathering at our feet; we were hemmed in on all sides; some of it fell on the outer edges of our observation platform where it lay thickly. Another area of cloud melted and fell as rain on Versailles and Paris.

The barometer had fallen 9 inches and the thermometer 16 degrees. Since we were interested in ascertaining the maximum height to which our machine could rise, we resolved to encourage as fierce a fire as possible, by lifting up the furnace and holding the faggots on the tips of our forks. When we reached the highest among these mountains of ice and were unable to rise any further, we drifted for a time in this savage scenery: scenery which man was seeing for the first time. Isolated and cut off from all nature, beneath our feet we could see nothing but these vast expanses of snow, which, reflecting the light of the sun, were illuminating the void through which we were travelling. We drifted on the top of these sheer-sided hills for 8 minutes, 11,732 feet from the ground in a temperature of 5 degrees below freezing. We were no longer able to estimate our speed as we had lost all points of reference by which to judge it. This situation, which a talented artist would doubtless find to his liking, did not seem to hold much of interest to a physicist; this led us to decide,

18 minutes after our departure, to return to a level below the clouds so that we might once more see the ground. Scarcely had we emerged from this sort of chasm, than the most sparkling view took the place of the most tiring of sceneries. All at once we saw the most marvellous sight; the countryside appeared to us in all its splendour; everything was so bright that we thought the sun to have dispersed the storm; and, as though the curtain hiding nature had been drawn back, we suddenly discovered a thousand different things spread over an area which, to our eyes, almost defied measure. Only the horizon was overcast with a few clouds which seemed to touch the ground. Some were diaphanous, others reflected the light in a myriad different shapes; all around, everything was free of that browny hue which is conducive to melancholy. In the space of a minute we passed from winter into spring. We saw a vast expanse of land covered with towns and villages which seemed to merge into beautiful castles, splendid in their isolation and surrounded by gardens; the rivers, diversifying themselves and winding their way across the fields from all the points of the compass, were now no more than minute brooks which decorated the gardens of the palaces; the most immense of forests had become an orchard or a mere hedgerow: in short, the meadows and fields formed no more than the grass of the lawns which embellish our flowerbeds. This marvellous picture, to which no painter can do justice, brought to mind those miraculous metamorphoses of fairy stories; with this difference, that we saw on a large scale what even the most fertile imagination had only been able to envisage in miniature, and that we were relishing the fact born of the fiction. It is in this bewitched state that the soul rises, thoughts are exalted and follow one another on with amazing rapidity. While travelling at this height our fire had but little need of our attention, and we could walk about the platform without concern for it. My enthusiastic helper changed his position several times; we were as untroubled on our balcony as we would have been on the terrace of a tall house, enjoying all the constantly changing scenes without suffering the giddy spells which are feared by so many when at a great height. Since the vigour with which I had worked had broken my fork, I went to the stores for a replacement. I met M. Proust, but the Mongolfière was so well ballasted that it only listed to the slightest degree: from which we concluded that the accidents which were reported with so much ceremony in some newspapers should be attributed either to the faulty construction of the balloon in question, or to the panic of the travellers.

Although the wind was very strong, our edifice was carried along without the slightest sign of rolling; the only method of determining our speed was by watching the villages fly past beneath our feet; this, combined with the tranquility of our progress, led to the impression that we were being carried along in conjunction with the sun on its course. Several times we sought to near the ground in order to hear the import of the cries of those below, to whom we could easily have replied with the aid of a speaking-trumpet: in short, everything diverted us. The ease of the controls enabled us to trace horizontal and oblique lines through the sky, to rise and fall, rise and fall again, and to do this as often as we deemed it necessary. When we arrived at Luzarche, we decided to set foot on land there. Already the people were manifesting great pleasure, the crowd was swelling, some of them were stretching out their hands to seize the ropes and so to help to slow our descent, while animals of every kind fled from our shadow, terrified, as if they had taken the Montgolfière for some savage beast. But, since we soon perceived that our speed would bring us down on to the houses, we fanned the flames; by this means we skipped lightly over the rooftops and left behind our potential hosts, who stood dumbfounded. As we continued on our way, we came upon that enormous forest which borders on Compiègne; however, knowing little of the topography of that region and seeing no propitious spot for our descent within eyesight and fearing, moreover, that our supplies would run out before we had left the forest behind us, I thought it would be wiser to land at the last crossroads, thirteen leagues from Versailles, rather than to bring this experiment to an end by setting the forest alight. The bags hanging from our gallery helped to soften our descent. I seized hold of the flag and then went to the aid of M. Proust. We threw the remaining combustibles out of our vessel, our clothes and instruments we stowed away safely. Twenty minutes after we touched the ground, the wind, as I had forecast to the Chief Administrator in the presence of the Queen and of the Comte d'Haga, was blowing fiercely on the top of the Montgolfière, which, in its horizontal position, dragged the gallery and the brazier attached to it along in its wake. The flames were coming out of the brazier through the grille and were licking at some of the ropes on the gallery. The canvas was quite a distance away, and we tried to separate it from the lower portion; unfortunately, we were alone for more than half an hour, working furiously with a rather blunt knife. Time was of the essence: I feared that the fire, spreading as it was, might cause a general conflagration. My instrument could not keep pace with my patience; I threw it away; tearing at the material now I managed to throw it away from the flames but, when

40

it came to the ropes holding the two portions together, I could not apply myself to their severing without my knife, for which I looked in vain. Time was passing; the fire was going to spread to the ropes and then to the gallery, the substance of which was extremely inflammable. There was no time to lose—the essential parts had to be saved. The canopy and cylinder were new and we immediately took these pieces aside. Curiosity caused two men to run up whose willingness to help I encouraged by the hope of recompense. Resigned to the loss of the tapering end of the Montgolfière which had been used to great advantage during the first experiments at Versailles and la Muette, we carried the rescued portions to a safe distance. Gentlemen from the surrounding districts were arriving; the people were coming *en masse*. I distributed pieces of the lower part of the balloon among them to prevent a disturbance breaking out and to satisfy their curiosity. M. de Combemale, who did not tarry in keeping the crowd in hand, rushed to my aid; at the sound of his voice everyone obeyed orders and we took the Montgolfière to a nearby château.

Several people offered us the use of their houses; we rode on horseback to the house of M. de Bienville in the company of President Molé and M. de Nantouillet.

Official report to the Queen

The Montgolfière which left the Courtyard of Ministers at 4.45 pm, came down at 5.32 pm at a crossroads in the forest of Chantilly near to the Manon road, about 13 leagues from Versailles. The voyagers, feeling very well, had suffered no accident. The only damage incurred was to the gallery and to a portion of the conical part of the balloon half-an-hour after the descent, as de Rozier had the honour of pointing out to your Majesty before his departure. Signed: Louis-Joseph de Bourbon, Duke of Enghien; Louise-Adelaïde de Bourbon; Bienville, Captain of the Dragoons in the Bourbon Regiment; Franclieu.

THE FIRST AMERICAN ASCENT
Baltimore, 24 June 1784

"Yesterday the ingenious Peter Carnes, Esq., made his curious AERO-STATIC EXPERIMENTS within the Limits of this Town", wrote the reporter, "in the Presence of a numerous and respectable congress of people, whom the fame of his superb BALLOON had drawn together from the East, West, North and South, who, generally, appeared highly delighted with the awful Grandeur of so novel a scene, as a large Globe making repeated voyages into the airy Regions, which Mr. Carnes's Machine actually performed, in a Manner that reflected Honor on his Character as a Man of Genius, and could not fail to inspire solemn and exalted Ideas in every reflecting Mind. —Ambition, on this occasion, so fired the youthful Heart of a Lad (only 13 Years old!) of the name of *Edward Warren* that he bravely embarked as a Volunteer on the last *Trip* into the Air, and behaved with the steady Fortitude of an Old Voyager. The 'gazing Multitude below' wafted to him their loud Applause, the receipt of which, as he was 'Soaring aloof,' he politely acknowledged by a significant Wave of his Hat. —When he returned to our terrene Element, he met with a Reward, from some of the Spectators, which had a *solid*, instead of an *airy*, Foundation, and of a Species which is ever acceptable to the Residents of this *lower World*."

In January 1784, Professor Filling conducted a ballooning experiment in the grounds of Windsor Castle. King George III, quizzing-glass in hand, Queen Charlotte and their suite watched the ascent of a small balloon inflated with hot air.

AÉROSTAT DE 30 PIEDS 3 POUCES DE DIAMÉTRE

Elevé à Nantes le 14 Juin 1784.   a 6 heures 30 min. du Soir.

On la perdu de vue   en 18 Minuttes.

A FIRST ATTEMPT AT SCIENTIFIC OBSERVATIONS
Nantes, 14 June 1784

Journal de Paris, 26 June, 1784

At Nantes, on 14 June, an aerostatic experiment took place, under the direction of M. Levesque, Correspondent of the Académie Royale des Sciences. The aerostat, fashioned from oiled silk, had a diameter of 30 feet and 4 inches. It was constructed by M. Coustard de Massi, Chevalier de St Louis and M. Mouchet, a teacher of Physics at the Oratory. In the car with the two voyagers were placed the necessary instruments, clothes and 245 pounds of ballast. At 6.10 pm the machine left the platform. However, the weight it carried was not proportionate to the gas it contained and, consequently, the aerostat sank and touched the ground twice. This accident broke the instruments and thereby robbed the travellers of the possibility of making the proposed observations. They then disposed of some of the ballast and rose to more than 200 feet. They floated at this height for about half-an-hour; but having thrown out more ballast they rose higher and were lost in the clouds, so that at 6.27 pm they were no more to be seen. The travellers estimate the apex of their ascent to have been between 1500 and 1800 fathoms.

As they drew near to Valette, they saw that their machine was going down at an alarming speed and it did in fact touch the ground several times; they threw out all that remained in the form of ballast, to wit, their speaking-trumpets and two bottles. By means of this loss in weight, they climbed back to between 500 and 600 fathoms; but soon sank back to earth and touched the ground a few more times. They were thrown violently against some oak trees with no means of protecting themselves or of avoiding the danger. When they arrived at Geste after many detours and 58 minutes travelling in all, they threw themselves out of the car 9 leagues away from Nantes without any harm having come to their persons, but the balloon, being now approximately 300 pounds lighter, rose rapidly; within two minutes it had disappeared from sight and was found that same evening in Poitou, a village near Brefenaire and 22 leagues from Nantes.

M. Levesque states that in his apparatus he used M. Meunier's tank, which he considered to be the best. He even avers that zinc is more suitable than iron in these experiments and that one can consider it less costly if one intends to make use of Goslar's vitriol in developing the gas.

VINCENT LUNARDI'S FLIGHT
London, 14 September 1784

Sept. 15, at about five minutes after two, the last gun was fired, the cords divided, and the balloon rose, the company returning my signals of adieu with the most unfeigned acclamations and applauses. The effect was that of a miracle on the multitudes that surrounded the place; and they passed from incredulity and menace into the most extravagant expressions of approbation and joy.

At the height of 20 yards the balloon was a little depressed by the wind, which had a fine effect. It held me over the ground for a few seconds, and seemed to pause majestically before its departure.

On discharging a part of the ballast, it ascended to the height of two hundred yards. As a multitude lay before me of a hundred and fifty thousand people, who had not seen my ascent from the ground, I had recourse to every stratagem to let them know I was in the gallery, and they literally rent the air with their acclamations and applause. In these stratagems I devoted my flag, and worked with my oars, one of which was immediately broken, and fell from me. A pigeon too escaped, which, with a dog and cat, were the only companions of my excursion.

When the thermometer had fallen from 68° to 61°, I perceived a great difference in the temperature of the air. I became very cold, and found it necessary to take a few glasses of wine.

When the thermometer was at 50°, the effect of the atmosphere, and the combination of circumstances around, produced a calm delight, which is inexpressible, and which no situation on earth could give. The stillness, extent, and magnificence of the scene, rendered it highly awful. My horizon seemed a perfect circle; the terminating line several hundred miles in circumference. This I conjectured from the view of London, the extreme points of which formed an angle of only a few degrees. It was so reduced on the great scale before me, that I can find no simile to convey an idea of it. I could distinguish St Paul's, and other churches, from the houses. I saw the streets as lines, all animated with beings, whom I knew to be men and women, but which I should otherwise have had a difficulty in describing. It was an enormous beehive, but the industry of it was suspended. Indeed, the whole scene before me filled my mind with a sublime pleasure of which I never had a conception. I had soared from the apprehensions and anxieties of the Artillery Ground, and felt as if I had left behind me all the cares and passions that molest mankind.

I had not the slightest sense of motion from the machine. I knew not whether it went swiftly or slowly; whether it ascended or descended;

spotted with cities, towns, villages, and houses, pouring out their inhabitants; you will allow me some merit at not having been exceedingly intoxicated with my situation. To prolong the enjoyment of it, and to try the effect of my only oar, I kept myself in the same parallel respecting the earth for nearly half an hour. But the exercise having fatigued and the experiment having satisfied me, I laid aside my oar, and again had recourse to my bottle. This I emptied to the health of my friends and benefactors in the lower world. All my affections were alive, in a manner not easily to be conceived; and you may be assured that the sentiment, which seemed to me most congenial to that happy situation, was gratitude and friendship. I sat down and wrote four pages of desultory observations, and pinning them to a napkin, committed them to the mild winds of the region, to be convoyed to my honoured friend and patron, Prince Caramanico.

During this business I had ascended rapidly; for, on hearing the report of a gun, fired in the Artillery Ground, I was induced to examine the thermometer, and found it had fallen to 32°. The balloon was so much inflated as to assume the form of an oblong spheroid, the shortest diameter of which was in a line with me, though I had ascended with it in the shape of an inverted cone, and wanting nearly one third of its full complement of air. Having no valve, I could only open the neck of the balloon, thinking it barely possible that the strong rarefaction might force out some of the inflammable air. The condensed vapour around its neck was frozen, though I found no inconvenience from the cold. The earth, at this point, appeared like a boundless plain, whose surface had variegated shades, but on which no object could be accurately distinguished.

I then had recourse to the utmost use of my single oar; by hard and persevering labour I brought myself within three hundred yards of the earth, and, moving horizontally, spoke through my trumpet to some country people, from whom I heard a confused noise in reply.

At half after three o'clock I descended in a corn field on the common of South Mimms, where I landed the cat. The poor animal had been sensibly affected by the cold, during the former

whether it was agitated or tranquil, but by the appearance or disappearance of objects on the earth. I moved to different parts of the gallery. I adjusted the furniture and apparatus. I uncorked my bottle, ate, drank, and wrote, just as in my study. The height had not the effect which a much less degree of it has near the earth, that of producing giddiness. The gradual diminution of objects, and the masses of light and shade, are intelligible in oblique and common prospects. But here every thing wore a new appearance, and had a new effect. The face of the country had a mild and permanent verdure, to which Italy is a stranger. The sea glistening with the rays of the sun, the immense district beneath me

A young attaché of the Neopolitan Ambassador to London, Vincent Lunardi, organised a subscription to construct a balloon. In September 1784, the ascent took place from the Moorfields Artillery Ground. Lunardi was accompanied by a dog, a cat and a pigeon confined in little cages. They all survived the flight.

On his return to London, Lunardi was presented to the King. His balloon was shown in the Pantheon in London, and attracted an elegant and fashionable crowd from morning till night.

44

part of the voyage. Here I might have terminated my excursion with satisfaction and honour to myself; and the people about me were very ready to assist at my disembarkation. But my affections were afloat, and in unison with the whole country, whose transport and admiration seemed boundless. I bade them, therefore, keep clear, and I would gratify them by ascending directly in their view.

My general course to this place was something more than one point to the westward of the north. A gentleman on horseback approached me, but I could not speak to him, being intent on my reascension, which I effected after moving horizontally about forty yards. As I ascended, one of the ballustrades of the gallery gave way; but the circumstance excited no apprehension of danger. I threw out the remainder of my ballast and provisions, and again resumed my pen. My ascension was so rapid, that before I had written half a page, the thermometer had fallen to 29°. The drops of water that adhered to the neck of the balloon were become like chrystals. At this point of elevation, which was the highest I attained, I finished my letter, and fastening it with a corkscrew to my handkerchief, threw it down. I likewise threw down the plates, knives, and forks, the little sand that remained, and an empty bottle, which took some time in disappearing. I now wrote the last of my dispatches from the clouds, which I fixed to a leathern belt, and sent towards the earth. It was visible to me on its passage for several minutes; but I was myself insensible of motion from the machine itself during the whole voyage. The earth appeared as before, like an extensive plain, with the same variegated surface, but the objects rather less distinguishable. The clouds to the eastward rolled beneath me, in masses immensely larger than the waves of the ocean. I therefore did not mistake them for the sea. Contrasted with the effects of the sun on the earth and water beneath, they gave a grandeur to the whole scene which no fancy can describe. I again betook myself to my oar, in order to descend; and by the hard labour of fifteen or twenty minutes, I accomplished my design, when my strength was nearly exhausted. My principal care was, to avoid a violent concussion at landing, and in this my good fortune was my friend.

At twenty minutes past four I descended in a spacious meadow in the parish of Stondon, near Ware, in Hertfordshire.

After the widely-reported ascent of Lunardi, ballooning caught on. James Sadler was the first Englishman to fly. This engraving shows one of his balloons accidently burning in Lord Foley's gardens on 29 September 1784.

Billet d'entrée
pour les Expériences Aérostatiques au Luxembourg
de M.M. l'Abbé Miolan et Janinet.
le 11 juillet 1784 à midy.

A rather damaged ticket for the enclosure at the Luxembourg gardens for the attempt of Miollan and Janinet. Probably the ticket was torn up by its owner in disgust at the failure of the experiment.

In March 1784, a prospectus was issued announcing the building of the biggest montgolfière ever seen in Paris. Subscription tickets were sold well in advance, and the crowd was enormous. However, the balloon was a dismal failure, and the enraged crowd tore it to pieces.

QUITTANCE D'UNE SOUSCRIPTION
POUR LA PREMIERE ENCEINTE.

Reçu 6 liv. pour un Billet qui sera livré quelques jours avant les expériences, & qui donne le droit d'entrer dans la premiere enceinte.

A Paris, ce _____ 1784.

AN UNHAPPY EXPERIENCE

Paris, 11 July 1784

The reward of failure

The machine was both built and sent up at the Observatory. It measured 112 feet in height and 84 in diameter. Its total lifting force was about 140,000 (sic). It was tested twice, on 17 and 30 June 1784; on the latter occasion there were 9 people and 900 pounds of ballast in the car which would have escaped the twenty pairs of hands holding it down by ropes if the fire had not been extinguished. The experiment took place before a great number of people including the Duke of Chaumes, the Marquis de Cassini who was in the car with M. Jeaurat Méchain, and the Comte de Milli, members of the Académie des Sciences. Since the experiment the volume of the balloon had been increased by 40,000 cubic feet resulting in an increase of 800 pounds in lifting power (sic). The machine, thus constructed, was taken to the Luxembourg Gardens to be sent up publicly on 11 July at noon precisely. For several reasons which had not been foreseen, above all, the searing heat and the rays of the sun which made the temperature rise to more than 28 degrees in the open air, the machine did not swell out sufficiently, despite the trouble taken to make it do so, the advice of learned men and the different methods which were attempted.

Soon afterwards, the public forced an entry into the gardens, tore up the balloon, smashed the gallery and the enclosure, the chairs, the instruments, etc., burned whatever could not be carried away and thereby put the authors of this experiment in a position whence they could not fulfil their obligations.

The death of Pilâtre de Rozier
15 June 1785,
related by Frédéric-Melchior Grimm

Be that as it may, Pilâtre des Rosiers (sic) decided on the Tuesday evening to leave at daybreak next morning. The preparations for the journey were lengthy; there were several holes in the machine which needed repair. At 7.7 am all was ready; there were 30 pounds of lifting power and the Montgolfière rose majestically at an angle of 60 degrees to the ground. At 200 feet, the south-east wind seemed to be controlling the direction of the machine and soon it was over the sea. Different currents pulled at it then for three minutes; the south-west wind proved to be the most forceful and the sphere was blown back to the French coast. According to some accounts, at 7.35 am a column of flame was seen to shoot up from the balloon; at the same moment the machine seemed to shudder two or three times and the subsequent fall was both violent and rapid. The two unhappy travellers, M. Pilâtre and M. Romain, the latter one of those involved in the construction of the machine, fell with the balloon. Pilâtre was killed instantly but his hapless companion survived this monstrous fall for ten minutes; he could not speak and gave but slight signs of recognising his surroundings. The Montgolfière was intact, having been neither burned nor even torn. At the time of its fall the machine might have been some 1,600 feet in the air, it came down 1¼ leagues and 300 paces from the shore, off the Tower of Croy.

Determined not to be outdone by Blanchard, Pilâtre de Rozier attempted a crossing of the Channel starting from Boulogne. His "Aéro-Montgolfière" (left) was a dangerous combination of a hydrogen and a fire-balloon, and exploded soon after its ascent, killing Rozier and his companion.

At Dover, Blanchard and Jeffries' balloon, flying the flags of England and France, was saluted by a fleet of small boats.

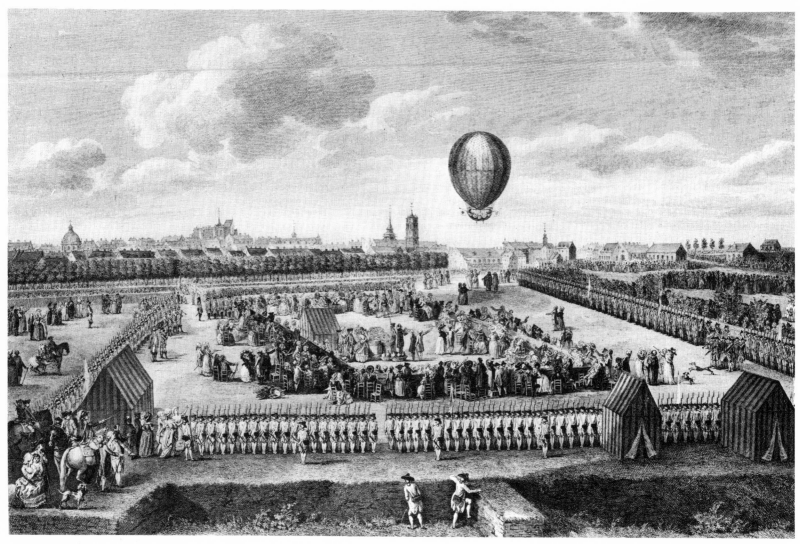

On 26 August 1785, Blanchard and the Chevalier de l'Epinard made an ascent from Lille. Blanchard used this flight to make the first parachute trials from a balloon, dropping a dog fastened to his device from 3,937 ft. The dog landed safe and sound.

The flight of Blanchard from Lille was, without question, the longest made solely within France. The aeronauts landed at Servon, not far from Challons sur Marne, after covering 157 miles in 7 hours. Earlier, in June, Lunardi covered 162 miles in 4 hours.

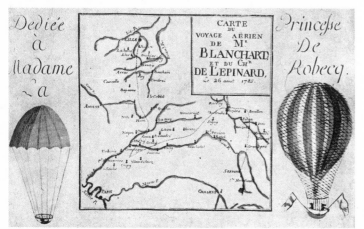

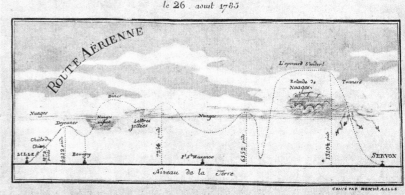

THE EXTENSIVE FLIGHT MADE BY BLANCHARD AND THE CHEVALIER DE L'EPINARD
Lille, 26 August 1785

M. Blanchard had completed the filling of the balloon at 9.45 am and he then applied himself to the various preparations for the departure and the testing of his parachute. At 10.45 am he entered the car with the Chevalier de l'Epinard, at which juncture the people who were assembled on the esplanade — the point of departure — cheered and applauded heartily. At 10.55 am the ropes were cut and the balloon rose majestically into the sky. The aeronauts waved to the onlookers with their flags on which the arms of the town were painted. The balloon travelled southwards as it ascended, the wind being north-westerly. After four minutes the balloon was seen to sink a few fathoms and rise as quickly. At this point M. Blanchard released the parachute, to which a dog was fastened, which seemed to fall very slowly; the animal came down three quarters of a league from the town, quite unharmed. The balloon was in sight for three quarters of an hour, always travelling southward, in which direction, not far away, lay Paris. There is no need to describe the feelings of the public at the moment when the balloon lifted off; they differed in no way from those of all men of sensibility.

M. Blanchard and the Chevalier de l'Epinard came down at 6 pm in the evening of 26 August at Senon in the region of Clermont. The next day they repaired to Sainte Menehould. The Municipal Officers, who had been informed of their impending arrival by a letter from the two aeronauts, welcomed them at the gates of the town, accompanied by the Knights of the Arquebus in full armour. They presented the honorary draught of wine to the two gentlemen and invited them to go down to the Town Hall where food and drink were awaiting them. They were led through a throng of cheering citizens to the Hall where they dined.

The Magistrates of Lille felicitated MM. Blanchard and l'Epinard on their aerial voyage when they went down into the town; a record of the event was entered in the registers. M. Blanchard had been granted the sum of 1200 pounds French on his departure; they issued an order that he be granted a similar sum for his return, unless he prefer a box of gold decorated with the insignia of the town, of the same value and with a suitable inscription. As for the Chevalier de l'Epinard, the Magistrates reserved the right to offer him a gift.

On 31 August 1785, five days after their ascent, Blanchard and the Chevalier de l'Epinard made a triumphal entry into Lille.

CES PHYSICIENS
MERVEILLEUX...

This caricature of the "amazing physicists" shows the saucy "physicienne" meeting the dandyfied "physicien" face to face, both clothed in balloon-shaped garments. The positions given to these shapely aids to dress underlines the satirical intent, for what lady would dress herself so, and what gentlemen could fail to realise the ridiculous impression he gave. Many of the prints of this period treated this theme in a similar way.

Journal de Paris:

THE AEROSTATIC GRAPE-PICKER

Lord Lhomond has built a figure thirteen feet high in gold-beater's skin, which he calls the Great Aerostatic Grape-picker, and which has on its head a balloon in the shape of a tub or a barrel; he intends to send it up permanently into the sky having first filled it with inflammable air. This figure is at present on show in the former concert hall of the Tuileries, where tickets are being sold for the day of departure at an average price of 24 francs; bearers of these tickets will be permitted to view the figure from this day onwards.

We shall give notice of the place and date of this event when they are available...

The test of Lord Lhomond's great Aerostatic Grape-picker took place yesterday in the Tuileries at the specified hour. The departure of this sort of mannequin was preceded by the explosion of a sphere containing inflammable air and dephlogisticated air. The physicist's intention was that the sphere should explode at a great height; but he was deceived in his intent. Soon afterwards we saw the great Grape-picker float through the window of the old concert hall into the open air. The different attitudes which he seemed to assume as he rose, his rocking motions, were somewhat picturesque; he had soon attained some considerable height, but he remained there for only a few minutes: driven before a fierce northerly wind, he ended his journey in the countryside around Grenelle.

◁ *The balloon fashion also swept Spain. In 1784, a Spanish engraver humourously imagined an aerial bullfight. The bull and the picador confront one another hanging from captive balloons.*

Toy balloons, made from gold-beaters skins, ▷ were then popular. In 1785, Lhomond and Roger sent up from the Tuileries "the great aerial grape-picker", more than 15 ft high, which created a sensation in town and country.

The interest in balloons even showed itself in the games of the times. The "New Aerial Balloon Game for Elevated Minds" was a typical example. At each throw of the dice, the player landed on a space that depicted a ballooning event of 1783 or 1784.

◁ Balloons soon found their way into the house. They were used as decorations on vases, on fans, and on calendars. "The Aerostatic Almanack" for 1785 shown here gave a retrospective list of all the most interesting ascents made up to its issue. In the centre, the Robert brothers and Colin-Hullin are depicted rising from the Tuileries gardens on 19 September 1784. Marshal Richelieu and Marshal Biron, the Bailli de Suffren and the Duke of Chaulnes are shown holding the four ropes of the balloon.

After his abortive attempt to steer his balloon, Blanchard became the target of numerous satirical quatrains. Ironic play was made on his motto "Sic itur ad astra" (It is thus one reaches the stars), and the French sang:

> From the Champ-de-Mars he flew
> Into the next field he fell
> Plenty of money he gained
> Sirs—sic itur ad astra.

Affronted, the aeronaut took ship for England. Unfortunately, his experiences there were no happier, as is shown by this English engraving. Shaped like a fool's head, the montgolfière depicted here referred to an ascent made on 30 November 1784 from London. Blanchard and Jeffries tried to control their balloon with oars, without any effect. Alexander Pope's verses, printed in the engraving, cruelly underline the ridiculous aspect of the proceedings.

Free balloons were at the mercy of the winds, and it was this that ▷ Blanchard and Guyton de Morveau struggled to overcome. However, the author of this "Almanack of Laughter" for 1785 put forward a simple solution to their problem. His "Infallible Method for Controlling Balloons" was simply to draw them along with animals like a post-chaise, complete with horn-blowing guard.

vers 1786.

MOYEN INFAILLIBLE DE DIRIGER LES BALLONS.

Air : Pierrot fur le bord
d'un ruiffeau.

L'art de voler affurément,
N'eft point un art comme on croit, fi futile:
Mais il faudroit préfentement
Se diriger adroitement.
Pour que la chofe foit facile,
Attellez-moi deux courfiers en avant.
Voilà, Meffieurs, & voilà juftement
Comme on fe rend maître du vent.

PROPHÉTIES.

Suivant des obfervations aftronomiques très-exactes, un jeune Phyficien profitera inceffamment de l'invention des Ballons pour enlever une jeune étrangere ; heureufement que le pere averti partira fur le champ dans un autre ballon : alors il y aura un combat fanglant. La fuite des obfervations nous inftruira fans doute du réfultat de cet événement. Ce qu'il y a de certain, c'eft que l'aftronome affure que le jeune homme eft en route pour cela ; & il eft bien fâcheux qu'il ne puiffe pas indiquer le lieu où l'enlévement fe fera, parce qu'au moins toute la Phyfique fe tiendroit fur fes gardes.

JUILLET		AOUST		SEPTEMBRE		OCTOBRE		NOVEMBRE		DECEMBRE	
V	1 Martial	L	1 Pier. es Li.	J	1 Lou. Gille	D	1 Remi	M	1 Touffaint	V	1 Eloi
S	2 Vifit. N. D.	M	2 Etienne P.	V	2 Lazare	L	2 Ange G.	J	2 Morts	S	2 Françoife
D	3 Anatole	M	3 Inv. S. Et.	S	3 Gregoire	M	3 Denis Ar.	V	3 Marcel	D	3 Fulgence
L	4 Tr. S. Mart.	J	4 Dominiq.	D	4 Rofalie	M	4 François	S	4 Charle	L	4 Barbe
M	5 Zoe	V	5 Yon	L	5 Victorin	J	5 Aure	D	5 Bertile	M	5 Sabas
M	6 Goar	S	6 Tranf. N. S.	M	6 Oneffipre	V	6 Brune	L	6 Leonard	M	6 Nicolas
J	7 Aubierge	D	7 Gaetan	M	7 Clsud	S	7 Serge	M	7 Achille	J	7 Ewo
V	8 Elizabeth	L	8 Juftin	J	8 Nativité	D	8 Brigitte	M	8 Reliques	V	8 Concept.
S	9 Cyrille	M	9 Spire	V	9 omer	L	9 Denis	J	9 Maturin	S	9 Leocade
D	10 S. Frene	M	10 Laurent	S	10 Nicolas T.	M	10 Tefchule	V	10 Leon	D	10 Valere
L	11 Tr. S. Ben.	J	11 S. C. AE.	D	11 Patient	M	11 Pion	S	11 Martin	L	11 Valery
M	12 Jean Ab.	V	12 Claire	L	12 Sordet	J	12 Gerard	D	12 Rene	M	12 Damafe
M	13 Turifi	S	13 Hippolite	M	13 Maurille	V	13 Edouard	L	13 Brice	M	13 Luce
J	14 Bonavent	D	14 Eu. S. Crif	M	14 Ex. S. Croi	S	14 Calfte	M	14 Laurent	J	14 Mefmin
V	15 Henri	L	15 Affomption	J	15 Nicomed.	D	15 Terefe	M	15 Machu	V	15 Jeffe
S	16 Euftat.	M	16 Roch	V	16 Cyprien	L	16 Bertrand	J	16 Eline	S	16 Tavare
D	17 Sperat	M	17 Mamas	S	17 Lambert	M	17 Corbenay	V	17 Agnant	D	17 Gation
L	18 Clair	J	18 Helene	D	18 Jean Chr.	M	18 Luc Ev.	S	18 Odon	L	18 Gemband
M	19 Vinc. de P.	V	19 Louis Ev.	L	19 Eupheme	J	19 Saumien	D	19 Elizabeth	M	19 Timoleon
M	20 Jean Ab.	S	20 Bernard	M	20 Euftache	V	20 Cyprii	L	20 Edmont	M	20 Thomas
J	21 Victor	D	21 Privat	M	21 Mathieu	S	21 Ffoule	M	21 Prif. N. D.	J	21 Honorat
V	22 Ma. Elain	L	22 Simphor	J	22 Maurice	D	22 Melon	M	22 Cecile	V	22 Victoire
S	23 Apolin	M	23 Brien	V	23 Thecle	L	23 Hilarion	J	23 Clement	S	23 Vic. con.
D	24 Chriftine	M	24 Barthel	S	24 Andoche	M	24 Maslore	V	24 Severin	D	24 Noel
L	25 Jacq. Chr.	J	25 S. Louis	D	25 Firmin	M	25 Crep. Cr.	S	25 Catherine	L	25 Etienne
M	26 Anne	V	26 Zephirin	L	26 Juftine	J	26 Celine	D	26 Gen. Ar.	M	26 Jean Ev.
M	27 Pantalon	S	27 Cesaire	M	27 Como e D.	V	27 Fromen	L	27 Avant	M	27 Innocent
J	28 Anne	D	28 Auguftin	M	28 Ceran	S	28 Sim. S. Ju.	M	28 Maxime	J	28 Thom. C.
V	29 Marthe	L	29 Mederie	J	29 Michel	D	29 Narciffe	M	29 Saturnin	V	29 Roger
S	30 Ours	M	30 Fiacre	V	30 Jerome	L	30 Lucain V. S.	M	30 Andre	S	30 Silveftre
D	31 Germain	M	31 Ovide			M	31 Quentin			D	31

Air : Pierrot fur le bord
d'un ruiffeau.

Tels que les Dieux de l'Opéra,
Fendez les airs, volez par méchanique,
Le Ciel, l'enfer, & cætera,
Tout y va bien moyennant ça.
Car fans elle, Danfe & Mufique,
Avec l'Auteur tomberoient fort fouvent.
Voilà, Meffieurs, & voilà juftement
Comme on fe rend maître du vent.

Suite des Prophéties.

Il y aura cette année un déluge épouvantable de farcafmes & de critiques : Thalie fur-tout fera déchirée à belles dents, fi elle s'avife de traiter, encore en enfant gâté la famille de Figaro ; & l'ami, qui a introduit chez elle cet intriguant, aura beau s'en moquer, on lui fera rendre gorge pour indemnifer tant de beaux-efprits qu'il a fait fécher fur pieds à attendre leur tour.

Mandement d'un Docteur à un Chirurgien pour l'emploi de chaque femaine.

Le Lundi, je vifiterai ; le Mardi, vous feignerez ; le Mercredi, je reviendrai ; le Jeudi, vous purgerez ; le Vendredi, il déclinera ; le Samedi, il teftera ; & Dimanche, on l'enterrera.

B. The cock is a symbol of vigilance, it is also the highest point of the aerostat; and observer placed on a level with the cock's eye can watch over all that takes place in the upper half of the balloon; he also tells the hour.

. Weather-cock or streamer for ascertaining the direction of the balloon's course when necessary.

The watchmen's quarters.

Needle which indicates the expansion and the condensation of the gas in the sphere.

. The observatory where compasses, astronomical instruments and quadrants for establishing the latitude are housed.

G. Hall reserved for recreation, walking and gymnastics.

K. Lecture hall for scientific conferences.

L. The chemistry laboratory.

M. The valve.

N. Sail which shows the aeronauts when they descend or rise.

O. Silken ladders providing ease of communication between all points of the sphere.

P. Small ship, equipped with sails and tackle, capable of floating on the water, so that, should the balloon be in a state of decay, the travellers would have the means to separate themselves from the balloon and return by sea.

Q. Large store to keep water, wine and all nutritive substances for the expedition.

R. Quarters for a few interested ladies; this part is set at a distance from the body of the construction, lest the learned travellers be distracted in their observations.

S. The kitchen; it has no chimney and is placed as far away as possible from the balloon.

U. Room for musical activities, organ etc.

X. Workshop for carpentry, iron work, machine work and laundry.

Y. Study, for physics and modern studies.

Z. Small balloon to be filled while suspended; it can be thought of as the tender to the balloon and is meant to be its subsidiary. When it is empty the gas can be replaced through the top.

Each aeronaut will be obliged to carry a parachute on his person throughout the journey.

Stoupy Bijou put forward seriously a project entitled "The Real Aerial Navigator". His machine flew by means of 5 balloons fastened along a mast 60 ft high. Tubes led from them to the nacelle, and served to "circulate the gas as may be desired by the navigator". In order to control this monster, the inventor fixed to it a gigantic moveable triangular rudder, of which the upper part was to be "a blade to cleave the air". Two 12 ft oars and two polygonal vanes controlled the rise and fall of the machine. Bijou showed more imagination than knowledge of physics in his invention, although he stated that construction would be begun as soon as finance was forthcoming.

In 1803, a Flemish physicist, Etienne G. Robertson, produced a splendid, if impractical, design. His "Minerva" was an "aerial ship, designed for exploration, and offered to all the Aacademies of Europe". Here is the description of it that he himself wrote :

Robertson's fantastic Minerva

A. Balloon, 150 feet in diameter, fashioned of raw silk produced especially for this use in Lyons, coated on the inside and outside with rubber.

In 1794, when France was at war with most of Europe, the Committee of Public Safety created a commission composed of Monge, Berthollet, Carnot, Poucroy and Guyton de Morveau. They were to find means of utilising the latest scientific discoveries to aid the war effort. Guyton de Morveau put forward a plan for constructing captive balloons as observation posts for the armies. The physicist Jean-Marie-Joseph Coutelle undertook the first trials at Meudon, the future home of the Ecole Nationale Aéronautique. His balloon, "L'Entreprenant", was attached to the Armée du Nord (Sambre et Meuse). The first true military ascent took place from Maubeuge, then besieged by the Austrians. It had a most demoralising effect on the besiegers. On 23 June, the balloon was taken secretly to Charleroi. Coutelle took notes of all the Austrian positions revealed to him from the balloon, and they capitulated next day. The battle of Fleurus (above) was fought on 26 June. During the whole duration of the battle—9 hours—Coutelle and Morlot constantly kept the French General Staff informed as to the enemy's movements, this information contributing to the eventual victory.

THE DESCENT ON ENGLAND

On 18 October 1797, the Treaty of Campo Formio put a temporary end to the war between France and Austria. Bonaparte, made Commander-in-Chief of the Armée d'Angleterre, contemplated an invasion of the British Isles. The British, however, were masters of the seas and barred the Channel to him. Some rather unrealistic inventors submitted many ideas to Bonaparte for aerial invasions. On 3 December 1797 "L'Etoile de Bruxelles" announced that "a numerous army was preparing to cross the sea and force the Cabinet in London to see reason . . . a mobile camp is being constructed, with a vast mongolfière to lift it and an army (100,000 men) and transport them across to England to effect the conquest". This project only existed on paper; in fact, it remained a manoeuvre to intimidate that had no effect. Still, however, the imaginations of the inventors continued to seeth. In 1805, Napoleon assembled 180,000 men at Boulogne, Brest and in Holland, and the construction of artificial harbours and invasion barges all along the coast gave the impression of imminent invasion. It was then that an Advocate, Thilorier, produced his "Thilorière" idea (left). This montgolfière, theoretically, was to cross the Channel by night, an enormous oil-lamp hanging beneath the platform keeping the air hot in flight. The author of the engraving below went even further, projecting a triple invasion by sea, by air, and underground. While an armada of small craft and balloons distracted the English, another army hacked a tunnel under the Channel. The battle of Trafalgar was to put an end to these impractical follies.

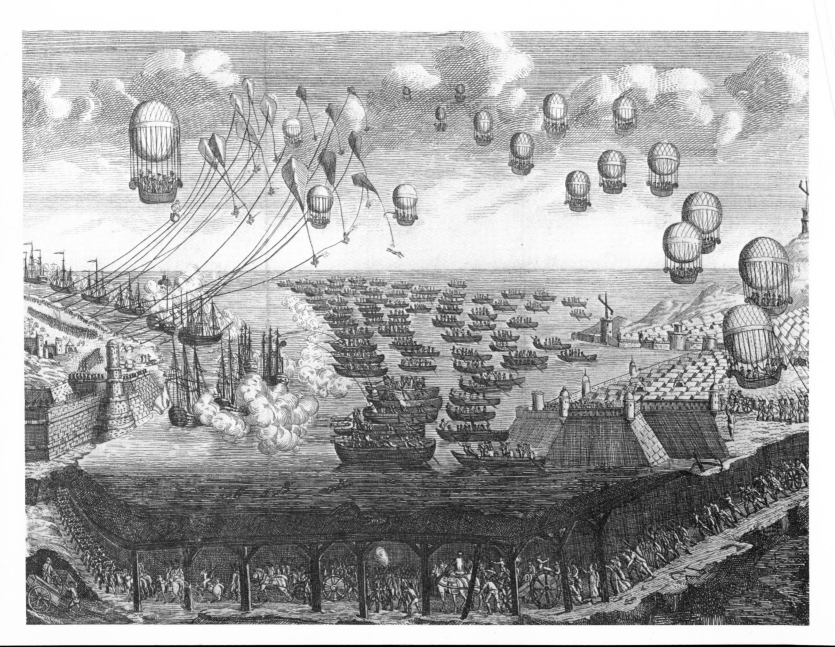

Folgen von der Erfindung der Luftmaschin
La Suite de la envention de la Machine
Aerostatique.

This German caricature, made by Johann Martin Will, gave a preview of another military use for balloons. By placing batteries of guns aboard huge balloons, it would, thought the author, be possible to mow down an enemy from the skies. The results of such a bombardment can be easily imagined, especially if it is remembered that troops were then drawn up in dense ranks. Happily, guns were far too heavy for the limited lifting forces then available, and it was left for the twentieth century to make Will's dream a reality.

The author of the caricature (left) prudently placed his "aerial battle between two vessels" towards the end of the nineteenth century. Of course, his idea was impossible to realise in this shape, but it does not lack an analogy with certain aspects of warfare today. His "aerostatic ships" were armed with 100 guns and manned by 1,000 soldiers. The author foresaw different types of flying machines, such as the "Dinghy, or polygonal balloon with rudder, oars, sails and other devices for large crews", shown on the right in the engraving. He thought, too, that if one of his aerial vessels lost gas, it would be able to drop into the water and continue the fight as an ordinary sailing vessel.

A HALF CENTURY OF FREE BALLOONS

1786-1845

24 August 1786	Abortive attempt at an ascent by Baron Lütgendorf at Augsburg.
5 May 1788	Ascent of Blanchard from Basle in Switzerland.
27 September 1788	Ascent of Blanchard from Berlin before Frederick the Great.
9 January 1793	Blanchard's ascent in Philadelphia before George Washington.
26 June 1794	Captain Coutelle, a French officer, ascended in the captive balloon "L'Entreprenant" to observe the battle of Fleurus, and transmitted many observations to the General Staff.
31 October 1794	The French Committee of Public Safety created the Ecole Nationale Aéronautique at Meudon by the decree of 10 Brumaire, Year III.
15 October 1798	Pierre Testu-Brissy made a remarkable ascent on horseback from Meudon.
4 October 1803	Francesco Zambeccari, Andreoli and Grassetti were nearly drowned when their "Aéromontgolfière" came down in the Adriatic. They were rescued at the last moment by fishermen.
22 August 1804	Zambeccari repeated his exploit of 1803. His balloon caught fire and he later fell into the sea. He was badly hurt.
3 December 1804	Five unmanned balloons were released from Paris on the occasion of the coronation of Napoleon. The balloon sent up by Jacques Garnerin was recovered near Rome.
4 June 1810	Mme Blanchard ascended from the Champ-de-Mars, Paris, before Napoleon and Marie-Louise in honour of their marriage.
21 September 1812	Zambeccari was killed at Bologna when his ballon caught fire.
4 May 1814	Mme Blanchard, in a balloon decorated with fleurs de lys, greeted the return of the Bourbons to Paris.
15 July 1814	Ascent of James Sadler and his son from the Burlington Gardens, London. When they attained an altitude of 5 miles, the aeronauts suffered violent headaches.
6 July 1819	Death of Mme Blanchard after her balloon caught fire.
1 October 1820	The ascent of Wilhelmine Reichardt during the Oktoberfest in Munich.
7 November 1836	Charles Green left London on board the "Royal Vauxhall", crossed the Channel, and landed not far from Nassau in Holland, having made a record flight of 373 miles in 18 hours.
24 July 1837	Robert Cocking made a parachute jump from the "Nassau" balloon, piloted by Charles Green, and fell to his death.
16 July 1843	A montgolfière escaped unmanned from Nantes. Its grapnel caught a youth named Guérin and dragged him up in the air.

This very attractive engraving made at Augsbourg conceals a failure : the Baron Lütgendorf was lucky to find an artist to save his self-respect, for his ascent, announced for 24 August 1786, had to be abandoned due to contrary winds, rain and the poor quality of the gas used. The spectators, present in force, went away disappointed.

THE INTERNATIONAL
EXPLOITS OF
JEAN-PIERRE BLANCHARD

During his travels, Jean-Pierre Blanchard (1753-1809) introduced aerostatics into many of the countries of Europe.

Blanchard's ascent of 5 May 1788 from Basle was much more dangerous than is shown by the engraving. The balloon was not sufficiently inflated, and Blanchard, in order not to break his promise, removed the car from its attachments and rose held only by four cords. Badly hurt by his landing, he was forced to spend fifteen days in bed.

Extract from: Wochentliche Nachrichten aus dem Bericht-Haus zu Basel: 8 May 1788

(Weekly report from the news-agency in Basle)

None of those who did not fully appreciate the dangerous situation in which M. Blanchard found himself will stop to ask themselves whether his courageous and energetic attitude which so gratified the honoured public, did not merit admiration. But those who were thrilled by the ascent and who at the time expressed the wholehearted wish to add a supplement to the amount they had already donated, will by this gesture reply to the question of whether this courage is amply rewarded by M. Blanchard's method of recompense. If these admirers and benefactors are still firm in their desire, they will find in the building of this company a small sealed box into which each person may put a supplementary donation. This will be delivered to M. Blanchard, who clearly will have deserved it.

Some friends have had the box brought along; their integrity may be relied upon; they will deposit it and its contents with the authorities. If sealed letters or small parcels are brought, they also will be delivered safely and faithfully to M. Blanchard. The honoured public will be happy to learn that M. Blanchard knows nothing of these additional gifts; when he receives them, his joy and gratitude will be all the greater.

On 27 September 1788, Blanchard made his 33rd ascent, rising from the military exercise ground of the Tiergarten in Berlin. He dropped a dog on a parachute.

Berlin, 27 September 1788

BLANCHARD'S ACCOUNT

After placing my instruments in the car, and calculating the lifting power of the balloon, I made my bow to the King and Queen, and saluted the numerous assembly. I then calculated the point when equilibrium would be upset, and threw out the necessary ballast, leaving the ground at 3.10 p.m. The wind, which was West-South-West, was violent and it was necessary to have a substantial lifting-force in order not to be forced down...

Soon all the objects on the ground shrank before my eyes, the large and splendid town of Berlin appeared to me to be like a model, while the ground seemed to me to be a greyish map. I noticed particularly a swirling cloud of dust set up by the infinite number of carriages and horses which dashed after the balloon, this nearly reaching to the clouds themselves. I had completely forgotten my balloon in studying the immense panorama that my eyes em-

73

braced. The sky, which was clear at my departure, was covered with dense clouds to the horizon...

Keeping then at an altitude of 160 feet, I scudded along at great speed; I wished to slow down and regain the ground, and to do this, I tried to open the valve, but the cord broke away from the upper part and fell into my hand.

Now my balloon, like a maddened horse, becoming uncontrollable, redoubled its speed, and carried me towards a nearby forest, so I attached a sharp tool to my flag pole, to cut open the middle of the balloon; it was the only way left for me to land. I was just about to tear the envelope when I saw the ground covered with horsemen who arrived from every direction. They found it difficult to approach me, for their horses, filled with terror at the sight of my enormous machine, backed away in fear. In the end, many of the riders forced the horses forward, and were able to seize the anchor cable, and, combining their strength, pulled me down to earth in spite of the wind.

SIC ITUR AD ASTRA..

45.ᵗʰ Ascension and the first made in America January 9.ᵗʰ 1793. at Philadelphia 39°56′ N. Latitude by M.ʳ J. P. Blanchard.

45.ᵉ ascension et la premiere faite en Amerique le 9 Janvier 1793 a Philadelphie 39° 56′ Latitude N. par M.ʳ J.P. Blanchard.

Philadelphia, 9 January 1793

At 9 minutes after 10, the sky being clear, serene and propitious, little wind and nearly calm at the surface of the earth... The moment of my departure was announced by the last discharge of the artillery; I then ascended my car, studied the proportions of aerial gravities, and threw out as much of my ballast as appeared necessary to leave the aerostat at liberty, and to render my ascent certain. I soon found myself possessed of every requisite; I felt myself balanced at 15 inches from the ground. This was all I wished for; I requested Messieurs Nassy and Legaux, who held the aerostat, to let it loose...

At 10 h. 36-37-38 m. I found that I was in a state of perfect equilibrium in the midst of a stagnant fluid; I made haste to avail myself of this happy circumstance, in order to execute the commissions I had charged myself with.

1 st. I began with emptying the six bottles which Doctor Wistar had put into my car, containing divers liquors; they were all filled with that atmospherical air wherein I was floating, and were stopped up hermetically, as the accuracy of the experiment required.

2 dly. I passed on to the observation which Doctor Ruth had requested me to make upon the pulsation of the artery, when I should be arrived at my greatest height. I found it impossible to make use of the quarter-minute glass which he had provided for that purpose, but I supplied its place by an excellent second-watch; and the result of my observations gave me 92 pulsations in the minute (the average of 4 observations made at the place of my highest elevation) whereas on the ground I had experienced no more than 84 in the same given time, average of 4 observations: difference 8 pulsations more at the height of 5812 English feet, where I then was.

3 dly. I had been requested by Doctor Glentworth to make experiments in the ethereal regions with a load-stone, which he had lent me: on the ground it raised 5½ ounces averdupois; but at the aforesaid height it would hardly bear 4 ounces.

4 thly. The lowest state of the mercury in the barometer after having brought its surface in its lower reservoir to its proper level and corrected its dilatation, was 69 lines 9/16 French measure, or 74 lines 3/16 English measure, which according to Mariot, Boyle, Deluc and Father Côte gives an elevation of 905 toises 1 foot and 6 inches (the toise at 6 feet) or 5431 feet 6 inches French measure, and at the usual reduction 963 fathoms 4 feet, or 5812 feet English measure. This was the highest elevation of my balloon, without having thrown out any of my ballast, except the liquor contained in the 6 bottles given to me by Doctor Wistar...

These may certify, that we the subscribers saw the bearer, Mr. Blanchard, settle in his balloon in Deptford township, country of Gloucester, in the state of New-Jersey, about fifteen miles from Philadelphia, about 10 o'clock 56 minutes, A. M. Witness our hands the ninth day of January, Anno Domini, 1793.

Everald Bolton,
Joseph Griffith,
Joseph Cheesman,
Samuel Toggart,
Amos Castell,
Zara North.

On the approach of the French Revolution, Blanchard set sail for the United States. He made an ascent from Philadelphia on January 1793 in the presence of George Washington.

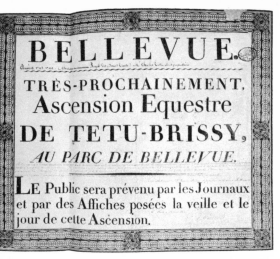

BELLEVUE.
TRÈS-PROCHAINEMENT,
Ascension Equestre
DE TETU-BRISSY,
AU PARC DE BELLEVUE.
LE Public sera prévenu par les Journaux
et par des Affiches posées la veille et le
jour de cette Ascension.

A poster for Testu-Brissy's ascent.

Citizen Testu-Brissy's amazing ascent

At Bellevue yesterday, citizen Testu-Brissy at last effected his equestrian ascent which had been so long delayed. He did not have an unqualified success and moreover he ran many risks. Since the balloon had not been filled to a sufficient extent it was unable to clear the right-hand wing of the castle; it was thrown against a chimney-stack which tore a large hole in the envelope and consequently gas began to escape. The aeronaut, calm and undaunted, threw out a rope by the aid of which he was brought safely to ground. During these dangerous moments in the manœuvres the horse did not move. Citizen Brissy, having repaired the rent, wished to go up once more, but the public were not in favour of this plan. Whatever the result of the experiment, citizen Testu proved nonetheless that those who had thrown doubts on his courage were mistaken.

A very interesting report by a lofty patriot

To the glory of the French nation, in the name and under the auspices of the municipality of Paris, on the second day of the third month of the third year of liberty and the Age of the Common Man, 18 September 1791, the day of the proclamation of the Constitution, at 5.45 in the afternoon.

Having suffered all the agonies of a man who is eager and more than willing to satisfy those waiting for a happy and successful event, my balloon measuring 30 feet in diameter, being three-quarters full, depicting, on 4 medallions Liberty, Love of the Fatherland, France and the Law.

My car, in the shape of a cock, eleven feet long by three feet wide by three feet high, carried me up, together with about 220 pounds of ballast, an anchor, a compass, a host of copies of the Constitution, a piece of bread, a bottle of wine, two legs of poultry; my lifting power was about 60 pounds, while the wind was in the west.

I then floated over the end of the Champs-Elysées, in the centre of a storm, to the admiration of all Paris. Then, bare-headed, with the Constitution in my hand, I passed straight over the Champs-Elysées, the Tuileries, Le Louvre, and the street and district of St Antoine. An immense crowd accompanied me with their cheers.

Extract from the Journal des Débats, 3 August 1800

Paris 16 Thermidor. Throughout this season there has not been a more populous and more brilliant meeting than that which took place yesterday at the Tivoli Gardens. Seven or eight thousand people attended to see the ascent of the *Temple of Olympus* and its *Fifteen Great Gods*. The ascent was majestic and the one regret was that it was too late in the day for the spectators to be able to follow closely the progress of this enormous balloon. A young lady in her eighteenth year and the citizen Garnerin took up this aerial vehicle, which came down much more quickly than was expected. Garnerin attempted to reach the Luxembourg Gardens but he could not stay aloft beyond the Rue de Tournon which, happily enough for himself and his companions, was wide enough to accommodate the Montgolfière with its vast circumference, and from which sparks were continually falling in great quantities. Had it chanced to fall into a narrower street, the balloon would have, of necessity, come down upon the houses, and leaving aside the danger of a general conflagration, the voyagers would themselves have run the greatest risk of either falling, or of fire engulfing the balloon. Two police officers and some firemen ran up the Rue de Tournon at the moment of the Montgolfière's descent. The young lady seemed to have remained calm in the midst of the danger which had threatened the travellers...

In October 1798, all Paris could talk of nothing but the extraordinary "equestrian ascent" of Testu-Brissy at Bellevue. The aeronaut performed this rash exploit mounted on a horse, which stood on a rectangular platform suspended from the balloon.

This engraving by Francesco Piranesi, son of the famous architect, depicts a fête given on the occasion of the peace arranged between the French and the Germans in 1803. General Berthier, then Minister of War, organised the festivities held in the Ministry garden. Garnerin (above) the official Government aeronaut, conceived an aerial spectacle that aroused the admiration of the guests — the illuminated car of his balloon was lit up and carried the words "A LA PAIX".

77

Neither the French Revolutionary Government, nor Napoleon, showed very great interest in balloons. After the utilisation of balloons in the campaign of 1794 and the Egyptian theatre in 1798, Napoleon had the École Nationale Aéronautique closed. Ballooning was relegated to public entertainment. Jacques Garnerin, who became "balloonist to public festivals" was responsible for most of the ascents of the time. The montgolfière which was sent up from the Tivoli gardens on 3 August 1800 (above) was probably carrying Garnerin.

THE ADVENTURES
& MISADVENTURES
OF FRANCESCO ZAMBECCARI

On 4 October 1804, Zambeccari's balloon came down in the Adriatic. Although partly deflated, the material of the envelope acted as a sail, and propelled itself through the water at a dizzy speed. The three passengers, half submerged, were finally rescued by fishermen.

The Police report of Zambeccari's ascent

Bologna, 4 October 1803

The announcement of an experiment in public of aerial flying by citizen Francesco Zambeccari of Bologna drew into this town a considerable crowd of followers; the date had been fixed for 4 September but the facts put before you in my other report prevented any attempt at a flight and greatly disappointed the assembled company.

Zambeccari, faithful to his engagement, promised another attempt on 5 September, but the weather was not favourable

for his plan and it was necessary to postpone it yet again despite the complaints which increased during the course of the morning of 7 September and which were made all the stronger by the promise of a favourable day that a calm atmosphere seemed to give.

It was necessary to cut the delay by half; we therefore found it expedient to encourage the aeronaut to satisfy the public which was all the more worthy of respect in that it included numerous foreigners whom any delay might discourage from staying. According to Zambecarri ..., although the request was made on 4 September, the day was already far advanced and ... at one o'clock in the afternoon he commenced the chemical preparations with his fellow workers.

The extraordinary capacity of the machine combined with precautions which the chemical work necessitated, incurred preparations which took many hours and it was not until 8.30 pm that the necessary equilibrium was obtained.

The night was murky, despite torches which had been lit in various spots to illuminate the darkness; moreover, there were not enough torches to light fully the four thousand or so spectators who had been waiting for a long time and with unbelievable patience in an arena which had been built especially for this purpose on a promontary; more than twice this number were outside in the Place d'Armes and from this direction arose a unanimous appeal that the flight should be put back to the morning.

The aeronaut wished to comply with this desire, for he also wanted to put off his flight; indeed, it was not possible for him to carry out the observations and the experiments at night. He had promised to rise to fifty feet and to stay there until dawn.

Moreover, if the machine stayed in the air all night, there must needs be considerable loss of gas, especially since the first test had damaged the varnish. So, taking a stand on these facts, which were of no minor importance, he decided to increase the lifting power and this put back the estimated time of departure to 11.30 pm.

Having attained this desired end, Zambeccari, in the company of Grassetti,

Doctor of Physics, Giovanni (sic), Andreoli, both mathematicians, entered the car. The car rose to a height of forty feet and was held at this height by an anchor. Zambeccari tried three times to descend by the use of oars, and each attempt was crowned by success.

From the sky above, Zambeccari asked the spectators whether they would prefer that the flight be put off until the next morning or whether they should leave immediately. Since the spectators preferred to see the flight postponed, the aeronauts remained at anchor.

The inconstancy of the autumnal season was not slow in showing itself; the aeronauts, seeing that the wind was getting up, were obliged to take into account the dew which was falling and which was, of course, weighing down the machine to considerable degree. They decided that they could not stay attached to their anchor, and at 12.14 in the morning of 8 October, they weighed anchor to the delight and acclaim of the small number of spectators who had remained in their places. The aeronauts rose up; by throwing out a small amount of ballast, they miraculously avoided a sixty-foot high tree, towards which the wind was carrying them.

The light illuminating the voyagers made it possible to see that they were travelling in a north-westerly direction and not merely rising slowly, sometimes vertically and sometimes otherwise. After five minutes, clouds hid the sphere, which, during the ten minutes that followed, was seen four times by the attentive admirers; the last time it seemed that it could not be less than ten miles away.

We must not forget that during this interval the sphere had turned towards the west; we noted that, having lifted off, it had turned towards the north-west and had consequently travelled in a south-easterly direction; having then risen once more, it resumed its first direction and then disappeared from view.

If this report tends to eulogise citizen Zambeccari, may I say that as far as is possible, he gave proof of his unique discoveries: namely, that of wings and that of maintaining the equilibrium of the machine in any part of the atmosphere.

We also have cause to praise his companions, who, besides their great knowledge, have shown great perseverance; the chemists who busied themselves with similar tasks are no less worthy of praise.

Two basins, surrounded, one by sixteen and the other by seventeen tanks, one of which containing only iron filings, the others all containing zinc filings, formed the laboratory. Five of them were used again for the decomposition of the substance; they had not been able to use large enough tanks capable of holding a sufficient quantity for the production of all the indispensable gas.

There we could observe the ingenious new method of emptying the residue which remained in the small tanks by the means of eight cisterns, some of which were thirteen feet deep. Previous experiments had shown that this residue was altering the composition set forth below:

200 pounds of iron filings, 6,000 of zinc, 8,500 of sulphuric acid and a quantity of water five times greater, produced the hydrogen gas, that is to say a quantity approximating 14,000 cubic feet. Losses which must inevitably have occurred are not accounted for in this figure.

Here then, citizen Prefect, is the accurate report of all that preceded, accompanied and followed Zambeccari's ascent. Do not let us forget to note the admirable order and calm which reigned through all the parish and which was undisturbed throughout the ascent.

I am sure that you will be well pleased with the observations which I have felt it my duty to convey to you. I convey to you my deepest respects, and pledging my abiding consideration, remain

A. Mulazzani   Peregalli, Assessor

In conveying this report to the central authorities of Milan, the Prefect of the Department of the Rhine, Somenzari, wrote in his letter dated 9 October 1803: ... a commendation on the part of the Government would be gratefully received by the family and region which has produced this new celestial inhabitant. As for myself, I admire him and cannot refrain from commending him even to the Government; it would be fitting for the Government to be generous with its favours towards this gentleman.

DESCENT
INTO THE ADRIATIC

23 August 1804

We left Bologna yesterday, Wednesday the 22nd, at nine o'clock in the morning in an aerostatic machine which bore us, I think, into the neighbourhood of Mermorta, and there I decided to descend having carried out tests and shown that my method was perfectly efficient for travelling through the air; I thereby also proved that all the smaller parts can be used with success.

I therefore dropped anchor at about eleven o'clock in the morning. My anchor was attached to a rope about 42 fathoms long and was caught fast in a bush; but the shock which my car underwent when the rope became caught, resulted in the lamp, in which spirits of wine burned continually, tilting and spilling ignited spirits of wine on my clothes, on the fabric of the balloon and on the car ropes. Everything was ablaze; my companion Andreoli and myself sought to preserve our safety; for my part, I poured two or three measures of water on to my head from a flask, extinguishing the flames which were beginning to cause me pain. I looked for my companion who seemed to be no longer in the car; it occurred to me that, at its descent, the car could have hit the ground and that my companion might have chosen that moment to escape, or perhaps he had slid down the rope which was tied to the anchor. I prayed God he might not have fallen!

Because of my companion's departure, the lightened machine rose violently and the anchor tore through the bush and bore part of it into the air. The machine's ascent was rapid and it reached a height where the clouds seemed to be in a chasm below me. As in my experiment the previous year, 7 October 1803, I suffered great pain from the freezing conditions; my hands were frozen. Before long I saw the coast and soon came down in the neighbourhood of Porto di Magnavacca.

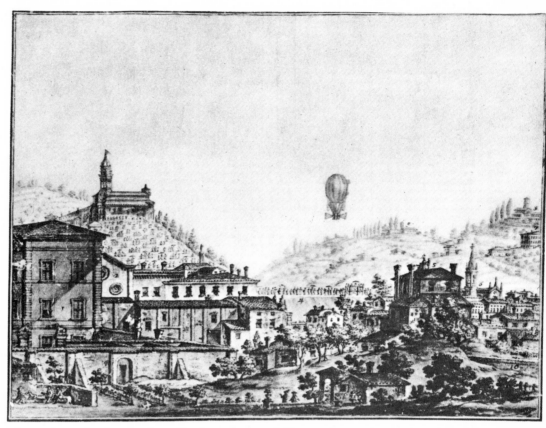

A year later, in August 1804, Zambeccari repeated his experiment. Rising from Bologna (above) in his "Aéromontgolfière", his balloon first caught fire, and later he was once again precipitated into the Adriatic.

I imagined that the wind had carried me towards the western seaboard because I saw the sail of a ship; I wanted to tie myself to the car so that I might rest during the night, which was falling rapidly. I gripped a silken rope which I recognised as that of the anchor; I took hold of it in my teeth for my hands were of no use to me in their present state, and I found that the rope was thwarting all my efforts to raise it and consequently I would be unable to make use of it in fastening myself to the car. I then, rightly, suspected that the hanging anchor had found a spot in the bed of the sea where it could take hold; I fear I was exceeding vexed for I had no sharp instrument with which to cut the rope; the idea occurred to me of breaking the glass of my spectacles; this I did and holding a fragment in my teeth, I sawed the rope with such effect that I succeeded in cut-

ting it. Then, my aerial vessel began to fly rapidly out to sea; I tried to row, sometimes with one arm, sometimes with the other and soon I saw boats in the distance. I believed that my machine had awoken the curiosity of some fishermen and that they were concerned for my safety, but it was not for many hours, three o'clock in the afternoon to be precise, that a fisherman, Giovanni Bovoli and his companion, Antonio Malta di Chiozza, steered towards me and saved me. When I had left the balloon it rose quickly to a height at which it was scarcely discernible with a naked eye and went on its way towards the East.

At the end of that day, 23 August, I found myself in Comacchio, at the house of the Superintendent of the Prefecture, a worthy gentleman, who brought me here where I am enjoying his incomparable hospitality.

THE CORONATION BALLOONS:

Extract from Le Moniteur of the 19th of Frimaire *

The inventiveness of Garnerin was again in demand for the Coronation of Napoleon. The watercolour (left) shows a model of one of the balloons conceived for the festivities. On 3 December 1804, at 11 pm, the great Coronation balloon ascended from the midst of fireworks, carrying an Imperial Crown up into the skies. The unmanned balloon was blown over Italy, and fell near Rome, after grazing the tomb of Nero and leaving a part of the crown on it. As a result of this rather ominous event, Garnerin fell into disfavour with the Emperor, and was replaced by Mᵐᵉ Blanchard.

Paris was en fête. For the Coronation celebrations, the Place de la Concorde was provided with four dance halls. At the moment when five wagons carrying musicians signalled the opening of the festivities, five balloons bearing allegorical devices were sent up into the Paris skies.

Paris, the 18th of Frimaire. Yesterday afternoon five balloons were sent up from the Place de la Concorde. Their departure was preceded by that of a small air balloon which rose with great speed and appeared in the sky as a shining point of light, coloured by all the rays of the sun. The largest of the five balloons, which was of a most majestic size, carried an eagle, the wings of which were outspread and which carried in its claws two large flags bearing the name of Napoleon, the Emperor. The five balloons rose up to a great height and burst into flames in a most spectacular manner; the eagle came down to earth, borne up by its wings and by the flags which it carried. The Place de la Concorde was covered by a vast crowd of onlookers.

* Frimaire—Third month of the Republican Calender (November-December)

As Napoleon's Coronation was celebrated with balloons, the Bourbon restoration had also to have its aerial festivities. On 4 May, Mme Blanchard saluted the return to Paris of Louis XVIII from a balloon decorated with fleurs de lys. The engraving above shows the King's second entry into Paris on 19 August. When the procession reached the Hôtel de Ville, the sky was filled with figures and animals sent up from the Ile Saint-Louis "in honour of the re-establishment of the Throne of the Bourbons".

83

Wilhelmine Reichardt's ascent, Munich, 1820

Mme Reichart rose into the air at sixteen minutes to four. She soon reached a considerable height; she could not have been less than 3,000 feet above the south of the town. At four o'clock she opened the valve to let some gas escape; the balloon immediately sank at least a thousand feet. The spectators no longer feared for the courageous woman, for, at this height, the balloon inflated itself well; so well, in fact, that one was quite prepared to think that it was going to bound upwards at any moment. Several times Mme Reichart threw some paper overboard. The balloon hardly wavered. At 4.4 pm she threw out some sand with the result that once more she rose to a great height ... Eventually, at 4.25 pm, she had decided to come down. The spectators could not but admire the expertise with which the brave woman controlled the height of her balloon, to avoid landing in the forest to the west of Perlach or of Strasstrudering. At 4.28 pm the balloon was shrouded by a cloud which was over Obersendling, at 4.30 pm the courageous woman came out of the clouds at a height which was not even three times that of the tower called "Frauenturm". At last the balloon began to come down more quickly and disappeared from the field of vision of the binoculars. It was behind the forest, in the Keferlohe district.

The beautiful Mrs L.A. Sage left London accompanied by Vincent Lunardi (standing, right) and George Biggins on 29 June 1785. She was the first English woman to fly in a balloon. After a 3 hrs flight, they landed in Middlesex.

This popular print (left) depicts an ascent made at Augsburg by Mme Bittorf. She was probably the wife of Bittorf, the aeronaut who, on 7 July 1812, died in a balloon near Mannheim.

In 1811, Wilhelmine Reichardt, a German, determinated to follow in the footsteps of Mme Blanchard. In 1820, at the Munich Oktoberfest, she made an ascent before a large crowd.

WOMEN AND BALLOONS

Madame Blanchard's accident

A deplorable occurrence changed the delightful festivities which took place on Tuesday evening in the Tivoli Gardens into a time of mourning; there, Mme Blanchard lost her life when she fell from her balloon, which had caught fire at a great height. Here are a few details of this terrible accident. At 9.30 in the evening the spectators assembled around the enclosure which fenced off the machine; although there was a slight wind, the weather was fine and augured a successful flight. At 10.15, Mme Blanchard got into the car, the fireworks were attached and a few minutes later the balloon left the ground: but since its load was apparently excessive, the machine could not rise and caught in the outer branches of the trees which bordered the enclo-

Elisa Garnerin, the niece of the aeronaut, and the first woman parachutist, is shown descending over the Champ-de-Mars on 25 August 1815. Jacques Garnerin's balloon is in the background. ▽

Blanchard's wife, Marie Madeleine Sophie, was killed on 6 July 1819, during her 67th ascent. The fireworks she carried set fire to her balloon, which crashed on to the Paris rooftops. ▷

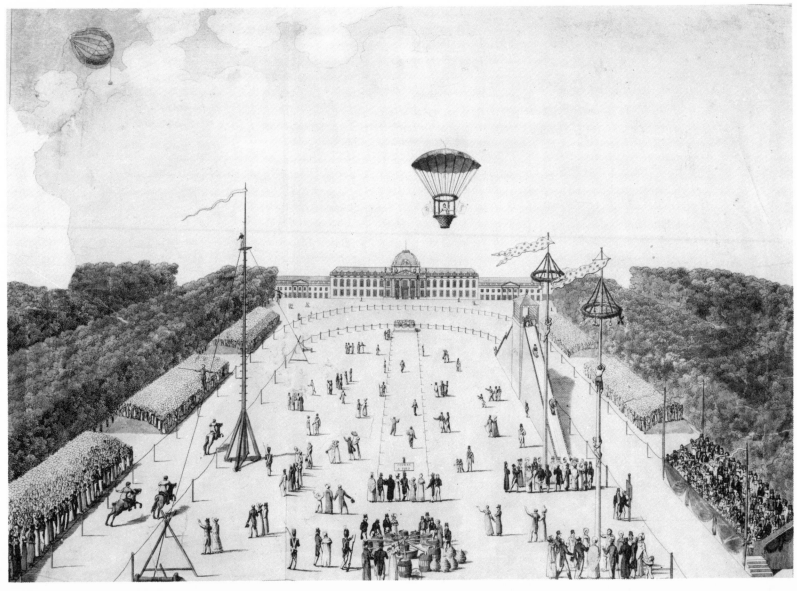

sure. Mme Blanchard jettisoned some ballast; relieved of this weight, the balloon continued on its way without anything untoward having occurred, other than that several small containers of spirits of wine were overturned. When the balloon had risen to a certain height, the fine effect of the fireworks could be fully appreciated, but something extraordinary also took place. Nevertheless, the bystanders, enchanted by the sight, paid no attention until the fire, which had spread to the body of the machine, threw down a vivid light and left no doubt as to the nature of the misfortune which had arisen. A spontaneous shout arose on all sides; some women felt unwell, and the terror which such a tragedy instils in the hearts of witnesses, soon spread throughout the assembly.

It was not long before we learned that the hapless aeronaut had fallen on to a house in the Rue de Provence, and had gone through the roof. Great haste was made to rush to her aid, but all succour was useless; she was without life; her body was found enmeshed in the remains of the ropes and of the car. She was examined by doctors when she had been carried back to the Tivoli Gardens; although her body was badly crushed, there was no disfiguration; the head was intact, as were the legs, so it seemed that the principle cause of death was asphyxiation.

Many suggestions have been put forward as to the cause of the fire on board the balloon. One cannot doubt that the personages chosen by Mme Blanchard, who presided over the ascent, did not do all that was possible to ensure a successful issue.

And, in fact, although the wind opposed the aeronaut's course to some slight degree, she was able, at a very great height, to light the fireworks beneath the balloon and the result was a perfect success. It was not until the fireworks were completely extinguished that we observed what was first seen as ignited vapour spread with amazing speed to the balloon; and then the fire caught a firm hold on the whole machine.

It has been suggested, and this seems quite probable, that the aeronaut wanted to descend in order to be in close proximity to the point of departure, and had not closed the appendix through which the gas had been introduced and through which it subsequently escaped; wishing to light another firework attached to a small parachute which she was meant to throw out of the balloon, the taper which she held ignited the escaping gas. Mme Blanchard was 45 years of age and leaves no children. This was her sixty-seventh ascent.

THE FIRST BRITISH AERONAUTS

JAMES SADLER'S ACCOUNT, 15 JULY 1814, BURLINGTON GARDENS

After the balloon had cleared the east wing of Burlington House, our ascent was slow, and only evidenced by the apparent receding of objects; for it was not we who seemed to rise, but every thing beneath us to retire; in a few minutes we were perpendicular with Leicester-square, and our prospect was at once grand and awful; the whole of London and its magnificent buildings lay below us, with its surrounding fields, canals, and parks; the beautiful serpentine form of the River, with its rich shipping, docks, and bridges. We enjoyed this scenery for about 15 minutes, and, at a quarter before four o'clock, entered a dense cloud, which completely shut us out from all sight of the earth; at this time we could sensibly perceive the balloon to be rising. When we had soared through this cloud, my son observed to me, that, from the variegated colours reflected and refracted from the multitudinous congregation of vapours around us, and the effulgence of different lights, he could scarcely see to any great distance, or make any distinct observations on the numberless forms around us; although, from the shadow of the balloon on the more opaque clouds, I could easily discover that we had already altered our course towards the south east. From the intense cold, and a most violent pain in my ears, which I never experienced before, our height could not be less, in my calculation, than five miles. The late Right Hon. W. Windham, about thirty years ago, indeed, experienced a similar attack in his ears, though we had not then ascended above two miles and a half; but, from my best observations, calculated upon former experience, we must have been about that height. My son soon after found the same effect, though in a much slighter degree.

THE AMAZING FLIGHT OF CHARLES GREEN

7 November 1836

Two months later, the same aeronaut, after the death of Cocking, accomplished the longest aerial voyage.

The balloon in which he travelled, with a capacity of 2,500 cubic metres, left London on 1 November 1836. With Mr Green were two other travellers: Messrs Holland and Monk-Mason; all three, not knowing where the wind would carry them, had supplied themselves with passports for all the States of Europe. At 1.30 pm, the balloon lifted off majestically, travelling in a south-easterly direction, and at 4 pm the travellers caught sight of the sea. The wind suddenly changed direction and bore them towards German waters. Since Mr Green thought it unwise to take that route, what with the night falling, he threw out some ballast. The balloon climbed until it met a current of wind which carried it over Dover; it was about to cross the Strait.

"It was twelve minutes to five," said one of the travellers, "when we saw the first line of waves break on the beach below us and we could say that we had in reality left the shores of our country to begin our journey over areas which had, so far, proved so formidable to the sea traveller. We could not but feel moved by the grandeur of the sight which met our eyes. Behind us was the English shoreline with its white cliffs half submerged in the dusk, shining with the sparkle of lights which increased at every moment, among which the Dover beacon was visible for a considerable length of time and served as a marker by which to judge our course. Below us on all sides we were confronted with the sight of the uninterrupted expanse of interlaced waves stretching into the shadows of night which were already covering the horizon, restricting our view. Before us, a barrier of thick cloud, like a fortress wall of which the battlements were topped in a strange fashion with parapets, towers, bastions, stretched up from the sea and seemed to be placed thus to obstruct our passage. It was only a few minutes before we were in the watery currents of cloud, surrounded by a gloom which deepened as the vapours around us grew thicker and the night began to fall. We could no longer hear a sound. The noise of waves breaking on the English strand had ceased and we were steadily being taken out of earshot of any sound from the land."

An hour later the Calais lighthouse was sighted by the voyagers.

"The darkness had fallen completely; it was only by the lights which shone beneath us, sometimes isolated, sometimes in clusters, that we could hope to gain any knowledge of the country over which we passed and form an idea of the towns and villages which continually came into view. The scene which followed defied description. The entire surface of the ground for several leagues around us, as far as the eye could see, showed naught but the scattered lights of people who were burning the candle late, and, spread out at our feet, an expanse which seemed to rival the lights of highest heaven. At every instant, during the first part of the night before men had gone to their beds, large patches of light, pointing to the existence of a sizeable population, came into view on the horizon, resembling fire in the distance. As we drew nearer, this confused mass of light seemed to increase in size and to spread itself over a wider area of land. When we came above this mass of lights, they seemed to divide themselves into different sections, and, stretching themselves into the form of roads or moving into the shapes of squares, they drew for us the plan of a town, diminished in proportion to the height from which we observed them at a given moment. It would be difficult to give an accurate idea of the effect which such a sight, in such circumstances, must have had on us. To find oneself carried into the shades of night, into the vast isolation of space, unknown and unseen, secretly and silently, travelling across kingdoms, exploring new territories, looking at towns which passed below us at such a speed and with such frequency that we could not examine them in detail, this is enough in itself to render sights which would not normally hold any interest sublime. If we add to this the uncertainty which governed this journey, an uncertainty which, increasing as we advanced through the night, covered everything with a veil of mystery and placed us in a position which was worse than that of complete ignorance, knowing not where we were, where we were going, what we were trying to discover, one can begin to form an idea of our extraordinary situation."

Covering more than ten leagues per hour, the balloon continued on its way. At midnight, it passed over Liège and the travellers were able to make out, by the brightness of the gas, the roads, the squares, the buildings; but the hour was drawing near when all grows dark, when everyone goes to rest, and soon the earth was drowned before their very eyes in the deepest of darknesses.

"Until dawn, everything which occurred was tinged with the intensity of night. Since the sight of nature was completely hidden from our eyes, we had to limit our observations to a collection of mixed sensations, of conjectures which were vague and surrounded by the untold mysteries which the darkness and uncertainty were bound to cast over our expedition. The moon did not appear. The sky, which is always darker when seen from the upper atmosphere than it is when seen by those who live below, seemed to us to be growing even blacker owing to the continuous deepening of the shadows. On the other hand, there was a great contrast in that the stars, increasing in their brilliance, shone in the sky like sparks sewn on to the ebony vault which encompassed us. In the event, nothing could be greater than the intensity of the night which ruled during this first part of our voyage. A black, plunging chasm was around us on all sides, and, as we tried to penetrate this mysterious gulf, we could not prevent the idea coming into our heads that *we were cutting a path through an immense block of black marble* by which we were enveloped, and which, a solid mass a few inches away from us, seemed to melt as we drew near, so that it might allow us to penetrate even further into its cold and dark embrace. The flares which we threw out of the car from time to time, instead of lightening the obscurity, intensified it, and, as they descended, one could imagine that they were cutting a path with the heat which emanated from them."...

"From time to time," Mr Mason goes on, "great foaming masses of clouds in the lower regions of the atmosphere, covering all the earth with

Charles Green made great contributions towards the popularisation of ballooning as a sport. He filled his balloons from the mains supplying domestic gas, and between 1821 and 1892, made 504 ascents. His "Royal Nassau" flies over the Thames on 5 September 1842.

Green's balloon, originally called the "Royal Vauxhall", of 2500 cu. m. capacity, served him for nearly 40 years. In 1836, he made a flight of more than 373 miles, during which he crossed the Channel. Some 18 hrs after leaving London, he landed at Niederhausen, not far from Nassau in Holland. To commemorate his magnificent flight, he re-christened his balloon the "Royal Nassau".

91

a whitish veil, came between ourselves and the ground and left us wondering whether this was not a continuation of those same snow-covered plains which we had already noticed. More than once during the night a noise came from this mass of vapour, resembling so much that of an enormous waterfall or that of waves breaking on a great stretch of shore, that we needed all our powers of reasoning, together with a definite knowledge of our route, to rid ourselves of the idea that we were approaching the sea and that, borne along by the wind, we had been brought as far as the shores of the North Sea or that we were very near to those even more distant shores of the Baltic Sea. As day drew nearer these symptoms disappeared. Instead of discovering the level surface of the sea, we gradually made out the uneven pattern of cultivated land, through which a stately river flowed. This river, when it had divided the countryside in two, split up, losing itself in the midst of the clouds which were still obscuring our view of the horizon."

This river was the Rhine, and the travellers came down at 7.30 in the morning in the Duchy of Nassau; by a strange coincidence, Blanchard had come down in the same spot, and the flags of the two aeronauts decorate the palace of the duke to this day.

Green and his companions had crossed England, France, Belgium, Belfort, and had passed over London, Canterbury, Dover, Calais, Ypres, Courtrai, Lille, Brussels, Namur, Liège and Coblenz. Their epic journey was not to be rivalled until the end of the century.

John Hampton was, with Sadler and Green, one of the most notable English aeronauts. The engraving below depicts an attempt at an ascent made at Maidstone, Kent, in 1837. The gas company was not able to provide enough gas to fill his balloon, so Hampton took it away by water.

THE ASCENT OF M. KIRSCH'S BALLOON CARRYING WITH IT A CHILD

16 July 1843

A certain aeronaut, M. Kirsch, had announced that his balloon would go up at Nantes on 16 July. An enormous crowd had gathered on the promenade de la Fosse; but, when the rope, attaching it to two poles, broke, the balloon rose violently, dragging along in its wake the car which was only attached on one side to the balloon, and the safety rope with its hook on the end, acting as an emergency anchor. This hook, sweeping along the paving-stones, came upon a child, twelve years of age, by the name of Guérin, an apprentice wheelwright who naturally tried to flee; however, the hook caught hold of the boy by his woollen trousers which it pierced above the left knee, coming out at the right thigh.

Caught up thus, and dragged along for a few moments before losing his footing, the child had no inkling of the fate which awaited him; meanwhile, by an instinctive movement, he took hold of the rope with both hands, and firmly secured in this position, as though he had prepared himself for this event with full fore-knowledge of the circumstances, he was borne up into the air, 1,000 ft above the ground. The onlookers were terrified; an awful disaster seemed inevitable. By some lucky chance, the balloon came down in a meadow, not far from the town, and the child came out of his terrible adventure unharmed. He was immediately restored to the arms of his mother, who knew nothing of what had happened. Here is an account of the divers feelings of the boy during his ascent.

His first thought was to say a prayer to Almighty God on behalf of his little sister and himself; next he shouted loudly for help; he felt neither dizzy nor faint. Glancing at the earth, he realised what had come to pass, noticing that the crowd, which looked to him like ants, was following the balloon and seemed to be running towards the probable landing-site.

Without having seriously considered the idea that he might be near the hour of his death, he avows nevertheless that he was very concerned about the possibility of his falling on to a house or into the Loire. Of the two fates he preferred the latter, thinking rightly that he would stand a greater chance of survival in the river. Glancing from the earth to the balloon and back again, he saw houses the size of his little finger, so he says, and the town of Nantes merging into one single point on the earth's surface.

Observing that the balloon was beginning to become a little flaccid, he gained heart, thinking that his adventure would soon be at an end; but, as the balloon descended, he was whirled round and round, and everything below him seemed to be doing likewise.

Eventually, just as he was about to touch the ground, he was once more a little perturbed by the manner of his descent and, seeing some people near a haystack in a meadow adjoining the Beau-Séjour land, he shouted: "Help me, my friends! Come to my aid, or I am lost!" They replied: "Never fear; we will save you."

Indeed, two men who had immediately come to his succour, caught him in their arms and the young Guérin asked that he be taken at once to one of his cousins who lived near to the Madeleine bridge.

His health suffered in no way as a result of his exploits. He was simply very restless during the following night: he imagined that he was still sailing along in his balloon, and called to his mother to help him.

On Independance Day, USA, 4 July 1873, John La Mountain was killed. He had the unfortunate idea of hanging the car of his balloon by ropes attached independently to a hoop fitted over the top of his montgolfière, and not to the usual net that covered the sphere. When he had risen above the clouds, the hoop broke away, liberating the balloon. La Mountain crashed to earth in front of thousands of spectators.

NOTABLE EXPLOITS

1 July 1859	The American aeronaut John Wise, accompanied by John La Mountain, made a dramatic flight in the balloon "Atlantic" from St Louis to Henderson, New York State, covering 803 miles in 20 hours 40 minutes. The flight was a trial run for their projected Atlantic crossing.
5 September 1862	The English metereologist James Glaisher, together with Henry Coxwell, undertook a dangerous ascent to a height of more than 26,246 ft. They both lost consciousness, and nearly died of asphyxiation.
9 October 1863	The first public ascent of Nadar's "Le Géant", of more than 6,000 cu m volume, took place from Paris. It ended prematurely at Meaux.
18 October 1863	The second and final voyage of "Le Géant". The balloon and its nine passengers were caught in a storm and dragged for 10 miles, coming to rest near Hanover.
23 September 1870	The "Neptune" was the first balloon sent off during the Siege of Paris. A survey was made of the Prussian positions, and the balloon landed in unoccupied territory. Some 64 balloons carrying about 100 passengers left the city during the siege.
30 September 1870	Gaston Tissandier passed over the enemy lines with his balloon "Céleste". He flew at a height of 5,249 ft and made a survey of the Prussian dispositions.
7 October 1870	Léon Gambetta, Minister of the Interior, escaped from Paris on board the balloon "L'Armand Barbès".
4 July 1873	The tragic death of the American aeronaut John La Mountain during an ascent.
15 April 1875	The sinister drama of the "Zenith". Théodore Sivel and Joseph Crocé-Spinelli died of asphyxiation during an ascent to 28,215 ft. The third occupant of the balloon, Gaston Tissandier, narrowly escaped.

WILLIAM HYDE'S ACCOUNT OF THE AMAZING FLIGHT OF THE "ATLANTIC", 1 JULY 1859

John Wise (1808-1879), an American, dreamt of founding a fast aerial service between America and Europe. Although he made some 479 ascents, he never actually made an Atlantic crossing by balloon.

At 10½ o'clock we had Lake Erie and Lake Ontario both in sight, a spectacle that could not be viewed without mingled sentiments of admiration and wonder. The balloon had now attained an altitude of nearly a mile. A terrible storm was surging beneath us, the trees waving and the mad waves dashing against the shore of Erie in an awfully tempestuous manner. But above the careering whirlpools and the thundering breakers swam the proud *Atlantic*, not a cord displaced, nor a breadth of silk disturbed, soaring aloft with her expectant crew and gaily heading for the salt crests which bound our vast Republic. Now, like a gurgle, comes the subdued roar of the plashing and headlong Cataract of Niagara.

At 11 o'clock, having skimmed over the Lake shore, still bound eastwardly, the balloon brought us in sight of Buffalo and Niagara Falls, as also of the celebrated Welland Canal. We had reached a height of more than a mile, the barometer marking 23,6 inches. At 12 o'clock we were nearly between the Falls and Buffalo, inclining rather to the left of the latter...

The famous Falls were quite insignificant, seen from our altitude. There was, to us, a descent of about two feet, and the water seemed to be perfectly motionless. The spray gave the whole appearance as of ice, and there was nothing grand or sublime about it. Passing the western terminus of the Erie Canal, the balloon was borne directly towards Lake Ontario. Our ballast was now nearly exhausted and to have determined on crossing the second lake would have been sheer recklessness and hardihood. At this point it was resolved to descend to the earth, land Mr. Gager and myself, in our stead take in a sufficient quantity of new ballast and again steer for the Atlantic Ocean. Could this have been done there is scarcely a doubt of Messrs. Wise and La Mountain's reaching their destination. The airship was lowered, but was immediately caught in the hurricane which was then raging and carried very near the tops of trees which were bending and swaying to and fro by the force of wind. Mr. La Mountain at once threw over the buckets and their

contents and the *lift* this gave us kept us from being crushed in the woods. Like a bullet we shot out into the lake. The machinery was got in readiness to be tossed out, and every possible preparation made for keeping out of the waves. For a while we cherished the hope that we would be able to pass the broad expanse of deep in safety, though we know we had nearly one hundred and ninety miles to traverse. But this hope died out in less than an hour, as the trooping winds bore down on us, it seemed, with greater and increasing fierceness. We had got far out and there was no land in sight. A dreary waste of nearly seven thousand square miles of water was before and around us. At length we neared the dashing billows, which were wildly flinging up their white laps and chasing one another towards the northeast. For me, a lifetime was concentrated in that awful, perilous moment. It was the first time since I had experienced fear as to my safety. I looked around at my companions: they were calm, but their countenances gave me no assurance. Plunge, Plunge, went the iron bars of the machinery into the waves, now rolling ten feet in height! And the *Atlantic*, obedient to this magic control, again bounded upward out of the way of the dark and hungry element. There was great relief in this, but the coolest reason could not have seen in the circumstance anything but momentary encouragement. I cannot recollect whether it was at this point, or before, that Mr. Gager climbed up into the car with Prof. Wise. Whenever it was he did so as much for the security of the entire party as for his own safety, for there is no selfishness in Mr. Gager, see him where you will.

For a time again our flying ship was buoyed up out of the way of hazard, but would frequently dart downward as though intent on burying us all. This movement was promptly checked by throwing out some article as ballast, and thus, carpet sacks containing clothing, overcoats, bundles of papers, provisions, were pitched out into the lake, and still we kept in almost hopeless proximity. Mr. La Mountain had said he desired to take care of the boat and advised me to get into the car above, with

Messrs. Wise and Gager, which I hastened to do. No sooner had I planted myself firmly in the wicker basket than down, down, down with a fearful speed went the balloon towards the lake. I closed my eyes involuntarily, but was quickly aroused by a crash and a lunge of the car forward. Three times were there a terrible clatter and splash. One moment more of life, thought I. Looking around I beheld a hat floating off, and the same instant the balloon darted out of the water. "Poor La Mountain" was in my heart to say, for I thought him gone; but a cheerful "All right, boys" stopped me and lightnened me of one grief. Now came a test of La Mountain's bravery, and nobly did he stand it. Taking a hatchet which was handed down to him from the car where it was slung, he began loosening the planks making the lining of the boat, which he sent overboard at every indication of another descent. When he had gone as far as possible this way he unscrewed the nuts which had been placed in the side of the boat by which to fasten the machinery. Gathering all articles, of no matter how little weight, together, he sent them with the rest. The oars went over next, and at last there was nothing in the boat. He had taken off his coat to it, and worked till the perspiration ran from his brow like rain— all the while speaking hopefully and endeavoring to quiet our apprehensions. When there was nothing more to be done below, Mr. La Mountain drew himself up by the rope into the car. Everything had now gone but an overcoat and two blankets, which were saved to be used as the final resort.

How wistfully did four persons strain their eyes that day in the direction of the shore; and would it never come in sight?

Mr. Gager's face bore an expression of mingled sadness and solicitude; perhaps he was thinking of a group of happy faces, all unconscious of his peril, away in Bennington, Vermont. Mr. La Mountain seemed more hopeful, and Prof. Wise talked as though we were certain of getting over the lake, though he warned us of danger as soon as we should be off the water. Prof. Wise's theory was, that if the boat should get swamped, the balloon would still have momentum and power sufficient to drag us to shore, which, happily, had by this time appeared in the dim distance. A propeller, called *Young America*, shortly afterwards bore down upon us to come to our relief, but we scudded some hundreds of feet before her bows, and so that hope failed.

Finally, after skimming within thirty feet of the dark waves, for a distance of not less than fifty miles, and perhaps more, we had the joy to know that we were out of danger of drowning; but a new peril was before us. Prof. Wise had been quite right in his prediction. The hurricane blew us immediately into a dense forest which skirted the lake, and threatened to tear us limb from limb. Mr. Gager had thrown out the anchor, a heavy iron one, with three hooks, each an inch and a quarter in thickness. So rapid was our flight that this stood out nearly straight from the car. As the grapnel swung against a tree of

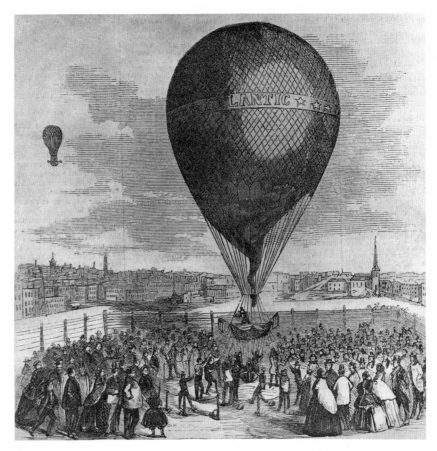

John Wise made his trial ascent from St Louis on 1 July 1859 to gain experience before undertaking the Atlantic crossing. His balloon, the "Atlantic", was fitted with two cars, one above the other. The lower was designed as a lifeboat. Wise was accompanied by his assistant, John La Mountain, by a Mr Gager, and by a journalist called Hyde who wrote up the adventure.

moderate size the velocity of the balloon and its terrible strength would tear it down and fling it to the ground. One by one the hooks broke off, and we were again at the mercy of the all-sweeping wind. Mr. La Mountain and I held on to the valve-rope, endeavouring to discharge the gas, but we quickly were compelled to release our grasp, and cling to the "concentrating hoop" to avoid being thrown out. It has been before stated that the meshes enveloping the silk of the *Atlantic* had an aggregate strength of one hundred and twenty tons. It is not strange that it was some time before these strong cords were broken. The balloon actually went through a mile of forest, and, tearing down trees and breaking branches, pursued its resistless course, dashing our party in the willow-car to and fro against trunks and limbs, until the stout netting had broke little by little, and the balloon itself had no longer any protection, when striking a tall tree the silk was punctured in a dozen places and rent into ribbons, leaving the car suspended by the net-work twenty feet above the ground. The course of the balloon through the woods left a path similar to that of a tornado. Trees half the size of a man's body were snapt in twain, as though they were pipe-stems, and huge limbs were scattered like leaves. It is difficult to see how any one of the quartette escaped with his life. It happened that the landing was made within one hundred and fifty yards of a settlement, and the crash was so great that the people ran to the spot to see what had happened. Singular as it would appear, there was only one of the four injured in the least— Mr. La Mountain receiving some slight contusions about one of his hips, and the remainder escaping without a scratch. When we got down, which was done partly by ropes and partly by means of a broken tree, several persons were standing around with open mouths and eyes staring out wonder. We then learned that we had landed on the place of Truman O. Whitney, near Sackett's Harbor, in the township of Henderson, Jefferson County, New-York. By Mr. La Mountain's watch, the time was 2 o'clock and twenty minutes. We had nineteen hours and forty minutes travelling a distance which cannot be less than nine hundred miles, and may reach as much as twelve hundred...

A storm blew the "Atlantic" and its four passengers down on to Lake Ontario. The aeronauts were forced to jettison clothing, provisions and the fittings of the lifeboat, but even so, narrowly escaped drowning. The hurricane then hurled them into a forest on the edge of the lake. In its headlong career, the balloon broke down trees and uprooted bushes before it crashed in a meadow. To the general amazement, Wise and his friends escaped alive from their adventure. Only John La Mountain was hurt.

COXWELL AND GLAISHER'S DANGEROUS ASCENT ON 5 SEPTEMBER 1862

James Glaisher, an English meteorologist (right), reached the greatest height that had yet been attained by man. In the course of an ascent from Wolverhampton on 5 September 1862, he passed the 26,000 ft mark. Glaisher and the aeronaut Henry Coxwell escaped asphyxiation by a miracle.

In this position my eyes were directed to Mr. Coxwell in the ring. When I shook my body I seemed to have full power over the muscles of the back, and considerably so over those of the neck, but none over either my arms or my legs. As in the case of the arms, so all muscular power was lost in an instant from my back and neck. I dimly saw Mr. Coxwell, and endeavoured to speak, but could not. In an instant intense darkness overcame me, so that the optic nerve lost power suddenly, but I was still conscious, with as active a brain as at the present moment whilst writing this. I thought I had been seized with asphyxia and believed I should experience nothing more, as death would come unless we speedily descended: other thoughts were entering my mind when suddenly I became unconscious as on going to sleep. I cannot tell anything of the sense of hearing, as no sound reaches the air to break the perfect stillness and silence of the regions between six and seven miles above the earth. My last observation was made at 1 h. 54 m. above 29,000 feet. I suppose two or three minutes to have elapsed between my eyes becoming insensible to seeing fine divisions and 1 h. 54 m., and then two or three minutes more to have passed till I was insensible, which I think, therefore, took place about 1 h. 56 m. or 57 m.

Whilst powerless I heard the words "temperature" and "observation", and I knew Mr. Coxwell was in the car, speaking to me and endeavouring to rouse me,—therefore consciousness and hearing had returned. I then heard him speak more emphatically, but could not see, speak or move. I heard him again say, "Do try; now do." Then the instru-

ments became dimly visible, then Mr. Coxwell, and very shortly I saw clearly. Next I arose in my seat and looked around as though waking from sleep, though not refreshed, and said to Mr. Coxwell, "I have been insensible." He said, "You have, and I too, very nearly." I then drew up my legs, and took a pencil in my hand to begin observations. Mr. Coxwell told me that he had lost the use of his hands, which were blackened, and I poured brandy over them.

I resumed my observations at 2 h. 7 m., recording the barometer reading at 11.53 inches and the temperature minus 2°. It is probable that three or four minutes passed from the time of my hearing the words "temperature" and "observation", till I began to observe; if so, returning conciousness came at 2 h. 4 m. P.M., and this gives seven minutes for total insensibility. I found the water in the vessel supplying the wet-bulb thermometer one solid mass of ice, though I had, by frequent disturbance, kept it from freezing. It did not all melt until we had been on the ground some time. Mr. Coxwell told me that while in the ring he felt it piercingly cold, that hoar frost was all round the neck of the balloon, and that on attempting to leave the ring he found his hands frozen. He had, therefore, to place his arms on the ring and drop down. ... He wished to approach me but could not; and when he felt insensibility coming over him too, he became anxious to open the valve. But in consequence of having lost the use of his hands he could not do this; ultimately he suceeded by seizing the cord with his teeth, and dipping his head two or three times, until the balloon took a decided turn downwards.

99

As they rose, the air rarified. The temperature
dropped to 20 below zero,
but still the balloon continued to climb. Glaisher
lost consciousness. Coxwell
managed to rally his
strength enough to climb up
to the hoop to open the valve,
but he was nearly overcome
by the cold and the lack of
air. His hands became
blackened, and he was
unable to move his fingers,
but he managed to pull the
valve-cord with his teeth.

100

THE DRAMA
OF NADAR'S "GÉANT"

Hanover, 18 October 1863

"Attention, please!... Hold tight!!..." Villages and orchards are passing beneath us... Flashing past dizzily.

"Hold on!!..."

A second shock, just as violent... the *Géant*, which only feels the reverberations, shakes with the force of it through all its mechanism...

The cable of our primary anchor, like a mere thread, has just snapped; we were not even aware of it having happened. The fierce wind which is carrying us away is redoubling its strength... our secondary anchor is already over the side, let down by Jules and Yon.

The sight of the cable strikes me:—Are these men mad?—This cable, which carries an anchor weighing 60 kilos, which tries to restrain the strength of several thousand horses, this cable is scarcely as thick as two fingers... And ten cables like this one, plaited together and what is more held together with coils, would barely suffice.

I lean over the edge and see our careering anchor pursuing its headlong course after us through the fields, bouncing along the ground and kicking up behind it a long cloud of dust... The balloon is nearing the ground.

"Hold on!..."

Everyone's muscles are tensed, hands gripping the ropes... another shock... then another, then another, blow after blow.

"The secondary anchor has gone," shouts Jules, "we are lost!" A more than fruitless cry! the evidence is clearly there, for—behaving as if it would add to the speed of this frantic rush, the lower part of the balloon, already empty and flaccid—about a third of it—no longer held back by the now broken appendix, is flattened against the full part and is acting as a sail.

The number of collisions increases, coming fast, one upon another, we can no longer count them...

Here at least, we can see each blow coming; we can, just in time, as we breathe in, gather our forces of resistance and, between two shocks—even if we only have a second—distend our contracted nerves, relax our hands and fore-arms which are braced against the safety cable.

From far away one isolated, lost tree rushes upon us—like a flash of lightning... we have just snapped it like a straw and felt not the slightest tremor... Two terrified horses, nostrils to the ground, manes flying in the wind, struggle at top speed to flee before us. But we are scorching distances. We have already left the horses far behind... A fold of frightened sheep passes below us, between bounces, as if in a dream...

But here is danger, real danger. At a time when we are already completely exhausted, when our companions must, like myself, be feeling this prickling sensation, these cramps which are deadening and paralysing my joints, we see before us, threatening us from the top of its embankment and travelling at ninety degrees to our course, a locomotive, drawing along its tender and its two coaches... A few more revolutions of the wheels and it must all be over... Only a

Nadar, whose real name was Felix Tournachon (1820-1910), was the first to take topographical photographs from a balloon. In 1863, he founded the "Société d'encouragement pour la navigation aérienne", and edited at his own expense a journal called "L'Aéronaute". Victor Hugo, George Sand, Jules Verne, Alexandre Dumas, Edmond About and Jacques Offenbach were among the subscribers.

few yards separate us from our enemy... A single cry escapes our throats, but what a cry!... They have heard us! The locomotive's whistle replies; it is slowing down; it stops as if hesitating, and finally reverses, just in time to allow us to pass... and the mechanic waves to us, his cap in his outstretched hand...

"Beware of the wires!"

Indeed, they are upon us, without our having seen them, the four wires of the electric telegraph, four guillotines... We have lowered our heads... Luckily we skim the ground at that precise moment; the meeting takes place at the level of the hoop and its lower small gabions; only one or two of our cables came against the razors, and these we drag behind us—like the tail of a wild comet—with the endless telegraphic wires and the uprooted poles which, but a little while ago supported them...

How much longer must it go on, the incredible agony of these bounces?"

The behaviour of "Le Géant"'s passengers was sometimes thoughtless. Floating above the clouds drinking champagne, they simply threw the empty bottles and glasses over the side. In the end, to avoid accidents and to maintain the necessary discipline, Nadar printed and enforced a set of rules.

RÈGLEMENT DE BORD

DE

L'AÉROSTAT LE GÉANT

Art. 1. — Tout voyageur, à quelque titre que ce soit, à bord du GÉANT, prend avant la montée connaissance du présent règlement, et s'engage sur l'honneur à le respecter et à le faire respecter, dans sa lettre et dans son esprit. Il accepte et conserve cette obligation jusqu'au retour inclusivement, à moins de congé acquis.

Art. 2. — Il n'y a, depuis le départ jusqu'au retour effectué, qu'un commandement : celui du capitaine. Ce commandement est absolu.

Art. 3. — A défaut de pénalité légale, le capitaine ayant seul la responsabilité de la vie des voyageurs, décide seul et sans appel, en toutes circonstances, des moyens d'assurer l'exécution de ses ordres, et le concours de tout voyageur lui est acquis. Le capitaine peut, dans certains cas, prendre l'avis de l'équipage, mais son autorité décide souverainement même contre l'unanimité.

Art. 4. — Tout voyageur affirme en montant à bord qu'il n'emporte avec lui aucune matière inflammable.

Art. 5. — Tout voyageur accepte, par le fait seul de sa présence à bord, sa part d'entière et parfaite coopération à toutes les manœuvres, et se soumet à toutes les nécessités du service sur toute et première réquisition du capitaine. — Il ne peut à terre s'écarter de l'aérostat sans autorisation, ni se retirer définitivement sans congé dûment acquis.

Art. 6. — Le silence doit être absolu au commandement du capitaine. Ce silence est de rigueur pendant toute manœuvre.

Art. 7. — Les vivres ou boissons quelconques qui pourraient être apportés par l'un des voyageurs sont déposés à la cantine commune. Le capitaine seul a la clef de la cantine et détermine les distributions. — Les vivres ne sont dus aux passagers qu'à bord seulement.

Art. 8. — La durée des voyages n'est jamais limitée. L'appréciation seule du capitaine décide de la limite. Cette même et unique appréciation décide sans appel de la mise à terre d'un ou de plusieurs voyageurs dans le courant du voyage.

Art. 9. — Tous jeux sont absolument interdits à bord.

Art. 10. — Il est rigoureusement interdit à tout voyageur de délester de quoi que ce soit à bord sous aucun prétexte.

Art. 11. — Le bagage total de chaque voyageur ne peut excéder en poids 15 kilog., et en volume celui d'un très-petit sac de nuit.

Art. 12. — Sauf de très-rares exceptions, dont le capitaine seul a l'appréciation, il est absolument interdit de fumer à bord et à terre en dedans de l'enceinte qui entoure le ballon.

Aucune de ces dispositions n'étant indifférente, et la moindre infraction, si puérile qu'elle paraisse, pouvant compromettre la vie de l'équipage, il est ici rappelé de nouveau que c'est à la conscience et à l'honneur de chaque voyageur qu'est confié le respect du présent règlement.

Paris, 5 octobre 1863 (jour du premier départ du GÉANT).

The "Le Géant" balloon, which Nadar had made in August 1863, was of 6000 cu m capacity. The car, which was fitted with glass windows, was very comfortable, for above all, Nadar wished to attract the wealthy and the fashionable. Among the first thirteen passengers were the Prince of Wittgenstein and the Princesse de la Tour d'Auvergne, who had paid 1000 francs for her place. The first ascent took place on 9 October 1863 from the Champ-de-Mars, Paris, and finished prematurely at Meaux, near Paris. The passengers were somewhat disillusioned.

Nadar's second flight, 18 October 1863, ended badly. The "Géant" was caught in a high wind, and blown at ground level across a railway line into the path of a train. Luckily, the driver was able to brake the train to let the balloon pass. The balloon broke its grapnel cables one after the other, and continued its mad career for 10 miles, knocking down everything that stood in its way. It was stopped finally by a small wood near Hanover ; by a miracle, no one was killed. Nadar, who can be seen (above right) under his wife at the lowest corner of the car, was covered with bruises and suffered a broken leg. The party, nearly all of whom were hurt, were taken to a nearby woodcutter's hut.

BALLOONS DURING THE SIEGE OF PARIS 1870-1871

Over the Prussian Lines, *14 October 1870*

"On 14 October, I left Paris," said my brother Albert, "in the car of the balloon, 'Jean Bart', at 1.15 pm in the afternoon. Besides the two travellers (MM Ranc and Ferrand) who had been entrusted to my care, I carried with me 400 kilos of mail; that is to say, 100,000 letters, 100,000 tokens of remembrance sent from Paris by 100,000 anxious families!

"Five carrier pigeons in a wicker cage were crushed pitifully, one on top of another, and we constantly heard their plaintive cooing.

"The sun beat down; we soon passed the line of fortifications at a height of 3,000 ft; we made out the enemy and saw hordes of Prussians preparing to shoot us down, but we were too far from the ground to be really concerned about the possibility of being hit by bullets; however, we could hear them humming like flies passing below our car as we continued on our way above the forest of Arman-villiers.

"There a sorrowful sight awaits us: the houses, the dwellings are deserted and abandoned; no sound reaches us but for the raucous, eerie barking of several abandoned dogs.

"At this moment I notice that the balloon is imperceptibly deflating, the lower part of the fabric is folding and making a noise similar to that of flapping silk. At the same time we feel a cool breeze and the barometer falls until we are hovering at 1,640 ft; as often happens, the effect of the forest's mass has been felt by the aerostat, which is forced down. I throw over a bag ballast to prevent us from drawing any nearer to the ground, for I can see a Prussian encampment in the forest.

"One could see their defences ably deployed to avoid any possibility of a surprise attack, the tents forming two parallel lines at the end of which had been erected fascines and gabions.

"Further on we see a huge convoy of munitions covering the road. Behind the convoy are an incalculable number of small carts protected by white covers. Uhlans escort the vehicles. When they see the aerostat they halt, and we can make out, despite the distance which separates us, that they are throwing glances full of hatred and resentment in our direction!

"Soon the sun warms the aerostat; as the gas expands it swells out the fabric of the balloon. The hot rays give us wings, we soar into the upper regions, we reach 8,200 ft and the earth disappears from view, obscured by the vaporous mists.

"What incomparable splendour, what indescribable magnificence is to be found in this sea of clouds, which seem to end in silvery fringes that sparkle with light! In the midst of silence and

During the Siege of Paris in 1870, the Postmaster, M. Rampont, established a regular balloon postal service between the beleaguered City and unoccupied France. The construction of the balloons was confided to Eugene and Jules Godard, who made their factory in the Gare d'Orléans (below). A second workshop, under Gabiel Yon and Camille Dartois, was set up in the Gare du Nord. Between September 1870 and January 1871, 64 balloons left Paris, of which only 5 fell into enemy hands, while 2 were lost at sea.

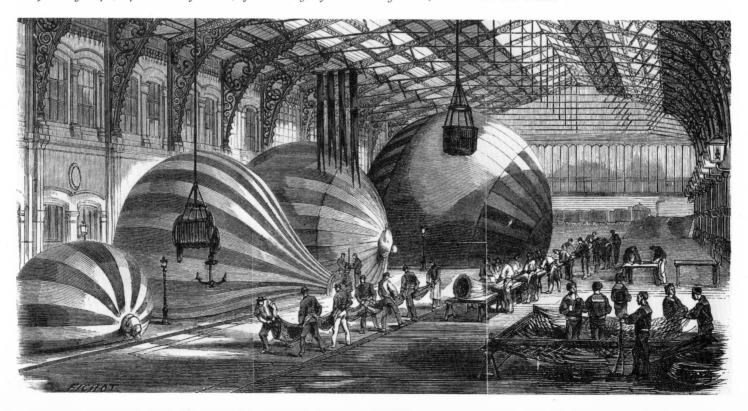

The aeronauts who escaped during the Siege of Paris were mostly ex-sailors. "The Aerial Wolf", painted on a plate by Draner, shows one of them sailing over the Prussian sentries, while making a derisive ▷ gesture at them.

peace we admire the sublime clarity of the sky, and I try to draw it so that the memory of it might not be effaced.

"Here comes the night, covering the sky and the countryside with its cloak. We must think of returning to land, of rejoining the defenders of our country. Our course, at departure, was a little disconcerting, for we were travelling in an easterly direction, that is to say, towards enemy occupied territory. I took care to bring the aerostat down very slowly, keeping back ballast in case we needed to climb rapidly. The wea-

ther was calm, the balloon was not losing gas; Everything was in our favour.

"Soon we see the ground where peasants are running up from all directions. We can hear their cries: 'There are no Prussians here, come down, come down.—You are at Nogent-sur-Seine, at Montpotier, come down!'

"Eventually, their cries, at first a little confused, become more distinct. I decide to land. The car, in a manner of speaking, falls into the arms of our compatriots. They surround us, full of emotion at welcoming us, eager for

news from Paris. They touch our bags of letters and our despatches with joy.

"We make haste to carry away the despatches and the balloon, for the Prussians are only a few kilometres away; they cannot have escaped seeing us and could come upon us at any moment. We have soon moved out, and, with all speed, present ourselves at Nogent. An enthusiastic reception awaits us at the Prefect's residence; we soon take our leave, wishing to lose no time in reaching Tours, to which city our duty calls us."

Albert Tissandier (above, left) narrowly avoided the enemy bullets during his perilous journey of 14 October 1870. He eventually ascended to 8,200 ft, as shown in the diagram, and landed at Montpotier after having surveyed the Prussian positions.

The Postmaster would hand over the packets of letters for the balloon post just before the ascent from the Place Saint-Pierre in Montmartre. M. Hervé-Mangon gave the aeronaut the latest meteorological information as to the wind direction and strength, and estimated the time the aeronaut would need to pass over the Prussian lines.

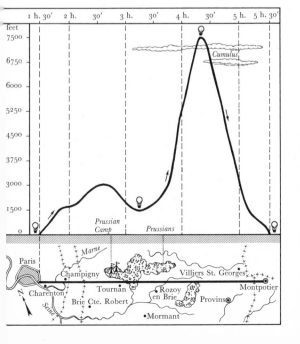

GAMBETTA'S ESCAPE FROM PARIS

Moniteur Universel (Tours Edition) - 7 October 1870

Balloons left Paris regularly every 48 hours. This infuriated Bismarck, who ordered from Krupps an "anti-balloon cannon", which proved to be virtually useless. Nevertheless, so that the balloons should not be too easy a target for the Prussians, they began to be despatched at night.

Borne along by a very slight wind, the two balloons left Saint-Denis behind them to their right, but scarcely had they passed the line of fortifications when they were welcomed by a fusillade from the Prussian outposts. They also received some cannon-fire. At this time the balloons were at 2,000 ft and the aerial travellers heard bullets whistling round their heads; they then rose to a height where they were out of the soldiers' range; but by some accident, or by some mistake in manoeuvring, the balloon carrying the Minister of the Interior began to go down rapidly and landed in a field across which, only a few hours before, enemy troops had marched, and which was very close to a German post. When ballast had been jettisoned they rose again and continued on their way. The balloon was only at an altitude of 700 ft when, near Creil, a second salvo was fired in their direction by some soldiers from Wurtemberg. At this moment they were in great peril: luckily, the arms of the enemy were piled; before they could take hold of them, the balloon, rid of some of its ballast, was climbing to 2,600 ft; the bullets, as the first occasion, did not find their target, but they passed very close to the travellers, and M. Gambetta even had his hand grazed by a projectile.

The adventures of the *Armand-Barbès* were not yet finished. Owing to lack of ballast, it could not maintain sufficient height; it was once more subjected to a salvo of rifle fire—this time from a Prussian encampment on the skirt of a wood; passing over the forest, the balloon entangled itself in the topmost branches of an oak-tree where it stayed hanging; some peasants ran up, and, with their help, the travellers reached the ground, near Mont-didier, at 2.45 pm. A local landowner was passing in his carriage; he made haste to offer the use of it to M. Gambetta and his friends, who had soon reached Montdidier and passed on towards Amiens. They arrived that evening in the town and spent the night there.

There were less mishaps during the journey of the second balloon. Having been subjected to the first fusillade it was able to stay at a sufficiently great height to escape the recurrence of another such incident; it came down at 4 pm at Cremery, near Roye, where they received a warm welcome from the townsfolk. M. Bertin, a sugar manufacturer and the mayor of Roye, offered his hospitality to the aeronaut for the night; the two Americans slept at the house of the Mayor's deputy.

The next day, a Saturday, the crew of the second balloon joined that of the first at Amiens, and they left again at mid-day. At Rouen, M. Gambetta was welcomed by the National Guard... and delivered a speech which fired the hearts of the crowd with enthusiasm. From Rouen, the Minister and his friends went to Le Mans where they slept, leaving the next day.

On 7 October 1870, the "Armand Barbès" balloon flew out Léon Gambetta, then Minister of the Interior, and his secretary, Spuller. The famous politician was charged with the raising and the organisation of an army in the unoccupied provinces to come to the relief of Paris.

Report of the arrival of Gambetta:

Extract from the official Journal: 11 October, Despatch brought by carrier-pigeon.—Montdidier (Somme), 8 pm in the evening.

Arrived after accident in forest at Epineuse. Balloon deflated, we were able escape from the Prussian rifle-fire and, thanks to the Mayor of Epineuse, come here, from whence we leave in one hour for Amiens, from there railway to Le Mans or Tours. The Prussian lines end at Clermont, Compiègne and Breteuil in the Oise. No Prussians in the Somme. Everywhere the people are rising. The government of La Défense Nationale is acclaimed on all sides.—Léon Gambetta.

Gambetta's departure, which took place from Montmartre, had a most encouraging effect on the morale of the Parisians. Gambetta landed at Montdidier, near Amiens. At the same time as his balloon took off, another, the "George Sand", was sent up. Nadar, Dartois and Yon directed operations.

107

No.	NAME OF BALLOON	PILOTS	DATE of FLIGHT	DEPARTURE PLACE	TIME h. min.	ARRIVAL PLACE	TIME h. min.	Weight of despatches kilos	REMARKS
1	LE NEPTUNE	J. Duruof, aeronaut	23 Sept.	Montmartre	8 » am	Craconville, n. Évreux (Eure)	11 » am	125	
2	VILLE-DE-FLORENCE	G. Mangin, aeronaut	25 »	Boulevard d'Italie	11 » »	Vernouillet (Seine-et-Oise)	1 » pm	300	
3	LES ÉTATS-UNIS	Louis Godard, aeronaut	29 »	Gas works, Villette	10 30 »	Mantes (Seine-et-Oise)	1 » »	58	Two balloons tied one to another.
4	LE CÉLESTE	G. Tissandier, chemist	30 »	Gas works, Vaugirard	9 30 »	Dreux (Eure-et-Loir)	11 50 am	80	Accidental descent. Pilot broke arm.
5	ARMAND-BARBÈS	Trichet, aeronaut	7 Oct.	Montmartre	11 » »	Montdidier, nr Amiens (Somme)	2 45 pm	10	Shot at near the ground.
6	GEORGE-SAND	J. Revilliod, landlord	7 »	Montmartre	11 » »	Crémery, nr Amiens (Somme)	4 » »	»	
7	WASHINGTON	Bertaux, writer	12 »	Gare d'Orléans	8 30 »	Cambrai (Nord)	11 » am	300	
8	LOUIS-BLANC	Farcot, mechanic	12 »	Montmartre	9 » »	Beclerc (Hainault) (Belgium)	12 30 pm	125	Dragged. Pilot hurt falling from nacelle.
9	G.-CAVAIGNAC	Godard père, aeronaut	14 »	Gare d'Orléans	10 15 am	Brillon (Meuse)	3 » »	170	Flew over the encircling Prussian lines.
10	JEAN-BART	A. Tissandier, architect	14 »	Gare d'Orléans	1 25 pm	Nogent-sur-Seine (Aube)	5 » pm	370	Bad landing. M. de Kératry hurt.
11	JULES-FAVRE	L. Godard jnr, aeronaut	16 »	Gare d'Orléans	7 20 »	Foix-Chapelle (Belgium)	12 20 pm	195	
12	LAFAYETTE	Labadie, sailor	16 »	Gare d'Orléans	9 50 »	Dinan (Belgium)	2 45 pm	270	Strong winds during landing. Pilot cut cords of nacelle
13	VICTOR-HUGO	Nadal	18 »	Jardin des Tuileries	11 45 »	Near Bar-le-Duc (Meuse)	5 30 »	440	Balloon lost.
14	RÉPUBLIQUE-UNIVERSELLE	Jossec, sailor	19 »	Gare d'Orléans	9 10 »	Mézières (Ardennes)	11 20 am	305	Dangerous landing in trees.
15	GARIBALDI	Iglésia, mechanic	22 »	Jardin des Tuileries	11 30 »	Quincy-Segy	1 30 pm	450	
16	MONTGOLFIER	Hervé, sailor	25 »	Gare d'Orléans	8 30 »	Holigenberg (Alsace)	12 30 pm	390	
17	LE VAUBAN	Guillaume, sailor	27 »	Gare d'Orléans	9 » »	Vignoles (Meuse)	1 » pm	270	
18	LA BRETAGNE	René Cuzon	27 »	Gas works, Villette	noon	Verdun (Meuse)	3 » »	»	Private flight. Taken by the Prussians.
19	COLONEL-CHARRAS	Gilles	29 »	Gare du Nord	noon	Montigny (Haute-Marne)	5 » »	460	
20	LE FULTON	Le Gloennec, sailor	2 Nov.	Gare du Nord	8 30 am	(Maine-et-Loire)	» »	250	Pilot died at Tours 8 days after landing.
21	FERDINAND-FLOCON	Vidal	4 »	Gare du Nord	9 » »	Nort, nr Châteaubriant (Loire-Inf.)	3 45 »	130	
22	LE GALILÉE	Husson, sailor	4 »	Gare du Nord	2 » pm	Near Chartres (Eure-et-Loir)	6 » »	420	Pilot and despatches taken by Prussians, passengers escape
23	VILLE-DE-CHÂTEAUDUN	Bosc, merchant	6 »	Gare du Nord	9 45 am	Réclainville, nr Voives	5 » »	455	
24	LA GIRONDE	Gallay, sailor	8 »	Gare d'Orléans	8 20 »	Granville (Eure)	3 40 »	60	
25	NIEPCE	Jubert, sailor	12 »	Gare d'Orléans	9.15 »	Vitry (Marne)	2 30 pm	260	Balloon taken by the Prussians.
26	DAGUERRE	Pagano, sailor	12 »	Gare d'Orléans	9 15 »	Ferrières (Seine-et-Marne)	3 40 »	»	Photographic equipment landed safely.
27	GÉNÉRAL-UHRICH	Lemoine, sailor	18 »	Gare du Nord	11 15 pm	Lusarche (Seine-et-Oise)	8 » am	80	Whole night spent in balloon.
28	ARCHIMÈDE	J. Buffet, sailor	21 »	Gare d'Orléans	midnight	Castelré (Holland)	6 45 »	220	Whole night spent in balloon.
29	VILLE-D'ORLÉANS	Rolier, engineer	21 »	Gare du Nord	11 » pm	Near Christiania (Norway)	1 » pm	250	15 hour flight. Crossed the North sea.
30	EGALITÉ	W. de Fonvielle, writer	24 »	Gas works, Vaugirard	10 » »	Louvain (Belgium)	2 » »	»	
31	LE JACQUARD	Prince, sailor	30 »	Gare d'Orléans	11 » »	Not known		250	Lost at sea.
32	JULES-FAVRE	Martin, merchant	30 »	Gare du Nord	11 30 »	Belle-Ile-en-Mer, Britanny		50	Crossed and arm of the sea. Pilot hurt.
33	BATAILLE-DE-PARIS	Poirrier, gymnast	1 Dec.	Gare du Nord	5 15 am	Grandchamp (Britanny)	noon	»	Dragged dangerously near the sea.
34	LE VOLTA	Chapelain, sailor	2 »	Gare d'Orléans	6 » »	Savenay (Loire-Inférieure)	11 30 am	»	Optical instruments carried to observe eclipse.
35	LE FRANKLIN	Marcia, sailor	4 »	Gare d'Orléans	1 » »	Nr Nantes (Loire-Inférieure)	8 » »	»	
36	ARMÉE-DE-BRETAGNE	Surrel	5 »	Gare d'Orléans	6 » »	Bouillet (Deux-Sèvres)	11 » »	400	Pilot suffered head wounds. Dangerous descent.
37	DENIS-PAPIN	Domalin, sailor	7 »	Gare d'Orléans	1 » »	Near le Mans (Sarthe)	7 » »	55	
38	GÉNÉRAL-RENAULT	Joygnerey, gymnast	11 »	Gare du Nord	2 15 »	(Seine-Inférieure)	5 30 »	100	Bad landing.
39	VILLE-DE-PARIS	Delamarne	15 »	Gare du Nord	4 » »	Wetzlar (Prussia)	1 » pm	65	Taken prisoner. Landed in Prussia.
40	PARMENTIER	Paul, sailor	17 »	Gare d'Orléans	1 15 »	Gourgansou (Marne)	9 » am	160	
41	GUTTEMBERG	Perruchon, sailor	17 »	Gare d'Orléans	1 30 »	Montpreux (Marne)	9 » »	»	
42	DAVY	Chaumont, sailor	18 »	Gare d'Orléans	5 » »	Chuney, nr Beaune (Côte-d'Or)	» »	25	
43	GÉNÉRAL-CHANZY	Werrecke, gymnast	20 »	Gare du Nord	2 30 »	Rottemberg (Bavaria)	10 45 am	25	Taken prisoner in Germany.
44	LAVOISIER	Ledret, sailor	22 »	Gare d'Orléans	2 30 »	Beaufort (Maine-et-Loire)	9 » »	175	
45	LA DÉLIVRANCE	Gauchet, tradesman	23 »	Gare du Nord	3 30 »	La Roche (Morbihan)	11 45 »	10	
46	ROUGET-DE-L'ISLE	Jahn, sailor	24 »	Gare d'Orléans	3 » »	Alençon (Orne)	9 » »	»	
47	TOURVILLE	Mouttet, sailor	27 »	Gare d'Orléans	4 » »	Eymoutiers (Haute-Vienne)	1 » pm	160	
48	LE BAYARD	Reginensi, sailor	29 »	Gare d'Orléans	4 » »	La Mothe-Achard (Vendée)	11 10 am	110	Balloon skimmed the sea but was brought back to land.
49	ARMÉE-DE-LA-LOIRE	Lemoine	30 »	Gare du Nord	5 » »	Le Mans (Sarthe)	1 » pm	250	
50	MERLIN-DE-DOUAI	L. Griseaux	3 Jan.	Gare du Nord	4 » »	Massay (Cher)	11 15 am	»	
51	NEWTON	Ours, sailor	4 »	Gare du Nord	4 » »	Digny (Eure-et-Loir)	» »	310	
52	DUQUESNE	Richard, QM & 3 sailors	9 »	Gare d'Orléans	3 50 »	Bizieu, near Reims (Marne)	11 » am		Screw rudder trials. A failure.
53	GAMBETTA	Duvivier, sailor	9 »	Gare d'Orléans	3 55 »	Clamecy, near Auxerre (Yonne)	2 30 pm	240	
54	KÉPLER	Roux, sailor	11 »	Gare d'Orléans	3 30 »	Laval (Mayenne)	9 15 am	160	Landed on trees. Pilot hurt hand.
55	LE MONGE	Raoul	13 »	Gare d'Orléans	12 50 pm	Harfeuille (Indre)	8 » »	»	
56	GÉNÉRAL-FAIDHERBE	Van Seymortier	13 »	Gare du Nord	3 30 am	Saint-Avit (Gironde)	2 » pm	60	Carried dogs trained to return to Paris with despatches.
57	VAUCANSON	Clariot, sailor	15 »	Gare d'Orléans	3 » »	Erquinghem (Belgium)	9 15 am	75	
58	STEENACKERS	Veibert, engineer	16 »	Gare du Nord	7 » »	Hynd (Holland)	» »	»	Two boxes of dynamite. Pilot hurt.
59	LA POSTE-DE-PARIS	Turbiaux, mechanic	18 »	Gare du Nord	3 » »	Venray (Flanders)	» »	70	
60	GÉNÉRAL-BOURBAKI	Mangin jnr	20 »	Gare du Nord	5 » »	Hasancourt, near Reims (Marne)	» »	125	Balloon burnt.
61	GÉNÉRAL-DAUMESNIL	Robin, sailor	22 »	Gare de l'Est	4 » »	Charleroi (Belgium)	8 20 am	280	
62	TORRICELLI	Bely, sailor	24 »	Gare de l'Est	3 » »	Fuchemont (Oise)	11 » »	230	
63	RICHARD-WALLACE	E. Lacaze	27 »	Gare du Nord	3 30 »	Not known		220	Lost at sea in sight of La Rochelle.
64	GÉNÉRAL-CAMBRONNE	Tristan, sailor	28 »	Gare de l'Est	6 » »	Mayenne (Mayenne)	1 » pm	20	

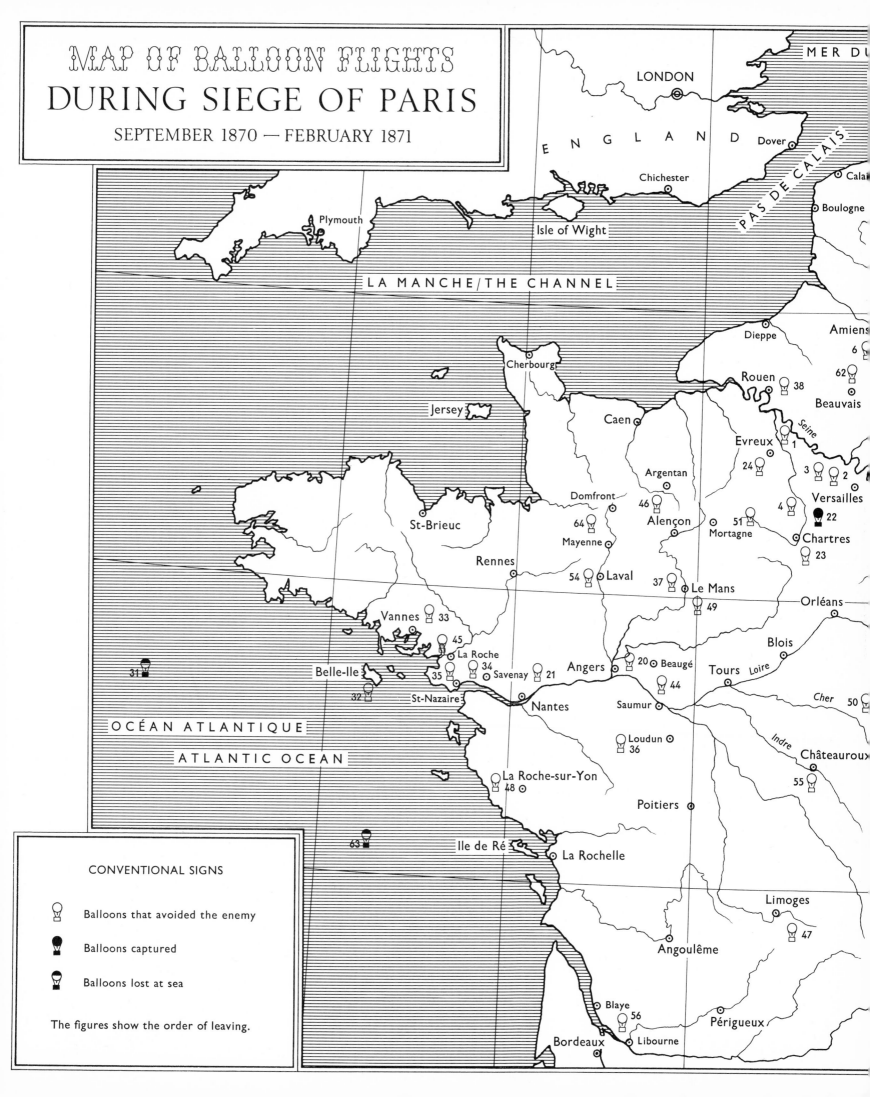

MAP OF BALLOON FLIGHTS
DURING SIEGE OF PARIS
SEPTEMBER 1870 — FEBRUARY 1871

MER DU

LONDON

ENGLAND   Dover

PAS DE CALAIS

Chichester

Calai

Boulogne

Plymouth

Isle of Wight

LA MANCHE/THE CHANNEL

Dieppe   Amiens

6

Cherbourg   Rouen   38   62   Beauvais

Jersey   Seine

Caen   Evreux   1

Argentan   24   3   2   Versailles

Domfront   46   4   22

64   Alençon   51   Chartres

Mayenne   Mortagne   23

St-Brieuc

Rennes   54   Laval   37   Le Mans   Orléans

49

Vannes   33   Blois

45   Beaugé   Tours   Loire

La Roche   34   Savenay   21   Angers   20   Cher   50

Belle-Ile   35   44

31   32   St-Nazaire   Saumur   Indre

Nantes   Châteauroux

OCÉAN ATLANTIQUE   Loudun   36   55

ATLANTIC OCEAN

La Roche-sur-Yon   Poitiers

48

63   Ile de Ré   La Rochelle   Limoges

47

Angoulême

CONVENTIONAL SIGNS

Balloons that avoided the enemy

Balloons captured

Balloons lost at sea

The figures show the order of leaving.

Blaye   56

Bordeaux   Libourne   Périgueux

THE TRAGEDY OF THE "ZENITH"

Narrated by Albert Tissandier, *15 April 1875*

At 11.32 am, on the morning of Thursday, 15 April 1875, the "Zenith" rose up from the grounds of the gas factory at la Villette. Crocé-Spinelli, Sivel and myself had taken our places in the car...

We have gone, rising through the centre of a pool of light, symbol of joy and hope!...

At 13,000 ft the sun blazes down, the sky is dazzling, numerous cirrus clouds stretch out to the horizon, dominating the opaline vapour which encircles our car. At 14,000 ft we begin to take some oxygen, not because we yet feel that we need to breathe the gaseous mixture, but simply because we want to be confident that the respiratory apparatus, which M. Limousin has constructed so well according to the proportions specified by M.B. Bert, is working efficiently...

Crocé-Spinelli had a passion for truth, and was incapable, he who was so frank and loyal, of supporting any doubt or question of his findings. It was at a height of 23,000 ft, at 1.20 pm, that I breathed the mixture of air and oxygen, and that I felt all my being, which was already sorely oppressed, come to life again from the effect of this cordial; at 23,000 ft I wrote in my log-book the following words: *I am breathing oxygen. First-class results.*

At this height Sivel, who was uncommonly strong as far as physique was concerned and of a sanguine temperament, was beginning to close his eyes and even doze and at the same time was growing a little pale. But this valiant soul did not succumb for long to this bout of weakness: he drew himself up, a determined expression on his face; he made me empty the liquid from my aspirator after I had tested it, and he threw ballast overboard so that we might rise to a greater height. The previous year, Sivel and Crocé-Spinelli had reached 24,000 ft. This year, Sivel wanted to climb to 26,246 ft, and when Sivel wanted something, it would have needed insurmountable obstacles to block his course...

I now come to the fatal hour when we were about to suffer from the effects of atmospheric depression. At 23,000 ft we are all on our feet in the car; Sivel, who for one moment became sluggish, is now fully recovered; Crocé-Spinelli stands impassively before me. "Look", the latter says to me, "How beautiful the cirrus are!" Indeed it was beautiful, this sublime sight before our eyes. Cirrus of differing shapes, some stretched out, others softly rounded, formed a circle of silvery white around us. By learning out of the car, we could see, as though it were at the bottom of a well of which the cirrus and the lower mists formed the inner wall, the surface of the earth which appeared in the chasms of the atmosphere. The sky, far from being dark and deep, was light blue and limpid; the scorching sun seared our faces. However, cold was beginning to creep up on us and we had already draped blankets around our shoulders. I felt sluggish, my hands were cold, frozen. I wanted to put on my fur gloves; but although I was not consciously aware of it, the action of putting my hands in my pocket and taking out my gloves, called for an effort on my part of which I was incapable.

At this height of 23,000 ft, I wrote mechanically in my notebook; I transcribe literally the following lines, which were written without my remembering clearly the action of writing; they are scarcely legible, having been formed by a hand which was trembling violently with cold:

"My hands are frozen. I am well. We are all well. Mist on the horizon with small rounded cirrus. We're climbing. Crocé is panting. We are breathing oxygen. Sivel's closing his eyes. Crocé is also closing his eyes. I empty the aspirator. Temp. —10°. 1.20 pm H. =320. Sivel is dozing... 1.25 pm, temp. —11° H = 300. Sivel jettisons ballast. Sivel jettisons ballast." (These last words are barely legible).

In fact, Sivel, who had stayed motionless and pensive for a few moments, occasionally closing his eyes, had evidently remembered that he wanted to rise higher than the level at which the *Zenith* was then floating. He draws himself up; his active face lights up suddenly with uncharacteristic animation; he turns towards me and says: "What is the pressure?" —300 (about 24,740 ft high).—"We have a lot of ballast, shall I throw some over?"—I reply: "Do as you wish."—He turns towards Crocé and puts the same question to him. Crocé nods his head in vigorous affirmation.

There were at least five bags of ballast in the car; there were about the same number hanging outside the car by their cords. These, I should add, were no longer completely full; Sivel had doubtlessly overestimated their weight, but we cannot make any categorical statement on this subject. Sivel takes hold of his knife and cuts three ropes in succession; the three bags empty out their contents and we climb at great speed. The last clear picture I have of the ascent is that of a few moments before this. Crocé-Spinelli was sitting down holding the wash-bottle of the oxygen in his hand; his head was drooping slightly and he seemed dejected. I still had the strength to tap the aneroid barometer with my finger to facilitate the movement of the needle; Sivel had just lifted his hand towards the sky, as if to point to the upper regions.

But I hadn't been long in becoming completely immobile without being aware that I had lost any ability to move. Towards 24,600 ft the state of inertia in which one finds oneself is remarkable. The body and mind grow gradually and imperceptibly weaker, without one realising it. There is no pain, rather the opposite. One feels an inner elation which is almost an effect of the shining light which surrounds one. You become indifferent; thinking neither of the perilous situation nor of any danger; you climb and are happy to climb. The vertigo of height is not an inapt expression. But, as far as I can judge from my own experience, this dizziness only comes during the last seconds; it immediately precedes extinction, sudden, unexpected, irresistible.

When Sivel had cut the three bags of ballast, at about 24,000 ft, that is to say, under the pressure 300 (this is the last figure which I noted at the time in notebook), I seem to remember that he sat down in the bottom of the car where I was holding myself up against the skiff. Soon I began to feel weak, so weak that I could not even turn my head to look at my companions.

Soon after, I want to grip hold of the oxygen tube, but I am incapable of lifting

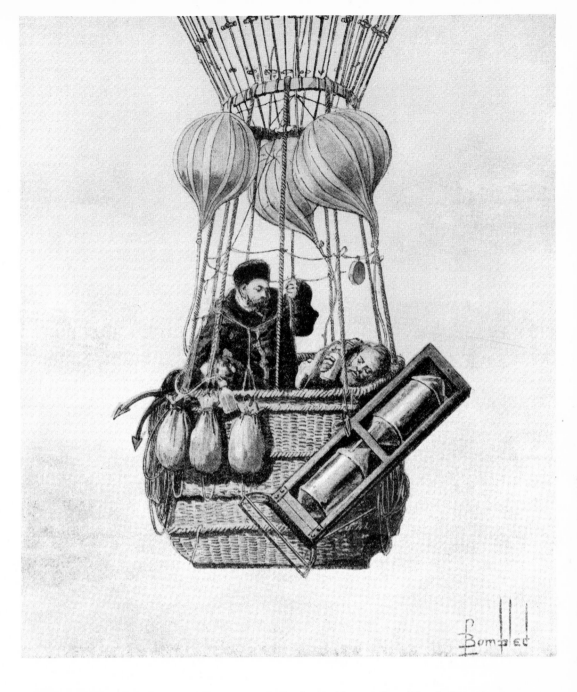

up my arm. Meanwhile, my mind is very clear. I am still watching the barometer; my eyes are glued to the needle which soon reaches the figure denoting pressure —200, then passes 280.

I want to shout out "We are at 26,246 ft!" But my tongue seems to be paralysed. Suddenly, I close my eyes and fall senseless to the ground, losing all consciousness. It was about 1.30 pm.

At 2.8 pm I came round for a minute. The balloon was going down rapidly. I managed to cut open a bag of ballast to slow down our speed, and to write in my logbook the following lines:

"We are going down; temperature —8°; I am jettisoning ballast, H.=315. We are going down. Sivel and Crocé still unconscious on the bottom of the car. We are going down rapidly." Scarcely had I written these words when a sort of tremor gripped me, and I fell once more, weakened, to the floor. The wind was blowing violently in a downwards direction which pointed to the speed of our descent. A few moments later, I can feel someone shaking my arm, and I recognize Crocé who has come round. "Throw

This diagram shows the course taken by the "Zenith" first to a height of 26,246 ft, which was followed by a short descent, and a second rise which was to prove fatal for two of the three aeronauts.

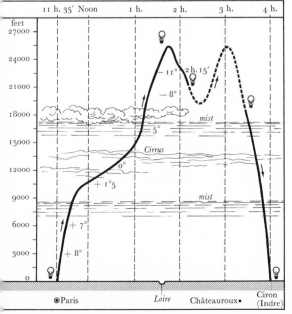

over some ballast," he says to me, "we are going down". But I can scarce open my eyes, and I have not been able to see whether Sivel is conscious or not.

I remember that Crocé detached the aspirator and threw it overboard, and that he jettisoned some ballast, blankets, etc. My memory of this is extremely confused and short-lived, for I soon fall even deeper into my state of inertia than before, and I have the impression of being in an eternal sleep.

What happened then? It is certain that once the balloon was rid of its ballast, since it was impermeable and very hot, it climbed once more into the upper regions of the atmosphere.

At about 3.30 pm, I open my eyes again; I feel numb, weakened, but my brain is working again. The balloon is descending at a terrifying speed; it is swaying strongly and is describing enormous arcs in the sky. I drag myself along on my knees and pull at Sivel's and Crocé's arms.

"Sivel! Crocé!" I shout, "Wake up!"

My two companions are crouching on the floor of the balloon under their travelling rugs. I gather my resources together and try to lift them up. Sivel's face was black, his eyes were dull, his mouth gaped and was full of blood. Crocé's eyes were closed and his mouth was bloody.

I cannot possibly describe what followed. I felt a fearful downward draught. We were still at 19,700 ft. There were two bags of ballast left in the car and I threw them overboard. Soon the ground

113

came up towards us, I wanted to snatch my knife to cut the anchor rope; impossible to find it. I was almost deranged, I carried on shouting: "Sivel! Sivel!"

Luckily, I was able to put a hand to my knife and cut the anchor adrift at the right moment. The shock on touching the ground was terrible. The balloon seemed to be lying on the ground, and I thought that it was going to stay in that position, but the strength of the wind dragged it along. The anchor was not taking any hold in the ground, and the car was sliding along the surface; the bodies of my unfortunate friends were jolted here and there; I thought that they would fall out of the skiff at any moment. However, I was able to take hold of the valve cord and soon the balloon was empty of its gas and flattened against a tree. It was 4 pm.

As I set foot on ground, I was seized by a feverish excitement and for a mo-

ment sank to the ground, livid. I thought that I was about to join my friends in the hereafter. The *Zenith* came down in the fields near Ciron (Indre), 155 miles from Paris as the crow flies...

Having gone over the story of the *Zenith*'s ascent, I come to the two important points which have so much preoccupied the attention of the learned world and of the public. What was the maximum height attained by the *Zenith*? What was the cause of the deaths of Crocé-Spinelli and Sivel?...

As, at the time of my falling into insenbility at 26,246 ft, the needle of the barometer was rapidly passing the figure of pressure 28 (26,262 ft) and thus was indicating a very rapid ascent. I am of the persuasion that we did indeed reach the height of 26,246 ft on the first ascent. But it was not the speed of the ascent which killed my two friends, for, after the

first descent, Crocé-Spinelli and certainly Sivel, were still alive. They were struck down dead when the balloon reached for a second time the heights which it had but recently left, but which it cannot have exceeded to a great degree, for its weight and volume could not have allowed it to rise much higher.

It does not seem unreasonable to me to suppose that the death of these hapless men came as a result of the lack of air, having its origins in the atmospheric depression; one can support this asphyxiation for a very short time; it is difficult to survive several of these experiences in rapid succession, during nearly two consecutive hours. Our sojourn in the upper regions was, in fact, much longer than any other which preceded it. May I add that the particular dryness of the air in these regions may perhaps have had a more than harmful effect.

The aeronauts took up with them small balloons filled with oxygen to compensate for the rarifaction of the air found at high altitudes. They did not seem to realise that they would become partially paralyzed, and unable to raise the breathing apparatus to their mouths. Left, Sivel cuts the cords holding a bag of ballast, while Tissandier reads the barometers and Crocé-Spinelli uses the breathing tube. After its ascent, the "Zenith" landed at Ciron (Indre). Tissandier alone, who was the strongest of the three, escaped asphyxiation. Below, he is shown looking with bowed head at the remains of his two companions. In the background is the "Zenith"'s car, which was caught by a branch of a tree.

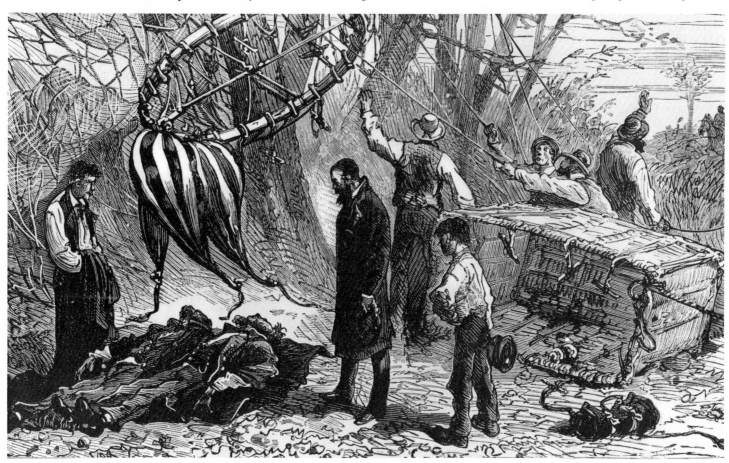

JULES VERNE

CINQ SEMAINES
EN
BALLON

VOYAGE DE DÉCOUVERTES EN AFRIQUE

PAR TROIS ANGLAIS

ILLUSTRATIONS PAR MM. RIOU ET DE MONTAUT

BIBLIOTHÈQUE
D'ÉDUCATION ET DE RÉCRÉATION
J. HETZEL ET Cⁱᵉ, 18, RUE JACOB
PARIS

Tous droits de traduction et de reproduction réservés

Jules Verne, a great friend of Nadar, was a devotee of aeronautics. His novel, "Un Drame dans les Airs", was his first published work. "Five Weeks in a Balloon", one of his first works to be illustrated, appeared in 1863, although at that time the author had not set foot in a balloon. He made only one short ascent, from Amiens, ten years later, with Eugène Godard.

The "Victoria"'s grapnel has caught in an elephant's tusks. Kennedy was forced to shoot many times before stopping the maddened career of the startled beast.

A FLIGHT OVER AFRICA - FICTION

(Five Weeks in a Balloon - Jules Verne)

At about 1,500 feet from the ground, they met an opaque mass of cloud and penetrated the thick mist, maintaining the same height; however, there was not even a breath of wind; the mist even seemed devoid of moisture, and the surfaces exposed to it were scarcely dampened. The *Victoria*, surrounded by this vapour, profited from its situation in that its movement was more perceptible.

The doctor was sadly surveying the lamentably unsuccessful result of his manoeuvre, when he heard Joe shout with surprise,

"Well, I never did!"

"What is it Joe?"

"Sir, Mr. Kennedy! what about that!"

"What on earth's the matter?"

"We're not the only ones up here! They're conspirators! They've stolen our invention!"

"Is he mad?" asked Kennedy.

Joe was the picture of stupefaction itself. He didn't move a muscle.

"Do you think the sun's affected the poor boy's mind?" asked the doctor, turning towards him.

"Will you tell me?..." he said.

"But look, sir!" exclaimed Joe, pointing across the void.

"By George!" shouted Kennedy in his turn, "It's not possible! Samuel, Samuel, just look at it!"

"I can see," the doctor replied calmly.

"Another balloon! Other travellers like us!"

Indeed, 200 feet away there was a balloon, with its car and its travellers floating in the air; it was following exactly the course of the *Victoria*.

"Well!" said the doctor, "We must signal it; fetch the flag, Kennedy, and show our colours."

It seems that the passengers in the second aerostat had had the same idea, for the same flag repeated the same movements in a hand which waved it in exactly the same way.

"What do they mean by that?" asked the hunter.

"They're nothing but apes," shouted Joe, "They're making fun of us."

"The meaning of this," replied Fergusson, laughingly, "Is that it is you yourself who is signalling, my dear Dick; it means that it is we ourselves who are in the other car, and that the balloon is simply our *Victoria*.".

"As for that, sir, with all due respect," said Joe, "I don't believe a word of it and you'll never make me."

"Climb on the edge, Joe, wave your arms, and you'll see."

Joe obeyed, and saw his every gesture reproduced instantaneously and exactly.

"It is a mere mirage," said the doctor, "Nothing more; a simple optical illusion; it's due to the unequal rarefaction of the layers of air, and there you have it."

"But it's marvellous!" exclaimed Joe who could not stop repeating the experiment of waving his arms.

"What a strange sight!" said Kennedy. "How delightful it is to see our gallant *Victoria*! See how fine she looks, and how majestically she moves!"

"You can explain it away in whatever way you like," replied Joe, "It's still an amazing effect."

But soon the image began to fade; the clouds rose to a greater height, leaving the *Victoria* behind, which no longer tried to follow them, and, at the end of an hour, they disappeared into the blue sky.

... Suddenly the balloon sustained a severe blow: the anchor had evidently hooked into a crack in a rock hidden beneath this vast stretch of greenery.

"We've anchored," said Joe.

"Well! throw down the ladder," replied the hunter. He had not finished speaking when a strident cry rent the air, and the following sentences, laced with exclamations, flew from the lips of the three travellers.

"What's that?"

"What a strange cry!"

"Hey! we're moving!"

"The anchor's free!"

"No! it's still stuck," said Joe, who was pulling on the rope.

"It's the rock that's moving!"

There was a large disturbance in the undergrowth, and soon a large sinuous form rose up out of it.

"A snake!" cried Joe.

"A snake!" shouted Kennedy, loading his rifle.

The elephant, brought down at last, fell at the edge of a forest. The travellers descended, and recovered the grapnel.

"No!" said the doctor, "It's the trunk of an elephant."

"An elephant, Samuel!"

And as he said this, Kennedy brought his gun to his shoulder.

"Wait, Dick, wait!"

"Of course! The animal is towing us."

"And in the right direction, Joe, in the right direction."

The elephant was moving with great speed; soon it came to a clearing where we could get a clear view of it; the doctor knew by its enormous size that it was a male, and a magnificent example of its species; it had two whitish tusks which curved impressively and might have measured anything up to eight feet in length; the anchor was held fast between these two tusks.

The beast was trying desperately and in vain with its trunk to rid itself of the cord which attached it to the car.

"Lead on!" cried Joe who was leaping with excitement, trying his best to urge on this strange crew. Here was a new method of travelling! Better than by horse! An elephant, if you please!

"But where is he taking us?" asked Kennedy, waving his gun, which he was itching to use, in the air.

"He's taking us where we want to go, my dear Dick! Be patient!"

"Wig a more! wig a more! as the Scottish peasants say," shouted the ecstatic Joe. "Onward! Onward!"

The animal broke into a rapid gallop; he waved his trunk in the air to right and left, and, as he bounded along, made the car shake violently. The doctor, axe in hand, was ready to cut the rope if need be.

"But," he said, "We will not cut ourselves off from the anchor until the very last moment."

This ride, in the wake of an elephant, lasted about an hour and a half; the beast did not seem in the least weary; these huge pachyderms are able to run for great distances, and in the space of one day, one can find them many miles from their original location, ressembling whales, whose mass and speed they possess.

"In fact," Joe was saying, "We've harpooned a whale, and we are doing nothing more than imitating the course of the whalers during their hunting."

However, a change in the nature of the terrain, obliged the doctor to change their mode of locomotion.

A thick forest of camwood came into sight to the north of the plain, about three miles away; this made it imperative that the balloon be separated from its guide.

Kennedy was therefore given the task of bringing the elephant to a halt; he brought his gun to his shoulder; but he was not in a favourable position for reaching the beast; the first bullet, fired towards the skull, had no more effect than if it had been fired at a sheet of metal; the animal was in no way affected by it, except that the report caused it to accelerate, so that it was travelling as fast as a horse galloping at full speed.

"Damn!" said Kennedy.

"What a thick skull!" said Joe.

"Let's try a few tapered bullets in the vulnerable part of the shoulder," said Dick, loading his rifle carefully, and he fired.

The beast let out a terrible cry, and ran even faster.

"Come on," said Joe, taking up one of the rifles, "I must give you a hand, Mr. Dick, or we'll never get it over with."

And two bullets found their home in the animal's side.

The elephant stopped, raised its trunk, and then continued his headlong flight

The aeronauts were unable to believe their eyes : an identical balloon appeared out of the mist. Was it a mirage . . .

towards the forest; he was shaking his enormous head, and blood was beginning to pour out of his wounds.

"Keep up the fire, Mr. Dick."

"And a well-sustained fire," added the doctor, "we're less than twenty fathoms from the woods!"

Ten more shots rang out. The elephant leaped into the air in a terrifying way; the car and the balloon made a cracking sound which made one think that they were falling to pieces; the tremor made the doctor let go of the axe, which fell to the ground below.

The situation was now perilous; the anchor cable which was tightly fastened could not be taken off, or affected by the travellers' knives; the balloon was rapidly approaching the forest, when a bullet penetrated the eye of the beast, at the moment when he was lifting his head; he stopped, hesitated; his legs buckled, and he lay down on his side.

"One more bullet in the heart," said the hunter, firing his rifle for the last time.

The elephant emitted a roar of distress and pain; he stood up for a moment, waving his trunk, then fell down with all his weight on to one of his tusks which snapped. He was dead.

117

SCIENTIFIC ASCENTS

18 June 1803	The first use of a balloon for purely scientific purposes. E. G. Robertson and Lhoest made an ascent from Hamburg. Their balloon, "L'Entreprenant", reached a height of 24,278 ft. They made observations on electricity.
30 June 1804	The ascent of Robertson and Saccharoff from St Petersburg. Robertson purported to have noticed a decrease in magnetism with height. He was violently attacked by Laplace at the Paris Académie des Sciences.
20 August 1804	Joseph-Louis Gay-Lussac and Jean-Baptiste Biot, members of l'Académie des Sciences, made an ascent of 12,548 ft in order to verify Robertson's theory and showed him to have been wrong.
16 September 1804	Gay-Lussac reached a height of 23,018 ft. He made a study of the composition of the air. The Institute decided to stop the researches.
29 June 1850	Resumption of the experiments. Barral and Bixio had to observe atmospheric phenomena during a violent storm. At a height of 19,685 ft their balloon expanded and pressed down on their car. They had to stop the flight.
27 July 1850	Barral and Bixio reached 23,127 ft, and noticed that the temperature had decreased to −39°, while it was still 9° 5 at the altitude of 19,685 ft.
1865-1885	Gaston Tissandier, Camille Flammarion and Jules Duruof made several ascents.
4 December 1894	Berson, a German physicist, made an ascent alone and observed a temperature of −47° 9.
11 July 1897	Three Swedish aeronauts: Salomon A. Andrée, Nils Strindberg and Knut Fraenkel departed from Danes Island aboard the "Örnen" in an attempt to reach the North Pole. Their bodies were found on White Island in 1930.
30 June 1901	Süring and Berson reached the height of 35,334 ft.
27 May 1931	Two Swiss, Auguste Piccard and Kipfer, aboard their balloon, "F.N.R.S.", made the first stratospheric ascent. Aided by their insulated car, they reached a height of 51,772 ft.
19 February 1932	The Germans Schultz and Sucksdorff attempted a stratospheric ascent aboard the "Ernest Brandeburg" but they could not go higher than 29,527 ft.
18 August 1932	Piccard and Max Cosyns' balloon, the "F.N.R.S.", reached an altitude of 53,149 ft.
30 September 1933	The Russians Prokofief, Birnbaum and Godunov, reached an altitude of 56,430 ft, aboard their balloon the "Osso-Aviachim".
30 January 1934	At a height of 65,616 ft, the cords of the car of the "Osso-Aviachim" broke and the aeronauts Fedossejenko, Vassenko and Oussyskine were killed.

Twenty years after Montgolfier's discoveries, scientists at last decided to make use of a balloon in the interests of pure science. On 16 September 1804, the Paris Académie des Sciences entrusted Joseph-Louis Gay-Lussac and Jean-Baptiste Biot with the task of studying the atmosphere 12,548 ft high. Their balloon ascended from the grounds of the Conservatoire des Arts et Métiers and landed 50 miles from Paris. The experiment was successful, but the Academy did not find it necessary to pursue these researches.

28 July 1934	The stratospheric balloon "Explorer" (U.S.A.) with W. Kepner, A.W. Stevens and O.A. Anderson aboard reached a height of 61,122 ft and became torn. The aeronauts aboard parachuted down from 984 ft.
18 August 1934	Cosyns and Van der Elst made a stratospheric ascent aboard the "F.N.R.S. II" and reached an altitude of 52,493 ft.
13 October 1934	Jean Piccard, brother of Auguste, reached a height of 51,480 ft.
11 November 1935	"Explorer II", a giant balloon, piloted by Anderson and Stevens, reached a height of 71,260 ft.
30 May 1954	Audouin and Charles Dollfus made an ascent by night and reached a height of 22,965 ft, carrying a telescope in their car.
2 June 1957	The American J.W. Kittinger reached a height of 96,128 ft in 1.15 hrs.
19 August 1957	Balloon "Man High II" enabled Major David G. Simon to reach a height of 101,509 ft in an ascent of 32 hrs.
22 April 1959	A system of 105 wind observation balloons grouped in threes around a nylon rope enabled Audouin and Charles Dollfus to reach a height of 44,291 ft They made telescopic observations of the Moon and Venus.
16 August 1960	Kittinger on board the "Excelsior II" reached the altitude of 101,181 ft and descended by parachute.

GAY-LUSSAC'S SCIENTIFIC ASCENT, *Paris, 16 September 1804*

"Having learned several useful things from our first ascent, we made some alterations in our instruments and firstly, so that the vibrations of the horizontal needle might be less affected by the balloon's rotation, we fashioned a new needle, only 15 centimetres (6 inches) long. Our intention was that, since the vibrations of the needle would be considerably more rapid than those of the balloon, it might be easier to judge their duration.

"When we reached 3,032 metres (10,000 feet) I began to induce vibrations in the horizontal needle and this time I obtained 20 vibrations in 83 seconds compared with 84.33 seconds on the ground in similar conditions to obtain the same number. Although my balloon was affected by the rotary movement which we had observed in the course of our first experiment, the rapidity of the movement of our needle enabled me to count up to 20, 30 and even 40 vibrations...

"Since only 15 kilogrammes of ballast remained, I decided to descend. At that time the thermometer measured 9.5° C below freezing and the barometer 32.88 centimetres which indicated the greatest height which I had yet attained over Paris, 6,977.37 metres, that is 7,016 metres (23,000 ft.) above sea-level.

"Although I was warmly clad, I began to feel cold, particularly as far as my hands were concerned, for I could not avoid exposing them to the air. My breathing was perceptibly impeded but I was still far from feeling sufficient discomfort to make me go down. My pulse and respiration were considerably increased: I should not have been surprised by the fact that my throat was so dry that I suffered pain when swallowing my bread, considering the fact that I was breathing rapidly in the dry air. Before leaving, I had a slight headache caused by the labour of the preceding day and the sleepless night and although this did not leave me, I was not aware that it was growing more severe. I suffered no greater inconveniences than these."

Louis-Joseph Gay-Lussac (1778-1850) a French physicist and also chemist (left) became famous at the age of twenty-four by publishing a treatise on the expansion of gases and vapours (1802). Gay-Lussac, ex-assistant of Berthollet and great friend of Humboldt, made two scientific ascents in 1804 : one to a height of 12,548 ft, and the other to 23,018 ft. His partner during the first ascent was (right) Jean-Baptiste Biot (1774-1862), author of essays on mathematics and astronomy.

François Arago's account of the ascent of Bixio and Barral, Paris,

29 June 1850

M. Arago gives his account, more or less in these words, of the aeronautical voyage of MM. Bixio and Barral.

MM. Bixio and Barral had conceived the notion to send a balloon up to a great height, in order to study, by means of the perfected instruments which science today possesses, a host of atmospheric phenomena which are still only partially understood.

The necessary instruments for such an interesting experiment had been prepared by M. Regnault with care and infinite precision. Bixio and Barral had entrusted the task of preparing the balloon and its accessories to an aeronaut with the experience of twenty-eight aerial voyages; all the arrangements had been made in the Observatory garden. The ascent took place on Saturday, 29 June at 10.27 am: the balloon was filled with pure hydrogen gas, prepared by the action of hydrochloric acid on iron. According to all the forecasts and calculations, the aeronauts were expected to be able to reach a height of 10,000 to 12,000 metres (33-40,000 feet). At the time of departure, it was evident that certain parts of the design of the aerostatic machine were unsuitable. It would have been more prudent not to have left; but MM. Bixio and Barral cast such a thought out of their minds. They entered the car and set off fearlessly into the sky without even taking the trouble to ascertain, by the use of a weight, the lifting power of the aerostat. Their upward movement was extremely violent: the whole assembly compared it to the flight of an arrow from the bow; soon MM. Bixio and Barral disappeared in the clouds, and it was above this curtain, which hid them from view, that the moving story which it falls to our lot to recount took its course.

The dilated balloon was applying great force to the mesh of the net, which was much too small; the balloon swelled out through all its length and pressed down on the travellers, whose car was suspended from it by ropes which were too short, and it covered them like a hat. At this time the two physicists found themselves in the most awkward of situations; one of them, in attempting to release the rope of the valve, caused a rent in the lower

On 29 June 1850, 46 years later, the scientists Barral and Bixio repeated the experiment. They rose from the court of the Paris Observatory, climbed to 19,685 ft, and landed near Lagny, narrowly avoiding an accident.

appendix of the balloon; the hydrogen gas, which was escaping at about the height of their heads, had an asphyxiating effect on first one of them and then the other, which caused them both to vomit copiously. On looking at the barometer, MM. Bixio and Barral realised that they were descending rapidly; they sought to discover the reason for this unexpected movement, and found that there was a rent, six feet in extent, in the equatorial part of the balloon. It was then that they realised, with a calm which could not be too much admired, that the most they could hope for was to come out of their bold venture alive; they came down more quickly that they had risen,

which was at no small speed. MM. Bixio and Barral disposed of all their remaining ballast, they threw overboard the blankets they had taken with them to keep out the cold, and even their fur boots, but they would not abandon their scientific instruments.

At 11.14 am, MM. Bixio and Barral fell into a vineyard in the parish of Dampart, near Lagny, where the ground was fortunately waterlogged. The labourers and vine growers ran up and found the two physicists holding on with their legs in an attempt to curtail the horizontal movement of the balloon to whatever degree possible. The new arrivals lent the aeronauts immediate succour.

THE ANDRÉE EXPEDITION

A short account taken from the logbook of Salomon A. Andrée

We let the balloon rise a little, until the hoop was a fair distance from the ground. The balloon was held down by three ropes. We then attached the car and in it placed the necessary quantity of ballast. The hour of departure had come. It was affectionate and moving, but with no trace of sentimentality. Andrée shouted: "Strindberg, Fraenkel, are you ready to go?"—"Yes."—They climbed into the car. For a few moments Strindberg's thoughts were with his fiancée and with those who were dear to him at home. How would the flight progress? The young man was almost overcome with emotion, but he regained control of himself. Machuron, of whom he was very fond, was near the car. Strindberg asked him to convey his regards to his fiancée. Now it was a matter of preparing the camera, throwing out some ballast and of doing many other things. The three travellers are standing on top of the car. A solemn silence reigns. Machuron says: "Wait for a calm moment!" The crucial moment is upon them. "Cast off!" cried Andrée. Three knives cut the three ropes holding down the hoop, the balloon rises, the spectators cheer, and the three occupants shout back: "Long live old Sweden!" The balloon leaves the enclosure. A strange, indescribable feeling takes hold of the polar navigators, but they have no time to let it possess them. Strindberg takes photographs. He notices that the balloon is falling. They throw out ballast but the car gently sinks into the water. But it soon rises again. Everything seems to be going well. The three friends can still hear the cheers of the spectators.

A Swedish scientist, Salomon August Andrée, planned to explore the North Pole by balloon. To do this, he had made in France the "Örnen" (Eagle), a balloon of 4500 cu. m. capacity. The car contained a sleeping compartment, provisions and scientific instruments. Equipment for returning across the icecap—sledges, a folding canoe, arms, and provisions for four months—was stored in a fabric cone between the car and the balloon. Andrée hoped to be able to control his balloon by means of two sails. On 11 July 1897, he took off from Danes Island, accompanied by his compatriots Knut Fraenkel and Nils Stringberg.

The balloon rises slowly, in fits and starts, to 160-320 ft and, under the auspices of the north-east wind, passes over the port where the "Virgo" is berthed. The trail lines slide over the water leaving on the surface a wide, deep mark similar to the wake of a boat. When they reach the middle of the port the balloon begins to go down, and after a brusque lurch the car is half-submerged in the water... The balloon soon rises once more and climbs higher and higher, looking like an immense ball, while the crew empty nine bags of sand and so lose 445 lbs of their valuable ballast during the departure alone.

Scarcely had the car touched the water than a sailor cried: "The ropes have been left behind on the shore", and this announcement caused them great concern, for they had planned to travel at a height of 500-650 ft, using the ropes to adjust their balloon's height to a certain extent. At first the spectators thought that the ropes had been torn off, but on looking closer, they saw that the screws had come away... This sad event must have taken place at the moment when the balloon received a great blow. So they added 1,168 lbs to the record of ballast which had been lost.

... From being a balloon with some means of control, the "Örnen" had become a free balloon destined to be subject to the caprices of the winds.

Three-quarters of an hour after their departure, the crew thought out a way of compensating to some extent for the

The "Örnen" set off in the direction of the North Pole—it was to be a one way trip. The balloon was supposed to keep up continually for 30 days, but their flight lasted only three days, from 11 July until 7 am on 14 July. For 33 years, the world was in ignorance of the fate of the expedition. Then in 1930 some sailors, visiting White Island, discovered the bodies of the unfortunate explorers.

loss of the lower portions of the cables. They untied a rope which was attached to a bag of ballast with the probable intention of lengthening a cable.

During the last few minutes, the balloon has once more gained an appreciable amount of height, for the crew note a loss of gas at an altitude of 1,640 ft. At this height, the balloon is travelling more distinctly in a northerly direction. Now, clouds surround it on most sides, except on the north-east side and on that facing Spitzbergen.

Spitzbergen disappears in the mist. A gull is still following the balloon. It is flying below the car. The "Örnen" is beginning to descend slowly. "Going down gently in a sine curve" writes Strindberg immediately after 17 h. 29 m. The sea's surface below the "Örnen" is covered with floating ice, of a beautiful dark-blue, quite different from that which has been noticed before. At 17 h. 36 m. the balloon is at a height of 87 ft. The first four carrier-pigeons are released. They fly off in a rough easterly direction. They never reached their destination.

At 15 h. 06 m., the ballon sinks so low that it bounces off the ice on two occasions.

During the hour which follows, it seems that the situation is critical. The crew attempt all means of making the balloon rise, throw overboard the grummets, 55 lbs of sand and some ropes. At 15 h. 16 m. a small iron anchor goes the same way... All these measures are in vain, the balloon is still very close to the ground, they fear that at any moment the balloon's car may smash in crashing against the ice. At 16 h. 51 m. the big buoy is thrown over with no message attached. This was perhaps the greatest sacrifice. The act of throwing it over expressed in no uncertain terms the doubts that the crew had of reaching their destination; they had just admitted the failure of the expedition. Every attempt at raising the balloon by lightening its load failed; indeed it was but a little time after Strindberg had made a note of the release of the large polar buoy, that the car bounced heavily along the ice for some distance. Their speed at this moment is approximately 9 ft per second, their bearing S 80°W. The "Örnen" cannot get airborne, the fog is pressing down on it too heavily.

Perilous times are now upon them. The balloon drags the car through the mists in a westerly direction over the ice

This photograph, and the one on p. 126, were taken from a film that was left in the ice for 33 years. It shows the Swedish camp, five days after their forced landing. Fraenkel, in the foreground, and Andrée, standing on the "Örnen"'s car, survey the horizon. On 21 July, the explorers struck camp, and set off on their tragic wanderings over the ice.

masses. The car is continually thrown against the frozen ground. At 17 h. 14 m. the crew note eight violent collisions with the ground in the course of 30 minutes... The fog is not dispersing. At 18 h. 33 m. they note that the car bounces off the ice once in every five minutes... The situation becomes more and more critical. The fog is thickening and the balloon sinking even lower, the car touches the ice every one or two minutes. They are travelling at 6½-9 ft per second. Every 150 ft the car scrapes the ice as it bounces off. The ice is 'stamped' says Andrée. At 22 h. the "Örnen" comes to a halt. The balloon itself is quite empty, everything on board is sodden.

"It is a strange experience being suspended in the air over the Arctic Sea. We are the first to travel in these regions in a balloon. When will someone follow in our path? Will we be thought fools by mankind or will they follow our example? I cannot deny that we three feel full of pride at our achievement. We are of the opinion that we can die in peace after this adventure. Perhaps we have an over-rated opinion of ourselves, perhaps we are unable to support the idea of living and dying side by side with the common race, of being forgotten. Does this mean that we are ambitious?"

13 July 1897

At 16.35 hrs it is noted that one of the pigeons which were released four hours before has come back and is wheeling round the balloon. The car touches the ice again, Strindberg writes that the collisions are becoming more frequent.

The situation continues to deteriorate:
"It is about 20.00 hrs. We decide to use all possible means of making the 'Örnen' rise and of steering her. When we have collected everything that is not strictly indispensable..., we throw it overboard. Since the first flight at an appreciable height, the cables have continously touched the ground. At last the 'Örnen' rises to a height where the stiff sails which have been erected across the vessel can carry us along and we can increase speed." The balloon has been travelling well since the sail has been erected and 110 lbs of superfluous ballast have been jettisoned. "It is a really wonderful flight" Andrée remarks.

This last, calm part of the journey did not last for long, apparently. At 22.30 hrs the balloon is already repeating its violent collision with the ice, and the fog is growing thicker. They notice sometimes the irregular surface of the ice and sometimes a smooth stretch; everywhere are pools of water or canals cutting through the frozen waste. To cap their misfortunes, the long cable breaks away half-an-hour before midnight. There is no sight of land, no birds, no seals, no walruses, only the vast expanse of ice and the canals of free flowing water which shine through the damp fog.

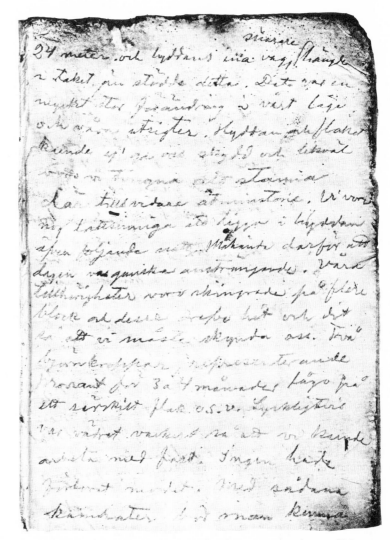

It is possible to reconstruct the tragedy that overcame the expedition from the fragments of Andrée's logbook recovered from White Island. After flying for 65 hours, the "Örnen", weighed down by a thick covering of ice from the Arctic drizzle, was forced down on to the ice cap. Andrée landed some 300 miles only from Danes Island and 500 miles from the Pole. The crucifixion began.

14 July 1897

From this moment onwards, their notes become few and far between. In stilted sentences, we learn that the ice forms a magnificently flat surface, that there are numerous canals, but that nowhere is there a sizeable extent of flowing water. During these last hours, when the fog is not dispersing, when the balloon is not rising, when there is no possibility of travelling under sail, when the car is being thrown against the ice at every turn and is moving slowly in a northerly direction, it seems that Andrée is thinking of interrupting their journey and landing. It is doubtless for this reason that he has been so interested in the condition of the ice and that he has been incessantly looking out for dry land.

Strindberg photographed Andrée and Fraenkel near their balloon. To avoid dying of cold, the explorers had to reach solid ground before the winter months. Their return was painful; their route had to be modified many times, for the sea-currents moved the ice floes about. After four months of terrible marching, Andrée and his companions gained White Island, and commenced their fatal wintering. The last entry in the expedition's journal was dated 17 October 1897.

The notes become shorter and shorter...

At the end we find: "06.20 hrs (= 05.28 hrs) the balloon has risen but we opened both the valves and at 06.29 hrs we descended once more. At 08.11 hrs we jumped out."

We do not know what happened during these 100 minutes. According to a note in Andrée's diary, dated 15 July, the balloon was covered in a thick layer of ice at the time of landing. The fog, falling as a fine drizzle, had turned into ice. The cables were also wrapped in a coating of ice which was thicker than Andrée had anticipated when he had made his preparations.

In the time which passed between the moment of landing and the departure, the balloon had lost 3,480 lbs of weight

of which 1,310 lbs were accounted for by the loss of gas. The weight of ice carried by the machine at landing must have been in the region of 2,200 lbs...

The cause of the failure of this attempt was the cold and the dampness of the arctic air. During the course of his preparations, Andrée had foreseen deposits of snow and rain. This is why he had placed a cap over the top of his balloon. But what he had not foreseen was that the mist would transform itself into ice.

The Arctic expedition of Andrée in the "Örnen" came to an end. Exhausted and hungry, the three men jumped on to the perilous ice floes at a latitude of about 82°56' and a longitude of 29°52' east.

AUGUSTE PICCARD CONQUERS THE STRATOSPHERE

Description of the F. R. N. S.

Our balloon must have differed in several ways from the traditional form of former free balloons. The effective load, that is to say, the weight of our cabin, its contents and of the necessary amount of ballast to allow the pilot to land, was about 1,000 kilos. This weight had to be carried up to a height where the air pressure is only 1/10 of the atmosphere, that is to say, 76 mm of mercury. This meant, therefore, that we had to use a very large balloon made out of very light fabric.

We could not use any other gas than hydrogen. It is true that helium has the advantage of being non-inflammable, but it is too expensive in Europe and moreover, as it is twice as heavy as hydrogen, its capacity for carrying weights is only 92.5% that of hydrogen. If a balloon is inflated with hydrogen it will invariably rise 400 metres above the level it would have reached had it been filled with helium.

Our calculations led us to design a balloon with a volume of 14,000 cubic metres and thus a diameter of 30 metres.

By completely filling a balloon of this size with hydrogen before departure, that is to say, obtaining the normal atmospheric pressure, it is possible to obtain a lifting power in the region of sixteen or seventeen tons; this power could necessitate the use of a very substantial fabric which would entail too great an increase in the weight of the balloon. Therefore, only a small part of the balloon should be filled with hydrogen before departure. Thus, the balloon would only contain gas in its upper part, with the rest of the envelope hanging in large slack folds (there is no question in this instance of the possibility of filling the lower part of the balloon with another gas which would be separated from the hydrogen by an impermeable membrane). The ballon only attains its spherical shape with the expansion of the gas during the ascent. This could be dangerous in the case of a bal-

loon covered with a net when it is taken into consideration the fact that the folds of the envelope could be caught up in the mesh. This would not merely cause a loss in the effective volume of the balloon and thereby a loss in height, but also there is the danger of possible excessive tension on the fabric which could cause tears.

To avoid this risk, I decided against using a net and opted for a loading belt. This was attached to the lower quarter of the balloon, 22.5 metres vertically below the valve. To the loading belt were fixed 128 ropes which, when joined together twice, formed 32 loading ropes.

We have seen in the foregoing that usually when filling a balloon without a net, a filling net is placed over the envelope and is taken off once the operation is completed. The considerable size and the shape of our balloon did not lend themselves to the use of such a net; to lift the net off before the balloon went up would have proved too difficult. I therefore decided against this type of net also and used instead a special belt which we shall call the "filling belt", fixed to the upper part of the balloon, 7.5 metres below the valve. Some 128 ropes are attached to the filling belt, and the ends of them, when joined into four thicknesses in two stages,

After a first stratospheric flight from Augsburg in 1931, Professor Auguste Piccard made a second ascent on 18 August 1932 from Dübendorf, near Zurich. The cabin weighed a ton, and Piccard had made a balloon of 14,000 cu. m. capacity and 30 m. diameter to lift it. The giant balloon, known as the "F.N.R.S." became thin and elongated during its inflation (below right), and was filled with hydrogen, which is twice as light as helium. Professor Piccard (left) inspected the gas cylinders before commencing operations.

127

The inflation took place during the night of the 17-18 July. As soon as the upper part of the balloon was filled with gas, the spherical cabin was attached to the 32 cords which led down from the carrying hoop.

form 32 loops through which 32 filling ropes are passed during inflation. The loops are placed half way along the filling ropes, which are 100 metres long.

The inflation

According to our plans, the inflation of the balloon and its subsequent departure were meant to take place in the following manner:

1) The envelope is spread out in such a way that the filling belt is flat on the ground in the shape of a circle. Its diameter is 26 metres; the upper quarter of the balloon is almost flat, while the other three-quarters is folded underneath.

The two valves of each filling rope are placed together and anchored to the ground, pointing directly away from the balloon. These 32 anchored ropes form a circle 80 metres in diameter around the balloon. Near to the loading belt the ropes are secured with bags of ballast;

2) The hydrogen is introduced into the balloon through a small filling neck near

the equatorial line of the balloon. The upper quarter of the envelope rises, forming part of a sphere, while the filling belt stays in contact with the ground. The filling neck is closed.

3) The bags of ballast are slowly let down the length of the ropes which are being paid out. The balloon rises slowly and the loading belt comes into view.

4) The cabin is brought underneath the balloon; the 32 loading ropes which hang from the loading belt are attached to 32 ropes coming down from the hoop, each of which measures 5 metres in length. Usually these loading ropes are attached directly to the hoop. This would have been very difficult in our case since the hoop is above the cabin and therefore the men would have had to climb up upon it. With its 32 ropes, 5 metres long, attached beforehand to the hoop, the manoeuvre is quite easy.

To the base of each alternate rope is fixed a manoeuvring rope. There are consequently sixteen of these ropes.

5) Some of the crew take hold of the manoeuvring ropes; the filling ropes are paid out until they no longer serve to hold the balloon down. At this moment the balloon is only restrained by the weight of the cabin and by the manoeuvring ropes. Now the filling ropes can be disposed of by releasing one end and pulling on the other;

6) The sixteen manoeuvring ropes are released simultaneously so that the balloon can rise. On the occasion of the second ascent, these sixteen ropes were attached directly to the hoop, and this gave greater stability to the whole operation. In fact, for the second ascent, we brought the balloon over the cabin rather than bringing the cabin under it...

The airtight cabin

Since we were hoping to rise to a height where the air pressure is less than that to which men had ever been subjected before, it was imperative that we should go up in a hermetically sealed cabin within which normal air pressure should be maintained as constantly as possible.

It is obvious that, by constructing the cabin in the form of a sphere, it is possible

to obtained the maximum volume with the minimum weight.

I specified a diameter of 2.1 metres for the sphere; it could not be any smaller and contain the necessary instruments without impeding the work of the two observers. We had decided on a circular, horizontal plank of wood, 120 cm in diameter, to cover the floor of the cabin...

The departure

At dawn, on 18 August 1932, the F.N.R.S. was ready to leave. The preparations were carried out so smoothly that we were ready one hour before the time scheduled for departure. I did not want to leave too soon before sunrise so that we would have enough light, and would not be too cold...

The weather was magnificent, there was no wind and the balloon stood erect above its cabin. Some slight wisps of fog lay across the plain; to the east the sky was becoming lighter above the hills of Wangen. The sun was about to show itself; it was time to go. As planned, the men brought down the loading hoop by pulling on the sixteen manoeuvring ropes; the four thick ropes which were now slack were quickly cut. The sixteen manoeuvring ropes were loosened slightly. Since the lifting power was not great enough, I threw out a little more ballast, and then Colonel Gerber gave the classic order "Hands off!". Slowly, majestically, the F.R.N.S. rose, for the second time, into the air. It appears that, through radiation, or perhaps even because of the evaporation of the moisture on the envelope of the balloon, the hydrogen cooled suddenly. I suppose that this is what led me to jettison some ballast on departure. Whatever the reason, the balloon was rising very slowly; soon it regained its balance and began to go down. It would have been easy for us to have avoided all this by leaving the ground with a greater lifting power. But in order to carry out our plans, we wanted to rise as slowly as possible, and to achieve this, it was essential that I did not throw out even one bag of ballast too many. This rather cumbersome departure would have been too dangerous in a closed cabin, as had been the case during our first ascent, since we

The spherical cabin was hermetically sealed. However, Piccard had fitted a manhole to make his control of the departure easier, and this manhole was not fastened until the balloon reached 1500 m. Right, the partially inflated balloon rose slowly. It reached an altitude of exactly 16,201 m (53,149 ft).

would not have been able to throw out ballast quickly enough at the instant when the balloon began to sink once more. However, at Dübendorf, with the manhole open, everything went off perfectly. While uncoiling the wireless aerial, I looked at the variometer which indicated that the balloon was descending; it was very easy then for me to throw out the necessary amount of ballast (three bags of 12.5 kilos) and the balloon began to rise again slowly and smoothly. At an altitude of 1,500 metres we were able to close the man-hole.

The work on board and our course

We could hardly have hoped for a more perfect journey; it was indeed so perfect that it became almost monotonous. If we had not had the pleasure of flying over the Alps, our day would have differed in no way from an ordinary working-day spent in Brussels, closed up in the laboratory. The instruments functioned nor-

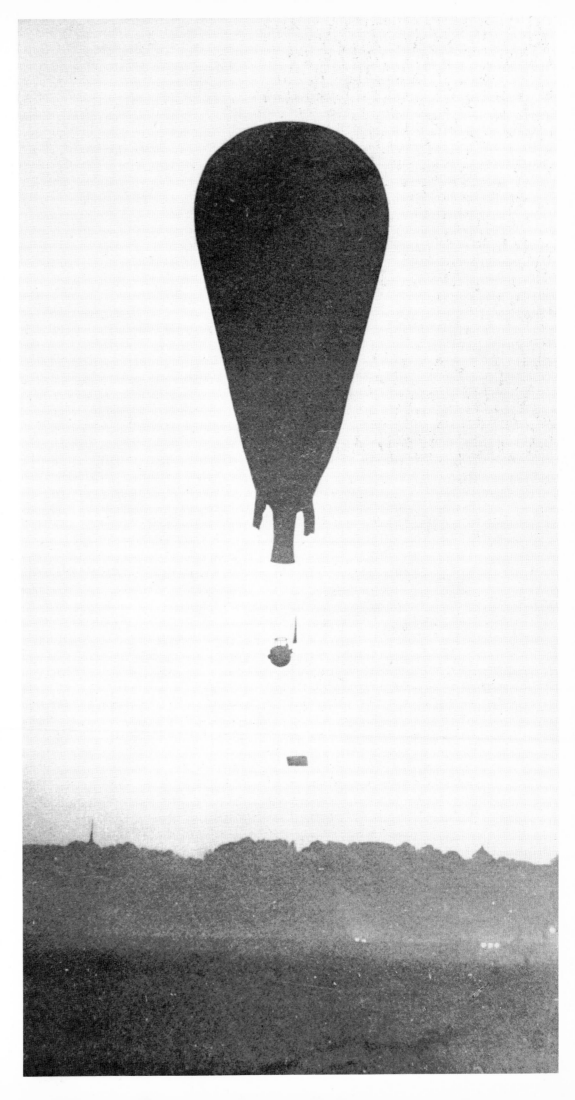

mally, M. Cosyns spent all his time making observations. For my part, I read the barometer, the variometer, and kept an eye on the Dräger appartus. Then I looked through the port-holes so that I could better plot our position. It is easy to establish position when it is possible to glance rapidly in all directions. But my every movement impeded M. Cosyns in his reading of the electrometers, as these instruments are extremely sensitive to movement. I was therefore obliged to keep as still as possible and could only use two portholes in determining our position, one of which was in the lower part of the cabin and only enabled me to glimpse a very restricted portion of the earth's surface directly below us; the other was on the side of the cabin which permitted me, thanks to the slow rotation of the balloon, to see out in all directions. I had no difficulty in determining our bearings with the aid of the lakes. I could easily recognize below us the Rapperswyl dyke, the elevated Lake of Zurich, the Wallensee and then we flew over the Rhine near Sargans. To the north I made out Lake Constance and, to our south-west, almost within a stone's throw, the Lake of the Four Cantons; then we flew right over the Canton of Grisons, all the while veering slowly to our right. I had to give up any hope of making a detailed plotting of our situation, but, since I frequently caught sight of the Glarus mountains, I ran no risk of losing track of our general bearings. Towards eleven o'clock I had the feeling that we should be above Engadine. I looked below to try to locate the lakes of Engadine; at the first glance I saw them below me, there was no mistaking them. We crossed the Inn below Samaden and soon found ourselves to the left of the Bernina pass. The Lago Blanco in all its milky whiteness surprised me for a moment; I had forgotten its existence, since in winter, at the time for ski-ing, it was always covered in a layer of snow and ice. Further to the south was the Lake of Tirano, a wonderful deep blue in colour. Even further to the south I saw a great lake; our large-scale maps did not cover this area, but the Lago di Garda is recognizable, even without the aid of a map. We never lost sight of it

during the last part of our journey, and its presence made the plotting of our position incalculably easier...

The temperature of the cabin

Naturally, at the time of our departure, at dawn on 18 August 1932, we were not too warm. During the ascent our little dwelling became even colder. We consoled ourselves with the thought that the sun would warm us up. Suddenly a circular red spot, 8 cm in diameter, appeared on the white lining of the cabin. Its source was the rising sun, the rays of which were passing through the opposite port-hole. Soon the shining ray turned white. Not long after sunrise, the golden orb was shining with all its strength. But the cabin remained cold (it was too white on the outside). Inside the cabin a layer of frost was forming; some of the frost on the lining exposed to the sun's rays melted, only to freeze again later in little crystals. Our dwelling sparkled like a castle in *A Thousand and One Nights*. The temperature stayed low throughout the day (0° at the top of the cabin and as little as −12° at the bottom). What a contrast with the first journey! It was a great delight for us to be able to put our heads outside the cabin through the man-hole, at about 4 pm and to go down gently towards the warm plain of Lombardy. Unfortunately, this pleasure did not last for long, for the heat to which we were subjected after landing was far worse than the cold. Luckily, it was already 5 pm. I would have preferred the icy cold of the Gurgl glacier.

The landing

At noon we decided to begin the procedure for landing by pulling on the valve rope. We could have stayed aloft for longer but we had accomplished our task. Before us stretched the wide plain of the Po river. Further away lay the Adriatic! There still remained 250 kilos of ballast, which is not excessive. If the F.R.N.S. is brought down very rapidly, 250 kilos of ballast would probably not be enough to stop the balloon (that is, to bring its speed down to zero before landing). If it is wished to come down slowly from 16,000 metres, it is necessary think about landing in time to effect it before the cold

period. A free balloon cools rapidly when the sun begins to sink near to the horizon. If a great quantity of ballast is disposed of, the subsequent fall of the balloon cannot be arrested, and it is forced to land where luck would have it, and this is more running aground than landing.

I believe, therefore, that if the pilot has no urgent reason for postponing the landing, noon is the best hour, in August, for putting into operation the landing of a stratospheric balloon.

We are therefore about to pull on the valve rope... Wisely, I pull the rope for 5 seconds. At first I cannot see whether the valve has opened or not, but Cosyns later informs me that at the moment when I pulled the rope, a ray of sunlight poured into the balloon. This reassures us, for the balloon is not reacting to this short pull. A pull of 10 seconds has no greater effect. We become bolder and pull for 30 seconds. Now the balloon descends at a speed of three metres a second, which corresponds (with air pressure 1/10 of the atmosphere) to a loss in lifting power of about twenty kilos. This loss is compensated for after a short interval.

It is a known fact that a free balloon which is sailing in its position of superior equilibrium, beneath the full force of the sun, only reacts very slowly to pressure on the valve. This phenomenon has not as yet today been fully explained.

We have to pull on the valve rope several times, sometimes for one minute and even for as long as two minutes. It is not too much of a chore when there are two to accomplish the task. I place the rope around the pulley and pull the other end down while Cosyns manipulates the winch. The strong friction of the rubber on the aluminum of the pulley makes my task easier, and Cosyns must not bring too much energy to bear on his actions for the crank arm is several times larger than that of the pulley. Now the descent of the balloon has been initiated. Meanwhile, we have crossed the Valtellina and are now above the mountains of the Adamello Massif. But we must not descend too quickly. At about 2 pm, we leave the mountains and arrive at the northern end of the Lago di Garda. We can now go down more rapidly, for before us is an area which is suitable for landing. Half-an-hour later, we are at a height of 11,000 metres. The aspect of the horizon changes suddenly. The layer of mist is less well defined. We are once more in the troposphere. We hear the throbbing of an aeroplane and we spot it through a port-hole, 4-5 kilometres below us.

Now come the manoeuvres which must be carried out by any pilot of a stratospheric balloon, if he wants to effect a normal landing. We turn a tap in the cabin and let the air escape slowly, just as we did last year over the Alps of Oetztal; but other emotions are governing our actions now. On that occasion it was night, there were high mountains, the uncertainty of a descent without recourse to the valve. Today, everything is fine and clear, failure is inconceivable! At 3.55 pm, we have balanced the pressure at a height of 3,900 metres. We open the man-holes. A marvellous expanse of countryside, in a land bathed in sunshine.

I had never before seen the Lago di Garda, but I recognized it thanks to numerous descriptions of it. There it is, then! Its northern extremity is closed in by mountains, while the different bays in its southern part spread into the plain. I tell Cosyns how the house of the poet-aviator, G. d'Annunzio, is somewhere in the vicinity. I did not suspect that three days later we would be invited to his home!

We are again visited by an aeroplane. A military Italian plane is circling round us. It is Colonel Bernasconi. I wave a handkerchief in greeting.

We approach the ground to the south of the Lago di Garda. It is flat country, some small humps, little fields and meadows separated by numerous hedges. The guide rope is rapidly paid out. The hoop of the drift-indicator, which it touches, is almost torn off.

All augurs well for the landing. We still have enough ballast and we are flying over open country. Close by, below us, we spot a small lake. Trees border the edge and are reflected in the surface, as if in a mirror. So, no waves and therefore no wind. What more could we wish for? The balloon is going down at a rate of 1½ to 2½ metres a second. We throw out a few bags of ballast through the man-holes, since the funnel is no longer being used. These small bags of lead shot are very pleasant to handle compared with the bags of sand which one usually sees hooked on to the cars of balloons. Sand is not so clean and so easy to use. You take hold of a closed bag in one hand (12½ kilos) and you throw it out of the cabin while still holding the ring... A small grey cloud falls towards the ground. The balloon is unballasted, but it is virtually inert. It does not move immediately. Is it still too heavy? We cannot tell. The ground is coming up to meet us. We throw out some more lead shot. People are running up on all sides. I bring out a few words of my meagre Italian vocabulary, shouting, "Prego tenere la corda." A reply comes in Swiss German, for below us is the engineer Zweifel from Glarus and Verona. He acts as our interpreter, which is a great help. The guide rope is now touching the ground. The inevitable effect of conducted electricity takes its toll. We must jettison more ballast. Have we thrown out too much or has the 'Spanish anchor' come away from its moorings?... It is difficult to make a decision after the event. (After we landed, the basket which had been hanging underneath us, laden with various objects, was missing). The fact is that our balloon does not want to land any longer. It has had a close-up view of the earth and wants to return to the stratosphere. It begins to climb again, very rapidly at that, and it is certain that it would have climbed to a height of 18 or 19,000 metres, had we not immediately pulled the valve rope. One must stop the ascent of the balloon before it has risen too high, otherwise the ensuing descent is too violent. We manage this manoeuvre very well. Soon we are once more nearing the ground. We have thrown out the last of the ballast. Below us, people take hold first of the guide rope and then of the sixteen loading ropes. The cabin touches the ground very gently. But the reactions of a balloon 14,000 cubic metres in volume are somewhat sluggish. It does not realise immediately that it is rid of its burden, and continues to descend, with the result that the loading ropes become slack. For a moment the cabin is its own master. The ground slopes away from us slightly and we are subjected to the effect of the gentle impetus gained by a slight lateral slide. The cabin suddenly remembers that it is a ball and... balls roll... and we roll with ours. This experience is not exactly pleasant, but there is nothing frightening about it. We are wearing our helmets. We hold on to the support rails so as not to be thrown against each other. At last everything comes to a halt. The

As soon as he had completed his study of cosmic rays, Piccard pulled the valve-cord. The "F.N.R.S." landed in Lombardy. It touched the ground very gently, but the cabin rolled about like a football. Fortunately, both Piccard and his assistant Max Cosyns were well padded. The local inhabitants helped to deflate the balloon by pulling the ripcord.

people are holding the balloon fast. We have landed. There are small hedges and acacia trees all around us. I am not very partial to the thorns as far as the balloon is concerned. Having made some inquiries, thanks to the generous help of our interpreter, I have the inflated balloon carried into a meadow. It is not a large meadow, but the barriers around it are by no means insurmountable. Here we can deflate the balloon. First of all, a long pull on the valve rope. Cosyns can get out, because there are plenty of people holding the ropes. He pulls the rip cord. The envelope leans over. For a moment it looks as though the balloon is going to collapse on to the cabin. I jump out, instinctively clutching the camera. Cosyns carries on pulling the rip cord. It is the first time that he has ripped a balloon...

Conclusions

Finally, here are the results obtained from our Geiger-counters:

1) Whether the axis of the counter is vertical or horizontal, the number of rays noted is the same. The average values of the numerous observations, during which the counters were alternately vertical and horizontal, tally with the percentage fractions just as much at 14,000 as at 16,000 metres. It is a known fact that a Geiger-counter is sensitive to changes in direction.

At sea-level we found that cosmic rays come from above. The fact that, above 14,000 metres, they seem to come from all sides in equal proportions is an important result of our observations in so far as the theory of cosmic rays is concerned.

2) If one compares the number of ions (measured in the ionisation chamber) with the number of rays (measured by the Geiger-counter) one finds that on average the cosmic rays over the same distance produce four times less ions than radium gamma rays with their subordinates.

We can conclude this chapter by saying: Nothing has been proved. We do not yet know the nature of cosmic rays, or where they originate. But the problem is more intriguing than ever and we can but hope that our knowledge of them will increase and that we are on the right road.

THE DRAMATIC END
OF THE "EXPLORER"

South Dakota, 28 July 1934

Although we were now in the warm rays of the sun, which should have expanded the gas and provided more lifting power, the *Explorer* was sluggish and seemed disinclined to move upward; in fact, it even settled a little. It became evident that, because we were dealing with an unusually large balloon, the responses were slow. Finally, Anderson discharged bag after bag of ballast through the air-locked hopper—nearly 400 pounds in all. Suddenly the balloon started to rise, and shortly the rate-of-climb meter indicated that we were ascending at 500 feet per minute...

We stayed at 40,000 feet, as scheduled, while the various instruments went through their cycles of operation. We started up the Geiger counter apparatus designed to record the directions of movement of cosmic rays. The magnetic relays of this instrument clicked when a cosmic ray passed through the apparatus in a certain narrow path...

We stopped valving gas and the *Explorer* again started to ascend. It was now nearly noon, mountain time, and for the next hour we moved steadily upward. At 1 o'clock we were approaching the 60,000 foot level, and Major Kepner prepared to bring the balloon again into equilibrium...

Suddenly a clattering noise was heard on top of the gondola.

Encouraged by Piccard's ascent, the Americans Albert W. Stevens, Orvil A. Anderson and William E. Kepner had made a stratospheric balloon of 84,000 cu. m, called "Explorer". Its car, which weighed a ton, was virtually a flying laboratory.

"Explorer" climbed to 61,122 ft. The aeronauts were quietly engaged in making their experiments, when suddenly an accident occurred. Three tears appeared in the envelope of the balloon. Gas escaped, and the balloon fell. At a height of 9,000 ft, the bottom of the balloon tore completely, and the remains of the envelope acted as a kind of parachute. The "Explorer" continued to fall. When they reached a height of 984 ft above the ground, the aeronauts parachuted to safety, while the cabin crashed to earth.

We looked upward through the three-inch upper port and saw that the noise had been caused by part of the appendix cord—a small rope—falling on the roof of the gondola.

What had caused the cord to drop? Looking still higher, we were startled to see a large rip in the balloon's lower surface. It was then a few minutes past 1. The gas had not expanded to fill out the balloon completely. Had the rip not occurred, the bottom of the bag should have become spherical at something over 65,000 feet. The hydrogen would have

poured out of the 8 foot appendix (an open sleeve of fabric at the bottom of the balloon) and the *Explorer* automatically would have stopped rising. From that point on, as we discharged ballast, we could have risen to 75,000 feet.

To go higher after the rip appeared was inadvisable. The gas was practically down to the open rip. We valved. But super-heat from the sun's rays was expanding the hydrogen so fast that the valve was just able to take care of the excess. It was twenty minutes before the bag started downward. In fact, it rose somewhat.

Imagine our feelings for a few minutes! It looked as though the valve hose had parted along with the torn fabric. Had this happened, we would have been help-less. But the valve did work! We oper-ated that valve altogether no less than 150 times during the flight. It never once failed us, though we could neither see it nor hear it working.

Through the overhead glass porthole we watched the rent in the fabric gra-dually becoming larger and larger. The minutes passed slowly by; the magnets of the cosmic ray instruments clattered on;

133

the buzzers hammered on the barometer box; the instrument cameras clicked in unison at regular intervals.

Above our heads were five glass flasks, each more than a foot in diameter, that had been pumped free from air. We had intended opening these at 75,000 feet to obtain samples of the air of the stratosphere, but now we opened them at 60,000 feet. We heard a faint hiss as each valve was cracked; methodically we shut the valves again, thus sealing the samples.

Across the gondola stood Major Kepner, his hand on the special lever that would release the 80 foot parachute installed by its designer, Major E. L. Hoffman.

Kepner was ready to turn the lever should the balloon suddenly disintegrate. However, when the balloon burst at a much lower altitude, no one was within reach of the lever to release the parachute.

Beside Major Kepner was Captain Anderson, with his hand on the control that led to the pneumatic balloon valve. Both officers looked in turn at the bag above, at the rate-of-climb meter (which had now become a rate-of-descent meter), and at the statoscopes, which also gave indication of the speed of descent.

At times we all talked briefly over the radio. But little other talking was done, for our ears were strained to get warning sounds from above us. Soft swishing noises came through the roof of the gondola from time to time. Each of these sounds meant a new rent, or an increase in length of a rip already there.

There was a temptation to shut off all the switches and quiet the instruments. The sharp drumming of the buzzer hammers on the barometer tubes was particularly irritating. But there was still a possibility of saving the records of the flight; so we let the mechanisms click on.

Below us was the brown, sun-baked earth, so far away that no roads, railroads, or houses could be made out. Our direction of drift was changing, but that was now a matter of little concern. The question now was not *where* we should get down, but *how*!

On 11 November 1935, one year after the accident to "Explorer", Stevens and Anderson made another attempt to reach the stratosphere. "Explorer II" was inflated at Rapid City with the help of the US Army.

At the top of our flight an extraordinary phenomenon was visible through the upper porthole. As we looked through the ports that were 45 degrees from the vertical the sky was the rich dark-blue color associated with high mountain views; but from the vertical port the sky was like black velvet on which ink has been spilled and dried—it was black with just the merest touch of dark blue. It looked as dark as the sky at the time of an eclipse of the sun when stars may be seen. However, it did not occur to us at the time to look for stars; our interest was in the increasing rents in the great white bag overhead.

But we could not fail to note the astounding brilliance of the sunlight and the intensity of the reflected light from the balloon rigging. Some of the ropes, especially those nearest the gondola, were so bright that they had a fluorescent appearance and looked larger than they really were. It is possible that the extreme contrast between the brilliantly lighted balloon envelope and rigging and the sky made the sky look darker than it was...

From our instruments we knew that outside it was almost 80 degrees below zero, Fahrenheit. We were in relatively warm air inside, about 10 degrees above freezing, but it was getting steadily colder. Already ice had formed in our gondola in a narrow band about two feet below the top. At first there had been condensation of moisture on the walls. This froze and accumulated still more frost until now there was a layer almost an eighth of an inch thick in places...

We still had to go about our routine duties. One was to watch the supply of liquid air, to keep it evaporating at the required rate, and to let air out of the gondola now and then to keep the internal pressure of the sphere to less than nine pounds per square inch...

Everything inside the gondola was working perfectly, so that it seemed strange to realize we were hurrying downward in the hope of escaping a very real danger.

Three quarters of an hour passed, and we were down to 40,000 feet. Our speed was increasing, and half an hour later we were down to 20,000 feet. Major Kepner and Captain Anderson each forced open a hatch, and for the first time we felt we were free.

It was good to know that we were in a position to use our parachutes if necessary.

We all climbed out on top and took a good look at the balloon. It was pretty badly torn. Many more tears and rips had appeared in it. The question was, how long would it hold together? As the enormous bag came downward through the air, large waves appeared in the lower fabric, sweeping across it and back again. With almost every wave the rents grew bigger and bigger.

Suddenly the entire bottom of the bag dropped out. We could look up into the whole bare inside of the balloon. Only the part above the lower catenary band now remained. The bottomless bag was acting largely as a parachute. It was a pretty sight, quite round and tight and symmetrical. But it was a bit too tight for safety!

We still had an enormous weight left in the gondola and it was urgent to lessen it. Kepner and Anderson cut loose the spectrograph and it floated down on its individual parachute.

I climbed back into the gondola and started discharging ballast. In accord with plans decided upon before the flight, all the liquid air that remained was first poured out. Then the two empty containers were fastened to a parachute and thrown overboard. These I followed with hundreds of pounds of lead ballast poured out through the hopper and in streams through the hatch, after opening each sack.

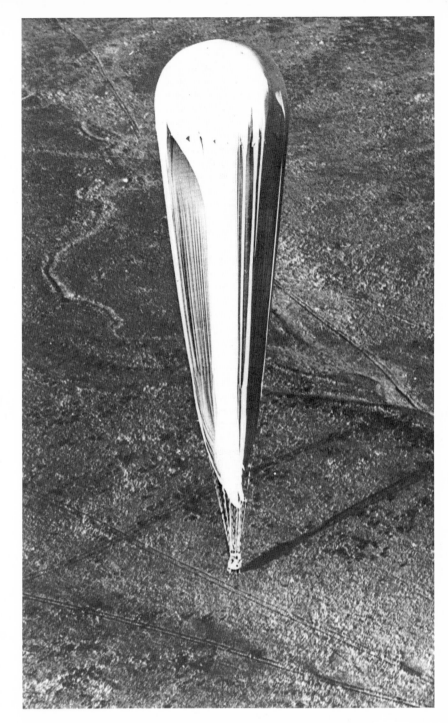

Stevens and Anderson reached a height of 71,260 ft. This photograph was taken at the moment when "Explorer II" touched ground. The rip cord is being pulled and the gas is escaping. This time, the flight was completely successful.

We could have disposed of the ballast much more rapidly if we had hurled it out in bulk, but at no time during the flight was anything thrown out in a way that might injure people on the ground.

We had worn our parachute harnesses constantly during the flight, and when things began to look bad we had each put on the detachable portion, or parachute proper.

We were ready, but we wanted to stay with the balloon as long as possible to avoid being distant from it when we landed.

135

On 16 August 1960, the American Joseph ▷
M. Kittinger jnr, reached a height of
17,454 ft He then made a free fall of
4 min. 30 sec., and at 101,181 ft opened his
parachute. This jump lasted 13 min.

Thanks to his stratospheric balloon "Man
High II", Major David G. Simon (below)
attained on 19 August 1957 the record height
of 101,509 ft. His ascent lasted 32 hours.
The technicians (opposite) waited until the
balloon was exactly vertical to the cabin
before releasing it.

136

At 10,000 feet we really should have left the balloon, but we did not wish to abandon the scientific apparatus. So we stayed on. At 6,000 feet we again talked the matter over and decided we had better leave. The last altimeter reading I gave was 5,000 feet above sea level.

Since this part of Nebraska was 2,000 feet above sea level, we were in reality only a little more than a half mile from the ground.

In the meantime Captain Anderson, atop the gondola, had been having difficulty with his parachute. The release handle had caught on something and the parachute pack had come open. It was a situation that might have been disconcerting to a less cool head. There was only one thing to do—that was to gather the folds of silk under one arm preparatory to leaping.

While getting the fabric together, Anderson stepped down until both his feet were in the hatch from which I planned to leap. Andy is a big man, but never before had I noticed that his feet were large. Now, looking up at the opening partially blocked by his pedal extremities, I shouted:

"Hey, get your big feet out of the way! I want to jump."

Whether Anderson heard me or not does not matter. Things started to happen fast. The feet disappeared, and I knew he had leaped. As he jumped, the balloon exploded.

The pressure suddenly became too great all over, and the fabric burst at once in hundreds of places.

The gondola dropped like a stone.

Twice I tried to push myself through the hatch of the gondola, but wind pressure around the rapidly falling sphere forced me back. So I backed up and plunged headlong at the opening. I managed to hit it fairly, and went out in a horizontal position, face down, with arms and legs outspread like a frog. By that time we had fallen 1,500 feet and were descending so fast that the wind pressure held me practically even with the gondola. In other words, I was not falling away from it, but moving downward at the same rate of speed. I turned over a half revolution and, as I came right side up, pulled my rip cord. The parachute opened instantly.

The jerk was like that made when one jumps from an airplane at 80 miles an hour. The folds of white silk opened in a large circle—and then a portion of the balloon fabric above the gondola fell on top of my parachute. For a second it looked as if the balloon would take my chute with it. The fabric covered it to the very center of the silk. And then luckily the parachute slid out from under and worked itself free.

How about Kepner and Anderson? I looked around and saw the other two parachutes in the air and knew they were safe. Directly below me, I heard the gondola hit with a tremendous thud, and saw a huge ring of dust shoot out. Forty seconds later I hit—fortunately with a much lighter thud—and the parachute dragged me a few feet on my face through the black dirt of a Nebraska cornfield.

In a very few minutes, Major Kepner, Captain Anderson, and I had rolled up our parachutes and hastened to the spot where the gondola had struck; already a score of people were present, seemingly rising out of the very ground, and in a few minutes hundreds more were coming across the fields to the wreck.

Lieut. J. F. Phillips already had landed his airplane in the adjoining field. He and Sergeant G. B. Gilbert had followed us, making pictures, all the way from South Dakota, had seen practically every detail of our flight up to the altitude they could reach, 25,000 feet, and had actually photographed the final collapse of the balloon as they circled us. We were in a cornfield not far from the town of Holdrege, Nebraska.

Things looked pretty black for scientific results when we walked up to the pile of balloon fabric that covered the fallen gondola, pulled it aside, and found that our beautiful black and white globe had been crushed like an eggshell. It had been almost flattened out, and gaping crevices ran in every direction across the irregularly curved top.

We borrowed an ax and cut through the few uncracked areas, removing sections of shell. Inside, the instruments of which we had been so proud were a heart-breaking mass of wreckage.

We realized, however, that since we had registered almost all of our records photographically, there still were chances that some of the recording negative could be salvaged.

On 30 September 1906, the first Gordon Bennett Cup competition was started from the Tuileries Gardens in Paris. The "Elfe" piloted by Alfredo Vonwiler took off at 4 pm to start the race. It rose slowly and gracefully displaying the Italian flag.

THE GORDON BENNETT AERONAUTIC CUP

The large balloon meetings organised at the 1900 Universal Exhibition in Paris marked the beginnings of aerial sport in France and abroad. In November 1905, the owner of the NEW YORK HERALD, James Gordon Bennett (1841-1918), announced the establishment of a new international competition, the Gordon Bennett Aeronautic Cup. This idea gave the world aeronautic movement a new and powerful direction. Some years before, in 1900, this wealthy patron of sport had contributed largely to the development of motor cars by means of the Gordon Bennett Automobile Cup. This was so successful that he decided to encourage aerial sport by the same method. The Cup, an artistic production valued then at 12,500 francs, was competed for the first time in Paris. The meeting was open to the Aero Clubs of all nations.

The meetings, which stopped just before the Second World War, gave rise to many extraordinary journeys, including the astonishing flight of the Swiss Schaeck. In 1923, five aeronauts—two Swiss, two Americans, and a Spaniard—were killed in pursuit of their sport. These were the only deaths caused by the competition.

RESULTS OF THE 26 MEETINGS

Date	Departure	Arrival	Duration	Distance	Winning balloons	Number of balloons
30. 9. 1906	Paris (France)	Fylingdales, Yorkshire (England)	22 hours	647 km	**United States**: Frank P. Lahm, H. B. Hersey (U.S.A.)	16
21. 10. 1907	St Louis (U.S.A.)	Bradley Beach, New Jersey (U.S.A.)	40 hours	1403 km	**Pommern**: Oskar Erbslöh, Henry P. Clayton (Germany)	9
1. 10. 1908	Berlin (Germany)	Bergest (Norway)	73 hours	1212 km	**Helvetia**: Col. Schaeck, Lt Messner (Switzerland)	23
3. 10. 1909	Zurich (Switzerland)	Ostrolenka (Poland)	35 hours	1121 km	**America II**: Edgar W. Mix, A. Roussel (U.S.A.)	17
7. 10. 1910	St Louis (U.S.A.)	Peribonka River, Quebec (Canada)	44 hours	1884 km	**America II**: Alan R. Hawley, August Post (U.S.A.)	10
9. 10. 1911	Kansas City (U.S.A.)	Halcombe, Wisconsin	12 hours	758 km	**Berlin II**: Lt Hans Gericke, O. Dunker (Germany)	7
7. 10. 1912	Stuttgart (Germany)	Riga (U.S.S.R.)	46 hours	2191 km	**La Picardie**: Maurice Bienaimé (France), R. Rumpelmayer	22
2. 10. 1913	Paris (France)	Bampton (England)	43 hours	618 km	**Goodyear**: Ralph H. Upson, R. A. L. Preston (U.S.A.)	18 28
1914-1919	No meetings	—	—	—	—	—
3. 10. 1920	Birmingham (U.S.A.)	North Hero Island, Vermont (U.S.A.)	40 hours	1760 km	**Belgica**: Ernest Demuyter, M. Labrousse (Belgium)	7
18. 9. 1921	Brussels (Belgium)	Lambay Island (Ireland)	27 hours	766 km	**Zurich**: Capt. Paul Armbruster, Ansermier (Switzerland)	15
6. 8. 1922	Geneva (Switzerland)	Ocnitza (Rumania)	25 hours	1372 km	**Belgica**: Ernest Demuyter, A. Veenstra (Belgium)	19
23. 9. 1923	Brussels (Belgium)	Sköllersta (Sweden)	21 hours	1115 km	**Belgica**: Ernest Demuyter, L. Coeckelbergh (Belgium)	16
15. 6. 1924	Brussels (Belgium)	St Abb's Head (Scotland)	43 hours	714 km	**Belgica**: Ernest Demuyter, L. Coeckelbergh (Belgium)	17
7. 6. 1925	Brussels (Belgium)	Cap Toriñana (Spain)	47 hours	1345 km	**Prince Léopold**: A. Veenstra, Ph. Quersin (Belgium)	19
30. 5. 1926	Antwerp (Belgium)	Sölvesborg (Sweden)	16 hours	861 km	**Goodyear III**: Ward T. Van Orman, Walter W. Morton (U.S.A.)	17
10. 9. 1927	Detroit (U.S.A.)	Baxley, Georgia (U.S.A.)	—	1198 km	**Detroit**: Edward J. Hill, A. G. Schlosser (U.S.A.)	15
30. 6. 1928	Detroit (U.S.A.)	Kenbridge, Virginia (U.S.A.)	48 hours	740 km	**U.S. Army**: Capt. W. E. Kepner, W. O. Earickson (U.S.A.)	12
28. 9. 1929	St Louis (U.S.A.)	Troy, Ohio (U.S.A.)	—	548 km	**Goodyear VIII**: Ward T. Van Orman, Alan L. MacCracken (U.S.A.)	9
1. 9. 1930	Cleveland, Ohio (U.S.A.)	Norfolk, Massachusetts (U.S.A.)	—	872 km	**Goodyear VIII**: Ward T. Van Orman, (U.S.A.) Alan L. MacCracken	6
1931	No meetings	—	—	—	—	—
25. 9. 1932	Basle (Switzerland)	Vilna (Poland)	41 hours	1536 km	**U.S. Navy**: T. G. M. Settle, W. Bushnell (U.S.A.)	17
2. 9. 1933	Chicago (U.S.A.)	Province of Quebec (Canada)	—	1361 km	**Kosciusko**: Franczyek Hynek, Zbigniew Burzynski (Poland)	7
23. 9. 1934	Warsaw (Poland)	Anna Woronez (U.S.S.R.)	44 hours	1331 km	**Kosciusko**: Franczyek Hynek, W. Pomaski (Poland)	8
15. 9. 1935	Warsaw (Poland)	Tiszkino Stalingrad (U.S.S.R.)	57 hours	1650 km	**Polonia II**: Zbigniew Burzynski, Wladyslaw Wysochi (Poland)	10
29. 8. 1936	Warsaw (Poland)	Archangel (U.S.S.R.)	—	1715 km	**Belgica**: Ernest Demuyter, P. Hoffmann (Belgium)	10
20. 6. 1937	Brussels (Belgium)	Tukumo (Lithuania)	46 hours	1396 km	**Belgica**: Ernest Demuyter, P. Hoffmann (Belgium)	12
11. 9. 1938	Liège (Belgium)	Trojan (Bulgaria)	37 hours	1692 km	**L.O.P.P.**: Antoni Janusz, Janik (Poland)	11

After 22 hours of flying, the "Elfe" landed on the roof of a small house at New Holland, Yorkshire. Vonwiler took the second prize. Above, his assistant Ettore Cianetti is recovering the car.

SEVENTY-THREE HOURS IN A BALLOON

Col. Schaeck, 1908

"We were in the air for precisely seventy-three hours, thirty hours above the land, forty-three above the sea, between sky and water, seeing nothing but the clouds, the sun, the heavens, and, from time to time, towering waves; hearing nothing but the sound of the raging storm which was beating on the North Sea at that time. We beat the endurance record, set up the previous year by Leblanc, of forty-four hours, three minutes. We could easily have carried on for another day, for we were in possession of all our faculties, as was the balloon... I believe, meanwhile, that we have set up a record which will stand for a long time.

"The distance, as the crow flies, from the point where we landed to Berlin is about 808 miles. But, in reality, we covered a much greater distance since before we came down near the Norwegian coast we had described a vast arc, the top of which

must have passed through a point beyond the arctic circle. And we did not approach the North Sea until we were to the south of the mouth of the Elbe and what is more, we had, on leaving Berlin, described a semi-circle around the south of the town. Therefore, our complete journey must have led us some 1,740 miles. Consequently we averaged a speed of 25 miles per hour...

"On Sunday, 11 October, we left Berlin at 3.59 pm, at the moment when we learned that our unhappy rivals in *The Conqueror* had crashed without hurting themselves. At first we were borne towards Kottbus and thought that our journey would be accomplished solely over dry land. So, we had not taken with us certain scientific instruments which would have been useful over the sea.

"Apart from that, the fittings of the balloon's car left nothing to be desired.

We had distributed the contents so that our actions might not be impeded and, even though we had 46 bags of ballast weighing 700 kilos with us, we could install ourselves comfortably in our improvised abode, which measured 3 ft 3 ins wide by 4 ft long. We could stretch out in it, by leaning our heads against the edge of the car, and, as in a ship, we made a point of resting at regular intervals. I slept in the evenings until midnight. At that time I relieved my second-in-command, who slept until the morning. When the sun had come up, and the expansion of the gas ensured a normal ascent, we dozed off and slept the sleep of the just until 9 am.

"We spent our first day in steadying the flight of our balloon, as one can clearly see on the records. Twelve hours after our departure, we reached a height of 820 ft and we stayed at that height for a long while. We were

21 October 1907. The flight of the "Pommern" piloted by Oskar Erbslöh, was halted by an insurmountable obstacle—the Atlantic. Erbslöh, who started from St Louis, made a flight of 870 miles, landing near New York (below). He won the cup.

On 3 October 1909, the competitors for the cup
started from Zurich. The winner was an American, Edgar W. Mix, who landed in Poland.

On the most remarkable flights for the Gordon Bennett Cup was that of Schaeck, a Swiss (above, taken in the car with his assistant Messner). Leaving Berlin on 11 October 1908, he landed in Norway, after an epic flight of more than 73hrs, in which he covered a distance of 753 miles from his starting point.

travelling in the direction of Magdeburg, and we passed close by at noon on the Monday. The fog, which had until then prevented us from catching sight of the land, parted, and we threw out a few messages, of which only one reached its destination...

"A little to the north of Bremen, as we were approaching the sea, my friend, who was on watch, heard people shouting: "Come down!" But he continued on his way and, without a moment's hesitation, set out across the waves of the North Sea, over which we were to spend the rest of our journey. When I awoke, we had been over the sea for several hours. I asked Lieutenant Messner whether he knew where we were. He answered merely: 'For two or three hours now, over the North Sea.'

"Not very much over, however. Since the previous day at 5 pm until the Tuesday at 6.30 am, for about fourteen hours, therefore, we sailed at a constant height of between 328 and 820 ft, and that was all.

"The sky was cloudless, the moon almost full. The sea murmured below us. The minutes we lived through then, we shall never forget.

"It was very cold early on Tuesday morning. A thick layer of cloud formed which impeded our view of the sea for almost the whole of the rest of our journey. A little before 7 am, our balloon began to climb, as it did each morning, and we gradually reached a height of nearly 11,483 ft...

"During the course of the afternoon we observed a curious phenomenon. We were sailing along the top of the clouds which were divided into glass frames, as it were. These frames formed a sort of screen, and, from moment to moment, we could see our balloon reflected in them in every detail, and sometimes there was even a three-dimensional effect.

"The temperature had been falling all the afternoon, and, a little before 3 pm, as we were crossing over the Gulf Stream, which we recognised when the clouds parted for a moment by the particular brown colour of the marine algae which is a distinguishing feature of this current, our balloon descended to such an extent that our guide rope touched the surface of the sea beneath the car.

"As we were still falling, my friend suddenly threw the heavy packing case, which was to contain the deflated balloon, into the water. I said: "You should have cut it up into small pieces. We'll climb much too high." He replied: "I didn't have time."

"Were we in danger then?"

"Merely that of getting wet, of sinking our provisions and of weighing down the balloon-car."

"We travelled at a height of 9,000 ft, but soon came down again. We decided that it would be wise to take some precautions in the event that the situation might become critical and we would have to abandon the car. Lieutenant Messner built me a small hemp ladder, so that I could climb up easily among the ropes, and to these ropes we attached all our ship's papers, carefully enclosed in thermos flasks,

for these documents were dearer to us than our lives.

"The night passed without incident, although a dreadful storm was whipping up the waves of the ocean throughout the hours of darkness. Our balloon running before the wind was carried along at a headlong speed, but rose and fell constantly, owing to the proximity of the Gulf Stream and the continual changes in temperature caused by this currant of water.

"Once more, a new day dawned, and we rose again. When we reached a height of nearly 13,131 ft, we began to be plagued by hallucinations. I could hear singing, the barking of a dog, bells ringing. We saw remarkable countryside, running water and very high mountains.

"We were still climbing; we reached the highest point of our journey, about 17,388 ft. At this moment, we wanted to test our strength: Lieutenant Messner lifted a bag of ballast on two occasions, and felt his heart beating violently. I did the same, only lifting the bag four times, with great ease. To tell the truth, we were both in perfect health, very pleased with our journey, trusting in our lucky star and in no way affected by the temperature, for the inflated rubber life-jackets which we had tied round our waists as soon as we had set out over the sea, were keeping us beautifully warm. And moreover, we were wearing capacious camelhair coats which were incredibly soft and warm.

"We had no notion of any possible danger we might meet. The wind had turned as we had forecast. It was coming from Iceland, and had gradually brought us down to the south; we should have been in the region of Norway. Shortly after having seen our fantastic mirages, and before we had risen to 17,388 ft, we caught sight of land.

"I must admit that we greeted this sight with shouts of joy.

"This time we were sure that our eyes were not deceiving us. We described what we could see in detail to each other, and our pictures matched perfectly. We were now absolutely sure.

"At 1 pm we sighted a ship: the *Cimbria*. We went down very rapidly and, soon, we were only 328 ft above the water; then, even nearer.

We decided at this point to carry on our way using the guide rope and following the coastline. We let our guide rope trail through the water...

"At 3 pm, the crew of the *Cimbria*, which had come very close to us, seized hold of the guide rope against our wishes. We could not make ourselves understood and were dragged along in tow, despite ourselves.

"This was the first time that we had come face to face with any sort of danger, in this case that of seeing our balloon explode. The vapour was travelling too quickly towards the ground and the atmospheric pressure was having a sorry effect on our aerostat which still contained gas.

"What is more, as we were travelling through islands which were very close to one another, the boat was making abrupt turns, which resulted in our car touching the water at one stage. I consequently went down on board the *Cimbria* to rid our balloon of some ballast, leaving my second-in-command, Messner, to pilot the balloon, as in the rule-book.

"At last, at 5 pm precisely, or seventy-three hours and one minute after our departure from Berlin, we landed at Ersholmen, a harbour near Bergseth, not far from Molde, some distance from Christiansund...

"A crowd of Norwegians had run up and lent willing hands to aid us. We then tried to telegraph our arrival. It took no less than two hours to send our message and it was not until 9 pm that we could refresh ourselves in the house of the schoolteacher of Molde...

The start of the 1922 Gordon Bennett race took place at Geneva (below). On 6 August, at 4.30 pm, the first competitors took off. The Belgian aeronaut Ernest Demuyter, who was to be winner five times, won the Cup for the first time in this race. Piloting the "Belgica", he made a flight lasting 25 hrs, landing at Ocnitza, Rumania, 852 miles from Geneva.

143

1945-1971

STOWAWAY IN THE SKY : ALBERT LAMORISSE

The film-maker Albert Lamorisse (1922-1970) managed to encapsule in film all that is the essence of ballooning. His film "The Red Balloon" (1956), an enchanting story of a little boy who has a "tame" toy balloon, which follows him everywhere like a dog, is almost poetry. Lamorisse became fascinated by the fairy-tale possibilities of aerial photography. He perfected a system he called "Hélivision", which neutralised the vibrations set up by helicopters, and made, in 1960, "Stowaway in the Sky".

For Lamorisse, it was the reality behind the Oriental tradition of the flying carpet, in which people had the ability to fly silently over the earth, and were able to view life from the skies. In his film, aimed at children of all ages, Lamorisse composed a portrait of France, revealed through the amusing adventures of an old inventor and his grandson, Pascal. The story begins...

Everything was ready. Pascal came up carrying his parrot and his little bag and wanted to climb into the car. But Grandpapa held him off. "No, Pascal", he said, "I can't take you with me!"—"But you promised, Grandpapa! And you've always said that your balloon is so easy to steer that I could do it myself."—"Of course, but this is my first test flight and we don't know that everything will be well. Listen: Go along with Antoine in the motor-car, like a good boy."

Pascal preferred not to hear this. His grandfather was a brilliant inventor and Pascal had been very excited for a long time, ever since his Grandpapa had given him permission to go with him on this marvellous adventure.

"Let go of the ropes!" cried Grandpapa, and the balloon rose into the sky.

In the hubbub of departure Pascal, who had been entirely forgotten, had hung on to one of the bags of sand and was now rising with the car. His position was by no means a comfortable or a secure one; he had to close his eyes. When he opened them again, the houses and people below were already minute.

Grandpapa examined his instruments. The needle on the altimeter was climbing the scale steadily but slowly. "Have I got too much ballast?" he asked himself. Suddenly, he caught sight of a small clutched hand appearing over the rim of the car. Grandpapa took hold of it immediately and hauled little Pascal into the shuddering basket; for a moment he could not speak with shock and fright. What a deadly fall Pascal would have taken if the bag of sand on which he had been sitting had suddenly come away!

Don't think that Grandpapa's balloon was a balloon like any other. Oh no! It was a balloon which one could steer as one wished. It was thus that its inventor had described it to the Aeronautic Club; a balloon which could be made to climb, to descend and to turn left or right at will. This balloon was very economical because it contained nothing but the air which we breathe. In short, in this case it was a question of a quite extraordinary invention which—there was no doubt about it—was going to open completely new perspectives on the field of transport and communications.

Grandpapa had built a special machine for inflating the balloon and had attached it to the engine of a car. The air passed first through a device which made it more fluid; it then passed through a cylinder where its new consistency was stabilized and thence into the balloon.

Antoine had been told in detail the sites where, each evening, he was to prepare for the landing and set up camp for the night.

This meant, of course, that he had to arrive before the balloon each time; at the moment, he could hardly manage to keep pace. His schedule was so tight that he could not even stop for lunch. This was the reason for his inventing a system of obtaining refreshment when he wished, without losing time.

Until now, he had always thought that his master and his master's friends in the Aeronautic Club were retrogressives who were living behind the times.

The idea that a return to simplicity could even enable one to overtake the progress of technology had never previously entered his head.

Now, he was near to admitting that in fact his master had—as he himself would say—discovered an ideal means of travel.

Meanwhile Pascal and his grandfather could themselves lunch when they so desired. They had evidently made up their differences, and Grandpapa had come to the conclusion that this journey was an excellent geography lesson for his grandson.

He was already imagining the day in the future when geography masters, with their pupils in the car of a balloon, would travel over continents, explaining

145

Antoine, Grandpapa's valet, follows the balloon in a splendid old car. Every evening, at a prearranged rendezvous, the aeronauts meet him (left). While they have breakfast in the morning, Antoine re-inflates the balloon with gas carried in the car.

Travelling in a balloon is a pleasant change from schoolroom geography lessons. Pascal, enraptured, learns to know his country from the height of the balloon car, for, map in hand, Grandpapa explains each new "discovery". ▷

Grandpapa's balloon sails peacefully over the sunny lands of the South of France. The village of Mallemort, near Arles, appears in the background.

The Mediterranean is in sight. The balloon flies over Eze, an old village perched on a rock not far from Nice on the Côte d'Azur. Pascal insists in having a paddle in the sea, suspended from the balloon by a rope.

Flying over the Breton coastline, Pascal and his Grandpapa are greeted by the guests at a traditional country wedding. They land not far away, and go to join in the fun.

what was to be seen below: the beauty of the mouths of rivers, valleys in all their different forms, the high, solitary plateaux, mountain chains with their folds, their crevices and the slow movement of their glaciers. The schoolboys would find that, seen from a certain height, man is transformed more and more into a fabulous animal, intelligent and beautiful to behold, whose life is spent purely in working the land, in sowing and harvesting. Thus he clothes the earth in a perpetually renewed mantle, the folds of which are sometimes wonderfully full, sometimes flat, which sparkles softly or throws off wondrous reflections like rich velvet; a mantle of a thousand colours, sometimes dark, sometimes light, beautiful from every angle.

At the end of the day, Antoine was nevertheless the first at their destination; for our two travellers had made a large detour in order to see the forests of the Vosges and the storks of Alsace. When they arrived, somewhat late, the camp was already prepared for the night.

At the moment of landing, something unexpected occurred. It was Antoine's fault. He was eager to help but did not know how to set about dealing with the aerostat. As soon as Pascal had jumped out of the car, the lightened balloon immediately lifted off again carrying Grandpapa who found himself, as one may well imagine, in an uncomfortable position.

However, it was not long before Grandpapa could write in his log-book that this first day had passed as planned, and that the balloon behaved admirably.

When the balloon appeared above Paris and passed over the roofs, so low that one could have touched it with a hand, wild enthusiasm caught hold of the members of the Aeronautic Club. All of them, even the out and out sceptics, were now convinced. The invention of a genius! At last one could dispense with lighter-than-air gases; at last the decline of all those noisy infernal machines had been announced. The era of the balloon had come into being. From now on, everyone, old men and children, could frolic in peace with their loved ones in the embrace of a calm Nature, in the purest of airs. Boldly, Grandpapa made the balloon pass close to the balcony of the Aeronautic Club; he wanted to show how easy it was to steer his machine. To land on the roof, as was his secret intention, did not seem very wise, however, as the roof, bristled with television aerials. In future, one would have to take care that they were removed. Leaving this aside, it was not the time for delicate

Before undertaking the flight over Mont Blanc, Grandpapa flies his balloon over Paris, wishing to show off his invention to his friends in the Club Aérostatique. The weather is splendid, and the aeronauts remain lost in admiration for the beauties of the French countryside. Plains, forests, lakes and picturesque villages stretch away beneath them to the horizon.

149

manoeuvres; the important thing was to bring their planned tour to a successful conclusion. For this reason, Grandpapa let his friends wish him 'bon voyage' and sailed off in the direction of the Loire...

On that day, they decided not to land for the night but to stay airborne.

The earth gradually became dark, while the balloon was still lit up by the rays of the sun.

When they woke up the next morning, the sea lay below them. Grandpapa was a little surprised at this. He made a few notes in his logbook and changed course for Brittany.

A wedding breakfast was taking place not far from the coast. The guests waved merrily to the balloon passing over their heads and invited its occupants to join the festivities. To the astonishment of all, Grandpapa landed. There was drinking and dancing...

Grandpapa and Pascal returned to the car and found themselves once more above the sea. All at once, Grandpapa caught sight of a marvellous sailing boat through his telescope. "Balloon to port!" shouted the man on watch. "What? A typhoon? All

hands on deck!" shouted the commanding officer. "No, it's a balloon! Look! up there."...

Grandpapa sailed on without a care in the world. He was above the Auvergne when he heard a strange noise, a sort of whistling sound which was not very reassuring.

Being a sensible man, he decided to land without delay. He was wise. For, at the moment when the balloon came into contact with the ground, it burst into flames. Pascal could feel the heat of the fire. It seemed to him that the sun had exploded.

Grandpapa wondered what the cause of the explosion might be. In his opinion, it was the result of a particular effect of static electricity; the chances of this happening were one in ten thousand.

In theory, there was therefore nothing to fear from the other nine thousand nine hundred and ninety-nine landings. Antoine had a spare balloon in the motor-car; the measuring and directional instruments were still intact, as the explosion had occurred at ground-level; Grandpapa therefore decided to leave without delay.

He rose into the air once more, with no idea of the dangers which threatened him, and set course for Mont Blanc, over which he intended to fly. This adventure would without doubt be the crowning glory of the journey.

As they continued over the summits of the mountains, the differences in pressure and temperature became more and more evident. Suddenly, the ominous whistling sound was heard again. But there was nowhere to land here! Pascal felt fear take hold of him. He

Their landings are not always so gentle. ▷
Grandpapa and Pascal are a little shaken when they make a heavy landing in a marsh near Paris. Their balloon is somewhat under-inflated, and they wait impatiently for Antoine to arrive with his tubes to inflate the balloon again.

The aeronauts travelled from Normandy to Provence. They interspersed their adventurous route with short trips, during which they saw, amongst other sights, a stag hunt and a bull run. Below, the balloon rests near a lake in the Jura, time for a picnic...

By mistake, the ballon escapes with only Pascal aboard. Grandpapa and Antoine are powerless to help him. The wind blows the balloon dangerously towards the sea. But Pascal takes advantage of a chance to jump to safety, and the abandoned balloon floats on on its flight over the water... Grandpapa has seen the last of it. Never mind, they feel, he will soon be making another.

stared fixedly at the balloon, to see whether it was going to explode again.

His stares were rewarded! He saw that there was a split in the balloon, and it was through this split that the whistling air was escaping instead of through the opening constructed for this purpose. It was this which obliged Grandpapa, 13,000 feet above the ground, to climb up the ropes and repair the split. May God be praised for this split! It saved both their lives, for it was only because of this leak that the balloon did not explode. But the two aeronauts had no inkling of the truth. They could still fly over Mont Blanc. It was bitterly cold and they could hear the wind roaring over the rocky ridges. However, Grandpapa was radiant with happiness. What a triumphant success!

During the night they spent on board, sailing peacefully through the air above the Mediterranean, Grandpapa thought of the improvements he could make to his balloon. He was already picturing a larger car with a cabin, a corridor and every comfort, in short! a proper little house of the clouds.

In the morning they were awoken by the singing of the cicadas and soon saw the sea. They came down near to the surface of the water and Pascal was determined to take a swim. Grandpapa was less than enthusiastic about this plan; however he tied a rope around Pascal and let him down into the water. Thus, Pascal could swim. His pleasure did not last for long; indeed, since the balloon no longer bore the weight of the child, it rose again. And there was Pascal, held up by the rope, kicking like a tree-frog.

As had been planned, Antoine had pitched camp for the night in the small square of a village in Provence. As he still had some time to wait before the arrival of the balloon, he went to see a bull race which was taking place a stone's throw away. It seemed to him the easiest thing in the world to beat a bull. And since he wanted to prove his prowess, he foolhardily went down into the arena. As a result of some difficulties which he had foolishly underestimated, at the moment of the balloon's arrival, Antoine was not alone at the rendezvous, the furious bull was hot on his heels. The people around the car of the balloon were seized by panic; they all ran for their lives: the balloon, with Pascal in it, climbed into the air again. Antoine followed in the motorcar, but in vain. Grandpapa was in despair.

Little Pascal was in seventh heaven. Now he dared touch anything and everything and steer the balloon in the direction which seemed best to him. Since he had always watched his grandfather's actions very carefully, he knew precisely how to go about it. He climbed, descended, and when he saw an animal fleeing on the ground, he gave chase in the balloon.

What Pascal did not understand was the map. He did not know how to read a map and therefore was completely ignorant of where he was going...

Suddenly he saw the sea. It was drawing nearer and nearer. He became afraid and decided to make a forced landing. When the balloon was near enough to the ground, he jumped.

The balloon, rid of his weight, did not take long to rise, and disappeared above the sea in the mist which was rising off the horizon.

It was lost for ever. But Pascal told himself that if Grandpapa found him here without the balloon, it was nevertheless better than not finding him at all. And anyway, Grandpapa would certainly build a new balloon!

(Taken from "Le voyage en ballon" Albert Lamorisse, Gallimard).

A FLIGHT OVER AFRICA - FACT   *Anthony Smith*

1862-1962—exactly 100 years after the publication of "Five Weeks in a Balloon", Anthony Smith undertook a flight similar to that described by Jules Verne in his novel. By a curious coincidence, Smith worked for the "Daily Telegraph", as did the hero of Verne's story. Anthony Smith hoped to be able to watch the African wild-life from the skies, and as a balloon is the only silent way of travel, he decided to make his safari by balloon. His expedition lasted from January to March 1962, starting from Zanzibar. Accompanied by Douglas Botting and Charl Pauw, he flew over some of the most inaccessible regions of Tanzania and Kenya in his balloon "Jambo".

Smith's East African travels demanded meticulous planning. The "Jambo" was followed at a distance by two Land Rovers carrying tents, food and gas, which had to be collected from Nairobi.   above, the dawn breaks over the traveller's camp in the Serengeti National Park. Their boy, Kiari, makes breakfast.

153

The main purpose of this first flight over part of the African continent was to assess the reaction of the animals in as wide a variety of habitats as possible. No one knew how they would behave below a balloon, but plainly their particular environment would influence them. The Manyara area was a complex of utterly different types of countryside....

The lake was swollen from all the rain of the recent months, and was probably 30 miles long and 10 miles wide....

People agreed it was probably about 300 square miles in extent, and were content to leave it at that. However, its swollen size did mean it was inadvisable for us to come down either in it or on its shores. It was normally possible to drive, or at least to progress, through the forest and the stretches of mud-flat beneath the Rift Valley's western wall; but now that was out of the question. The track had been passable for a mere 7 miles when we arrived, but the sudden and amazing flooding of the Marera River had knocked another 2 miles off even that diminutive journey.

Therefore, for the balloon flight, it was necessary to get well away from the lake before coming down. On the high ground to the west of the cliff wall there was a road, a frequently blocked one, but a road none the less, that led from Karatu southwards to Mbulu. From Mbulu there was a cross-road of sorts that led to the Great North Road, the north-south highway of Africa. Therefore our flight plan, so far as it could be predicted, was at least bounded by a rectangle of roads. It would plainly be advantageous if we landed near one of them. How, or where, or when was not in our control. Therefore, as we took off from Manyara, these crucial issues of the future were well at the back of our minds as we sailed, effortlessly, wonderfully, into the vast blue expanse of sky above our launching site....

The world was just as exciting in every direction but, in a balloon, it is almost impossible not to look forwards. What has passed is only interesting in that it indicates the line of travel, and therefore predicts the course that is still to come.

The balloon stabilized itself at 1,000 feet, rather better than at Zanzibar. In no time we were at the lake's northern edge, drifting over the huge and impenetrable wilderness of reed. It was Alan who first pointed out that certain blobs were buffaloes, the first animals we ever saw. There were thirty of them, doing absolutely nothing, and flapping their ears in the itchy heat. And then came two warthogs, snuffing along busily, and making much noise about it. At last, I said to myself, at last I was in a balloon, and having Africa pass by beneath me. For no reason beyond that, but that was more than enough, I grinned hugely at the others, and then laughed with the joy of it all.

With the lake coming along, and with so much of it to cross, this was no occasion for letting out gas to test the animals' reaction to us. I had not touched the six sacks of sand, but the lake looked long. So we left those buffaloes behind and, still at the height of 1,000 feet, moved out over the water. In theory, and at midday, a lake should bring a balloon down towards it; but this lake was so shallow, and consequently so much hotter than any normal lake, that we rose a little on reaching it. In fact, it was at about 1,500 feet that the three of us coasted down the Rift Valley

for the first part of the trip. We were comfortably in the shade from the balloon, and life was very pleasant...

For the first hour of that flight we floated over the lake, roughly parallel with the western cliff, and on a course of 200...

At the water's edge, and extending in clusters from it, were the pink streaks of thousands of flamingoes. Occasionally, a streak flew into the air, and a long skein of birds moved along the shore to settle somewhere else. It was all so remote. They were busily engaged in finding food, and had no relation with the woods behind them, or the open plains, or anything beyond the mud which supported them. They certainly took no heed of us.

When we were still a mile from the shore, a group of shapes suddenly appeared as giraffes. They edged out of the wood, and wandered across to the water. One even walked into it and then, spreading himself with legs astride, contrived to drink in the only manner possible for his species. At 600 feet we passed over these splendid creatures, and knew that had we been in an aircraft they would have scattered in every direction. As it was, they did nothing. In fact, one sat down, and folded his legs tidily beneath him. His 7-foot neck still stuck up like a pole pushed over, and at some 60 degrees to the ground...

The various overspills from Nairobi then vanished, and we moved instead over primitive farmland. We shouted at the Africans in the fields, and they would look everywhere for the voice except directly above them. Finally, we reached the soft slopes of the Ngongs. These are largely covered with a forest reserve, and we saw buffalo moving among the trees. There were eland, and we stalked quietly up on them at 300 feet above the ground. There was a hacking noise coming from somewhere, and suddenly we saw him. A man was helping himself to wood, and safely deep in the reserve.

"I see you," Alan shouted in Swahili. "And who said you could cut trees in a reserve?"

I have never seen anyone move so fast. He was under a bush in no time.

"I see you under that bush," said Alan. "You might as well give yourself up."

Naturally, this big talk on our part could not be sustained. At 30 miles an hour he and his bush were left rapidly behind, and the first piece of forestry surveillance by balloon was over.

There was no ocean span to cross, no jungle ahead, no distraught airstream; and it was still the calm of the morning. Well to the east of us were the Ngorongoro Highlands, now shrouded in cloud, and obviously a place where trouble could be expected. A few miles in their direction was the great crack of the Olduvai Gorge, a dry and arid scar across the ground. Beneath were the animals and the moon-shaped barkan, those shifting sands where we had spent that infantile afternoon. They had zebras cropping the grass near them, and a herd of eland further away. These big antelopes are the most timid of the lot, allegedly because they know their meat is prized. Some are being husbanded in captivity as an alternative to beef, and even from our height we could see the heavy folds of flesh. Those below us were wild, but every member of the species, whether being fattened or not, always seems to have plenty

154

of meat on board. Their long twisted horns reaching back over their necks must have saved them again and again. I looked down for too long and had to throw out sand hastily, for a descent had begun to build up.

Our shadow moved steadily ahead of us, and showed the way. It moved over the ground like some giant amoeba, undulating slightly at the edges with the unevenness of the earth, and then pushing out a pseudo-podium as it climbed up one side of an isolated rise in the ground. It became an exceedingly sensitive form of altimeter, for the eye is good at appreciating whether something is growing or shrinking before it. So I stared at that shadow leading us towards the herd, and threw out sand accordingly.

At last we came near, and as we did so an immensity of noise came up towards us. I had listened to that congregation on the ground, but when heard from the air it was far more deafening. The nasal grunts of the wildebeest were strung together so continuously that it sounded as if a swarm of buzzing bees had dropped their note an octave or

While flying calmly over Lake Manyara, in Tanzania, the balloon rose dangerously near large cumulo-nimbus storm clouds. However, this cloud formation was so common to African skies that Smith, quite rightly, ignored it. The flight was uneventful.

two. It was a raucous vibration coming from everywhere. It was the real noise of a migration on the move, not the half-hearted imitation of it we had heard when on the ground. It was one mighty impulse. It was a herd, and it was careering, walking, eating, and galloping on its way. It was magnificent.

The whole sight was so magical. To both sides there were ten miles of animals. To the front of us, and to the back, there were thousands of them. And above them all we floated with the simplicity that only a balloon can possess, provided the air is calm and the African day is young.

(Taken from "Throw Out Two Hands" Anthony Smith, George Allen & Unwin, London. USA: "Jambo; African Balloon Safari", E. P. Dutton & Co., Inc., New York.)

The sight of orange globe floating in the skies never failed to astound the natives. Opposite, left, three Masai hunters watch the "Jambo".

When an unusual animal was seen, Anthony Smith gently pulled the valve cord, letting a little gas escape (right). The balloon would then descend to an ideal height for observing the animals.

The balloon safari idea was successful. The travellers were able to film hundreds of wild animals in the acacia-dotted plains of Serengeti. It would be impossible to take pictures like these from an aircraft, for the noise would cause the animals to stampede.

The aeronauts were fortunate in avoiding the tops of the surrounding trees, and came down on an old rotting tree trunk. John Newbould, one of the discomfited passengers, contemplates the wreck. Luckily, the damage was repairable.

Smith had to deflate the balloon, for the trees made take-off impossible. With native help, he had the balloon and the basket carried out of the jungle back to his camp.

In an attempt to escape from threatening clouds, Smith lost control of the balloon, and made a heavy landing in the jungle not far from Ngorongoro, in Tanzania. Masai warriors lent a hand.

ALPINE FLIGHTS

On the 2 September 1849, the aeronaut François Ardan, a Frenchman, flew over the Alpes Maritimes in a free balloon. He left from Marseilles, and, after passing the night in the car of his balloon, landed the next day near Turin. His flight was then considered an unique achievement. The crossing of the Alpine range seemed particularly dangerous, for the metereological conditions varied at different points in the same valley so that aeronauts dared not take off, for fear of being caught in a storm and dashed against the rocks, or, somewhere else, the balloon might, if it were forced down, fall into a

Every year, a dozen balloons ascend from Mürren, situated at an altitude of 5,300 ft in the middle of the Alps. It is an ideal place for the start of a flight, for, surrounded by high mountains, it is sheltered from the violent winds which hinder the balloon ascents.

crevasse or lodge on an isolated peak from which the aeronaut would be unable to descend and where he would perish of exposure.

A Swiss, Eduard Spelterini, finally showed the way; on 3 October 1898, he took off from Sion, in the Valais, crossed the Alps, and landed on the outskirts of Dijon in France. Following this, Spelterini made more than ten flights over the Alps, during which he made a number of useful metereological observations. Profiting from these, the Italians Usuelli and Crespi set off in 1906 to fly over the Alps from east to west, passing over the Mont Blanc massif. Two years later, the Alpinist Victor de Beauclair crossed the Alps and the Jungfrau to the Tessin.

Thanks to the valuable observations recorded by the pioneers, and the extremely efficient cooperation of the Zurich Weather Station, an Alpine flight today is pleasure trip for many who have some sporting spirit. Indeed, since 1962, Fred Dolder, an accredited pilot with more than 380 flights logged, organises each year an International Ballooning Week in the Alps at Mürren, in the Bernese Oberland. During the week, which takes place in June—July, aeronauts from many countries gather and exchange ideas and experiences while waiting for the right weather conditions for take off. Free balloon enthusiasts have an opportunity to make an unforgetable Alpine flight as passengers.

The Swiss Captain Spelterini—alias Eduard Schweizer (1852-1931)—was the second, after Ardan, to venture to fly over the Alps. His famous flight in 1898 heralded the era of Alpine flights.

MOST IMPORTANT FLIGHTS OVER THE ALPS

Date	Pilot	Balloon	Route
2/3. 9. 1849	François Ardan	—	Marseilles – Pion-Poté, Turin.
3. 10. 1898	Eduard Spelterini	Wega	Sion – Vaud Alps – Rivière (between Dijon and Langres)
8. 5. 1900	Dr Stolberg, Prof Hergesell	—	Friedrichshafen/Lake Constance – Zugspitze – Fernpass
1. 8. 1900	Eduard Spelterini	Jupiter	Rigi-Furst – Central Switzerland – Alp Ennetseewen (Glarus)
16. 4. 1902	Cdt Hinterstoisser, Archduke Leopold Salvator	Meteor	Salzburg – Weissenkirchen – Judenburg
17/18. 8. 1903	Eduard Spelterini	Stella	Zermatt – Simplon massif – Bignasco (Tessin)
20. 9. 1904	Eduard Spelterini	Stella	Eiger Glacier – Jungfrau massif – Blümlisalp
27. 5. 1906	E. O. Frischknecht	Augusta II	Davos – Lower Engadine – Baladore
11. 11. 1906	Usuelli, Crespi	Città di Milano	Milan – Grand St Bernard – Mont Blanc – Aix les Bains
20. 7. 1907	Eduard Spelterini	Augusta	Andermatt – St Gothard – Tessin – Bergamo
22. 7. 1907	Dr Bröckelmann	—	Innsbruck – Zillertal Alps – Luttach (Taufertal)
29. 6. 1908	Victor de Beauclair	Cognac	Eiger Glacier – Simplon – Italian Alps – Gignese, west of Stresa
6. 9. 1908	Eduard Spelterini	Sirius	Interlaken – Rhône valley – Val d'Ayas
4. 12. 1908	Victor de Beauclair	Cognac	Bitterfeld (N. of Leipzig) – Pilsen – Moldau – Linz – Karstgebirge – Fiume – Casala Marittima
16. 3. 1909	Victor de Beauclair	Cognac	Davos – Zirbelkopf/Wetterstein
9. 8. 1909	Eduard Spelterini	Sirius	Chamonix – Mont Blanc – Pizzo di Ruscada (above Biasco)
21/22. 8. 1909	E. Messner	Helvetia	St Moritz – Lower Engadine – Regensburg – Weidmessgum – Karlsbad
9. 11. 1909	Victor de Beauclair	Cognac	Linthal (Glarus) – Tessin Alps – Barnero/Navarre
12. 2. 1910	Von Holthoff	Berlin	St Moritz – Bernina – Milan
30. 5. 1910	Von Sarley	Tirol	Innsbruck – Zillertal
29. 5. 1910	Hinterstoisser	Tirol	Innsbruck – Zillertal
12. 8. 1910	Eduard Spelterini	Sirius	Mürren – Rhône valley – Monte Basso/Turin
26/27. 3. 1911	Usuelli	—	Milan – Engadine – Filisur
17. 4. 1911	Victor de Beauclair	St Gotthard	Augsburg – Lake Trasimeno/Perugia
4/5. 4. 1912	Victor de Beauclair	St Gotthard	Augsburg – Lake Constance – San Benigno (near Turin)
14. 6. 1912	Lt Endtner	Cumulus	Berne – Kehrtal der Gaulistöcke
29/30. 8. 1912	Eduard Spelterini	Sirius	Interlaken – Unterammergau (Bavaria)
3. 8. 1913	Eduard Spelterini	Sirius	Kandersteg – Rhône valley – Alagna (Italy)
27. 5. 1931	Auguste Piccard, Paul Kipfer	F.N.R.S.	Augsburg – Gurgl glačier (Otztal)
18. 8. 1932	Auguste Piccard, Max Cosyns	F.N.R.S.	Zurich/Dübendorf – Volta/Mantua, near Desenzano

On 20 September 1904, Spelterini took off from the Eiger glacier station on board the balloon "Stella", here shown being prepared for the flight. He landed at Adelboden.

Before long, Spelterini discovered the advantages of Mürren, and made it his departure point for his Alpine flights. On 12 August 1910, he ascended from this future ballooning centre on board the "Sirius". He flew over the Rhône valley and landed near Turin.

FREE BALLOON ASCENTS FROM MÜRREN

Flight	Date		Pilot and passengers	Balloon	Vol. m³	Where landed
1.	1910	12. 8.	**Eduard Spelterini** (CH)	Sirius	1500	Lanzo Torinese (I)
			Baron L. Rothschild, Dr Ed. Etthofen (A)			
2.	1957	30. 8.	**Fred Dolder** (CH)	Zurich	2300	San Nazzaro, Lake Maggiore (CH)
			Dr Jürg Marmet (CH), Dölf Reist (CH)			
3.	1961	13. 8.	**Fred Dolder** (CH)	Bernina	1260	Besnate/Varese (I)
			E. A. Sautter (CH), Phil Walker (USA)			

DOLDER BALLOONING WEEK, MÜRREN

Flight	Date		Pilot and passengers	Balloon	Vol. m³	Where landed
4.	1962	20. 8.	**Conny Wolf** (USA), Fred R. Forrer (CH)	N 10 W	945	Brissago, Lake Maggiore (CH)
5.		20. 8.	**Fred Dolder** (CH), Hch. Appenzeller (CH)	Rapperswil	1050	Cimaimotto, Domodossola (I)
6.		20. 8.	**A. Vanden Bemden** (B), D. Heggemann (D)	OO-BSD	945	Monte Giove (I)
7.		23. 8.	**Mme Nini Boesman** (NL), Ruedy Meyer (CH)	Utrecht	630	Gorduno, Bellinzona (CH)
8.		23. 8.	**Habib Eskenasi** (B), G. W. Powell (CAN)	OO-BOB	945	Monte Piotta, Bellinzona (CH)
9.		23. 8.	**H. Jo. Scheer** (D)	Bernina	1260	Piazza Brembana, Bergamo (I)
			E. A. Sautter (CH), Phil Walker (USA)			
10.	1963	20. 8.	**Heinz Elckmeyer** (D), Franz-Josef Görtz (D)	Münster XX	945	Unterhiersee/Kufstein (A)
11.		20. 8.	**Hugo Elmermacher** (D)	Berlin	1680	Kreith/Innsbruck (A)
			Paul Riemer (D), Heinz Tödter (D)			
12.		20. 8.	**H. Jo. Scheer** (D), Willy Vlasdek (D)	Bernina	1260	Partenkirchen, Bavaria (D)
13.		20. 8.	**Fred R. Forrer** (CH), Solo	HB-BID	945	Bregenz (A)
14.		22. 8.	**Mme Nini Boesman** (NL), P. Verseveldt (NL)	Hanseat	945	Pontoglio, Bergamo (I)
15.		22. 8.	**F. Schmidbauer** (A), Phil Walker (USA)	Juventute	945	Grumello, Bergamo (I)
16.		24. 8.	**Anthony Smith** (GB), Douglas Botting (GB)	Jambo	800	Livigno (I)
17.		24. 8.	**Alfred Eckert** (D), Harry Valerien (D)	Rapperswil	1050	Santa Maria (CH)
18.		24. 8.	**Richard Jahre** (D), Butch Calderwood (AUS)	Tropi	945	Trafoi/Stilfserjoch
19.		26. 8.	**Fred Dolder** (CH)	Spelterini	1260	Vaduz, Liechtenstein (FL)
			Hch. Appenzeller (CH), E. A. Sautter (CH)			
20.	1964	17. 8.	**Fred R. Forrer** (CH), Solo	HB-BID	935	Weissenbach/Höfen, Tyrol (A)
21.		17. 8.	**Mme Regula Hug-Messner** (CH)	Rapperswil	1050	Bad Reichenhall (D)
			Dr Ch. Burckhardt (CH)			
22.		17. 8.	**Alfred Eckert** (D)	Bernina	1260	Sonthofen im Allgäu (D)
			E. A. Sautter (CH), Ruedy Meyer (CH)			
23.		20. 8.	**Richard Jahre** (D), Dieter Bertram (D)	Tropi	945	Piz d'Astra, Engadine (CH)
24.	1964	25. 8.	**Mme Regula Hug-Messner** (CH)	Juventute	945	Mont Rouge, Val de Nendaz (CH)
			Dr Ch. Burckhardt (CH)			
25.		25. 8.	**Fred Dolder** (CH)	Toblerone	1680	Barrage de Cleuson, Val de Nendaz (CH)
			Hch. Appenzeller (CH), Dr Charles Dollfus (F)			
26.	1965	19. 8.	**Peter Peterka** (CH), Franz Vlasak (CH)	Rapperswil	1050	Mittwald VS (CH)
27.		19. 8.	**Mme Nini Boesman** (NL)	Toblerone	1680	Nieder-Gampel VS (CH)
			J. Routh (GB), D. Davies (GB)			
28.		19. 8.	**Richard Jahre** (D), Jean Reitberger (USA)	Wickühler	945	Biberg/Kandersteg (CH)
29.		19. 8.	**Fred R. Forrer** (CH), Solo	HB-BID	945	Guttet/Leuk VS (CH)
30.		19. 8.	**H.-G. Bergmann** (A), Walter Eberl (A)	OE-DZG	945	Suldtal/Aeschi BE (CH)
31.		19. 8.	**Pierre Ladevèze** (F), Gérard Wurtz (F)	F-ANQX	900	Oberfeselalp, Gampel VS (CH)
32.		19. 8.	**Ernst Krauer** (CH)	Spelterini	1260	Weritz-Alp. Wiler VS (CH)
			Mme M. Krauer (CH), J. Guillon (F)			
33.		21. 9.	**Fred Dolder** (CH)	Spelterini	1260	Morrilon/Samoens Haute Savoie (F)
			Hch. Appenzeller (CH), E. A. Sautter (CH)			
34.	1966	18. 8.	**Ernst Krauer** (CH)	Spelterini	1260	Münsingen (CH)
			Mme M. Krauer (CH), G. Reddy (USA)			
35.		18. 8.	**Horst Hassold** (D)	Hanseat	945	Teuffenthal (CH)
			Meryll Darbley (USA)			
36.		18. 8.	**Peter Peterka** (CH), Willy Rüegg (CH)	Circus Knie	1050	Wimmis (CH)
37.		20. 8.	**Peter Pellegrino** (USA), M. Jasinski (B)	Rapperswil	1050	Trivero (I)
38.		20. 8.	**Richard Jahre** (D)	Uncle Ben	1260	Mollia (I)
			Pierre Monnier (F), V. M. Kavan (CAN)			
39.		26. 8.	**Wolfgang Haueisen** (D), W. Ledermann (CH)	Hanseat	945	Portomanegro (I)
40.		27. 8.	**Fred Dolder** (CH), Hch. Appenzeller (CH)	Spelterini	1260	Eriz (CH)
			Dewitt Powell (CAN)			
41.		9. 11.	**Fred Dolder** (CH), E. A. Sautter (CH)	Helvetia	1680	Blumberg (D)
42.	1967	14. 6.	**Peter Peterka** (CH), Willy Rüegg (CH)	Circus Knie	1050	Caluso/Torino (I)
43.		14. 6.	**Wolfgang Haueisen** (D), Frans Verbunt (NL)	Hanseat	945	Villa-Echalot/Aosta (I)
44.		14. 6.	**G. F. Turnbull** (GB), Tom Sage (GB)	G-ATXR	900	Verres/Aosta (I)
45.		16. 6.	**H. Hassold** (D), R. Laue (D), V. M. Kavan (CAN)	Bernina	1260	Bottenwil (CH)
46.		17. 6.	**F. L. Shields** (USA), Chs. Rathgeb (CAN)	Rapperswil	1050	Saxteen (CH)
47.		22. 6.	**Fred Dolder** (CH), F. L. Shields (USA)	Zurich	2300	Como (I)
			Dr V. Mangili (I), Bruno Brunello (I)			
48.	1967	22. 6.	**Wolfgang Haueisen** (D), A. de la Varre (USA)	Hanseat	945	Val Onsernone (CH)
49.		27. 9.	**Fred Dolder** (CH), Andy Jenkins (GB)	Circus Knie	1050	Giswil (CH)

On 13 August 1961, Fred Dolder, Erwin A. Sautter and the American film producer Phil Walker took off from Mürren on board the "Bernina" (right, shown over them Lötschental, alt. 12,450 ft). They landed in Italy at Besnate. This flight, made in memory of Spelterini, was the start of the International Free Balloon Week, which Dolder decided to organise the following year from Mürren.

FREE BALLOON ASCENTS FROM MÜRREN (Cont.)

Flight	Date		Pilot and passengers	Balloon	Vol. m³	Where landed
50.	1968	19.6.	**Wolfgang Haueisen** (D), Frans Verbunt (NL)	Hanseat	945	Oberkirch (CH)
51.		19.6.	**G. F. Turnbull** (GB), R. Cullen (GB)	CPA-Star	1260	Meerenschwand (CH)
52.		22.6.	**Richard Jahre** (D), Horst Hassold (D) Ruedy Meier (CH)	Ikarus	1245	Disentis (CH)
53.		22.6.	**Peter Peterka** (CH), Hakoon Mielche (DK) Malcolm Kirk (USA)	Ajoie	1360	Vals GB (CH)
54.		23.6.	**Emil Imhof** (CH), Anthony Fairbanks (USA) J.-P. Kuenzi (CH), E. A. Sautter (CH)	Zurich	2300	Unteriberg (CH)
55.		25.6.	**Wolfgang Haueisen** (D), Eugen Weber (D)	Hanseat	945	Seriate/Bergamo (I)
56.	1969	10.6.	**Fred Dolder** (CH), Otto Rüedlinger (CH) Kaspar von Almen, Allen O'Brien (USA), Jacques Huber (CH)	Vagabund	2300	Corcelles FR (CH)
57.		27.6.	**Horst Hassold** (D), Otto Oeckl (D) Eckhard Graf von Mandelsloh (D)	Martini	1260	Vicolungo-Novara (I)
58.		27.6.	**Emil Imhof** (CH), Oscar Meuli (CH)	Rapperswil	1050	Bivio Quinto-Vercelli (I)
59.		29.6.	**Wolfgang Haueisen** (D) Bernhard Kemper (D), Frans Verbunt (NL)	Ferdinand Eimermacher	1680	Loazolo-Acqui (I)
60.		29.6.	**Anthony Fairbanks** (USA), Bud Bombard Chalet Club, New York, N.Y. (USA)	Mürren	945	Salussola (I)
61.		29.6.	**Richard Jahre** (D) Dieter Bertram (D) Rudolf Laue (D)	Uncle Ben	1260	Tavigliano-Biella (I)
62.		29.6.	**Ernst Krauer** (CH), Mme M. Krauer (CH)	Quo Vadis	945	Sforcesca-Vigevano (I)
63.		3.7.	**Franco Segre** (I), Solo	Savoia	945	Morzine (F)
64.		3.7.	**Eugen Weber** (D), Josef Walzel (D)	Carl Götze	945	Haut de Cry (CH)
65.		3.7.	**Fred Dolder** (CH), Peter Peterka (CH) Toni Hiebeler (D), Dölf Reist (CH)	Zurich	2300	Chandolin VS (CH)
66.	1970	23.6.	**Mme Nini Boesman** (NL) Piet Verseveldt (NL)	Quo Vadis	945	Schwendi-Schattenhalb (CH)
67.		23.6.	**Ernst Krauer** (CH), Hiroshi Isogai (JAP) Rolf Ulrichsen (NOR)	Spelterini	1260	Grindelwald (CH)
68.	1970	23.6.	**Richard Jahre** (NL), Conte Raimondo di Sambuy (I), Peter Wälti (CH) Konrad Wolf (CH)	Toblerone	1680	Boden-Wengernalp (CH)
69.		26.6.	**Horst Hassold** (D), Josef Walzel (D) Paul D. Suloff (USA)	Martini	1260	Räterichsboden (CH)
70.		26.6.	**Eugen Weber** (D), Adolf Heineke (D)	Carl Götze	945	Gelmer Artificial Lake (CH)
71.		26.6.	**Emil Imhof** (CH), Oscar Meuli (CH)	BOE	945	Göscheneralp (CH)
72.		26.6.	**Peter Peterka** (CH), Derek Stevenson (GB)	Circus Knie	1050	Oberwald VS (CH)
73.		27.6.	**Wolfgang Haueisen** (D) Frans Verbunt (NL), Louis Mertens (B)	Hamburg	1680	Kriens LU (CH)
74.		6.7.	**Fred Dolder** (CH), Silvan Osterwalder (CH) Allen O'Brien (USA), Pierre Dysli (CH), Dr Luigi Brindicci (I)	Zurich	2300	Graglia-Biella (I)
75.		19.7.	**Fred Dolder** (CH), Alfred Nater (CH) Dipl. Ing. Carl Reuther (D)	Zurich	2300	S. Catarina di Lusiana, prov. Vincenza, Venizia (I)
76.	1971	2.3.	**Wolfgang Haueisen/Fred Dolder** Frans Verbunt (NL), Bernhard Kemper (D)	Zurich	2300	Magnano, prov. Vercelli (I)

FRED DOLDER FLIES THE ALPS

*Above : On 19 July 1970, at 7.40 am, the balloon "Zurich" is
ready to leave. It was inflated on the lawn of the Hotel Palace—
an operation that took more than four hours—while Fred Dolder
obtained the last minute weather situation and gave his final orders.*

*Leaving from Mürren, the aeronauts enjoyed a fantastic view,
discovering from their vantage point an immense ring of peaks.
Left, the higher balloon flies over the west of the Jungfrau, while
the other is about to pass over the Silberhorn (12,122 ft).*

"Salute!" cried the Padre, and a hundred enthusiastic children
added their greetings to his. For it was Sunday afternoon and all
the young people of the village were out at play. We had come
down like invaders from a clouded sky, to land on the slopes of a
lush green meadow. This was an unusual sight for the inhabitants of this little hamlet—the "occasion of the century"
for Conco and Lusiana. "Little Switzerland" is a land of valleys
and hills—comparable to the lower part of the Toggenburg—
between Asiago and Marostica, it consists of seven communes
and numerous hamlets; to the west flows the Astico and to the
east the Brenta; this country is 1,640 ft above the plain of
Venezia. It is a green land where the air is fresh and pure; the
main industry is agriculture but there is little profit in it. The
roads leading into it are good; as in the Tramola valley there are
some tortuous hairpin bends. At this season, in the height of
summer, all the rooms are taken; these holiday-makers are mostly
"homesick natives". They earn their living lower down in the
plains, or abroad, and come back every summer to spend a few
days or a few weeks in the land of their birth. Everyone knows
everyone else. A foreigner would not be able to find his way

165

into this attractive "Piccola Svizzera" peopled with working inhabitants worthy of our affection. Venice is too near...

If it were not for the balloon I should never have visited Santa Catarina di Lusiana. Had I had 90 kilos more ballast I should never have come to know this part of Italy—a real gem—and its likeable inhabitants. This is how it came to pass.

On Friday evening the meteorologist telephoned me: "It won't be long now. Everything will go well on Sunday. But you must leave early. With the evening will come the first disturbance in the weather!" A great commotion ensued. We had to bring together my companion for the flight, the co-pilot, the person who was going to follow us, the balloonist, the man who dealt with the gas (they hailed from Bazenheid, Berne, Oftringen and Wyl, in the canton of Saint-Gall in Switzerland). The rendezvous was planned for Saturday evening at Mürren, 5,300 ft above sea-level, at the foot of the Schilthorn (Piz Gloria) in the Bernese Oberland.

Some 150 cylinders of gas and a free balloon weighing 750 kilos (two heavy envelopes and a car) had been awaiting us there for weeks— together with nearly 9,000 letters.

However, on the Saturday the barometer fell with stubborn consistency. The summits of the Mönch, the Eiger and the Jungfrau were invisible when we arrived at Mürren. But according to our trusted prophet of the weather, the disturbances would not become evident for 24 hours. So we announced our imminent departure.

At 3 am on the Sunday morning, with the full moon shining brightly in the sky—we began to inflate the balloon. At 07.40 h, the *Zurich*, with a volume of 2,300 cubic metres was ready to leave and, at 07.55 h, the pilot cried: "Hands off!" The aerostat rose immediately and climbed into the cloudless sky at a speed of 9 ft per second. There were three men in the car. In addition, 12 sacks of mail and 19 bags of sand: the ballast, each bag weighing at least 18 kilos.

At first the balloon drifted slightly towards the Schilthorn. At 08.00 h, we were at a height of 6,890 ft. At 08.03 h, we were 8,200 ft above the ground. Then we veered towards the mountain mass of the Jungfrau. We accelerated our ascent by emptying a bag of ballast. At 08.10 h, we had reached a height of 11,500 ft. At 08.20 h, we were 15,900 ft above the Joch in a strong wind, a pressure gradient of 300°.

The glory of the freshly snow-covered Alps defies description, the ecstasy of travellers sailing noiselessly over the peaks is limitless! In this clear and transparent air one can see further than 190 miles, the panorama is breathtaking. At 08.30 h, Konkordiaplatz. At 08.45 h, at an altitude of 18,500 ft we cross the valley of Conches between Münster and Reckingen. At 10.00 h, height 13,300 ft, we are in the middle of the Verzasca valley. Charles is 'baptized' Baron of Verzasca. At 10.25 h, at a height of 15,100 ft, we fly over Arbedo. At 11.08 h, we find ourselves over Dongo at the upper extremity of Lake Como. At noon we no longer know where we are. Who could find his bearings in the midst of these peaks, these steep escarpments, these little mountain lakes and the green and blue dammed lakes, shining so brilliantly? Not far away, towards the north, should be the Valtellina. A little more to the east the ice cap of the Adamello is shimmering brightly, and to the north we can see the vast mass of the Bernina chain; eleven months previously we had flown over it at a height of 19,750 ft, when it had been covered in cloud. But we have difficulty in

Flight Report

In charge of balloon: Osterwalder & Nater
                                        (co-pilot)

Flight 19 July 1970

BALLOON
NUMBER & NAME

HB- BIX "ZÜRICH"

Volume 2300 m3 (inflated to 63% of vol)

Type of Gas hydrogen

Specific weight 0.07

Pilot*/Passengers

Dipl. Ing. C. Reuther
Mannheim
"Baron de Vercasca"

PILOT Fred Dolder (379./395.)*

* Comprises intermediate landings made 1967-1969.

Weather Conditions

Flight centre forecast   Timed at 07.00

General situation moving anticyclone

	Direction of Wind	Temp Deg C.
Terrain		
1500 m		
3000 m	330°	20 Knots
5000 m	330°	25 Knots

Weather conditions at time of departure (as observed by pilot)

Visibility 300 km Wind 300 - 280°

Clouds none

Barometer........mm/mb Temp 18 °C Air pressure........

Ballast

Departure (19 bags of 18 kg)	kg	342 *)
Max alt	kg	314
Used by max alt	kg	18
Average used per hr at max alt	kg	18
Used on leaving max alt to landing	kg	233

*) Plus c. 150 kg of mail

Pilot's signature   *Fred Dolder*

Departure

Time 0755
Place ....Mürren
Altitude 1650
Guiderope ....coiled

Landing

Time 1615
Place Conco/Lusiana
(Prov. d. Vicenza)
Altitude 640
Guiderope uncoiled

Performance

Duration ....8 hrs 20 min   Max altitude 5650 m

Flight distance ....303 km   Distance covered ....313 km

Notes

Time	Height	Place	Ballast (sacks)	Wind (dir)	Wind km/h	Clouds	Temp	Valve	Remarks
0300		Inflation commenced							3 bags of ballast dispensed with.
0740		Ready to depart, Mürren							
0755	1650	Departure from Palace	19	0	0	none	18		Climbed at + 3m/sec.
0800	2100	Over Lauterbrunnen	19	0	0				+ 2.7 Direction Schilthorn-Jungfrau 7m/sec.
0803	2500	Drift towards Jungfrau	18	0	0				+ 1.7 to accelerate climb 7m/sec threw out 1 bag ballast.
0804									+ 3m/sec.
0805	2800								+ 2.8m/sec.
0810	3500								+ 2.6m/sec radio call from Zurich.
0815	4000								
0820	4850	Passed the Jungfraujoch	18						+ 2.5m/sec.
0822	5100		18	300	40	"			Rather cold in the car.
0824	5200								Appendix turned. Everything O.K. at present + 4m/sec. - 1 to - 1.5m/sec.
0830	5500	Konkordiaplatz	18	300	40				- 1 to - 1.5m/sec.
0835		Galmihorn	18	300	40				South west of the Grimsel lakes.
0845	5630	Münster in Goms	18	290	30				Radio call. - 1.5 to - 2 m/sec.
0905	4800	South east of Haut Valais							Descended for some minutes - 1.5m/sec.
0910	4300	Lago Castel, Italy	18	300	40				- 0.3m/sec. Finished dropping ballast.
0915	3800	Upper part of Formazza val.	17	300	40				Temp. becomes agreeable. Descended rapidly, threw out 1 bag of ballast.
0940	3750	Pizze delle Peccore	16	300	40				Towards Bellinzona.
0950	3850	Val Vercasca, north of Brione	15					General	direction of upper Lake Como.
1000	4050	Middle of Val Vercasca	15	290	35				Aerial baptism.

All events taking place during flight, together with technical incidents, changes in the weather or meetings with other flying machines, should be recorded. The pilot should indicate his position at least every 20 minutes. The report should be forwarded to the Office de l'Air not later than 5 days after the flight.

Notes

Time	Height	Place	Ballast (sacks)	Wind (dir)	Wind km/h	Clouds	Temp	Valve	Remarks
1010	4300	North of artif. Lake Vercasca	15	290	40	none			No response from Milan.
1025	4600	Passed Arbedo	15	295					Radio contact with Magadino. Asked them to pass on our position moving towards Vicenza.
1050	5000	To the west of Lake Como	15	300	40				
1108	4600	Dongo/Lake Como	15	300	40				Opened valve a little. Asked Samedan-Tower to report our position to Zurich (was not done).
1135	3200	Mezzoldo, NW of Piazzatore	15	280	30				
1200	3300	Lost direction							change of course.
1205	3320	Monte Valrossa	14	270	30				
1225	3600	Branzi area	14	270	40				Deviation over the mountain.
1245	4100	To the north of Lake Iseo	14	290	40				Many small mountain lakes, some artificial.
1300	4300	Bienno, near Breno		280	40				Back on old course.
1340	3900	To the north of Ponte Cafarro	13	270	40				Val Camonica
1400	3700	Riva, Lake Garda	12	280	30				
1420	3650	5 km to south of Rovereto	12	280	30				Mist in front of us.
1450	3400	Col Santo	11	280	50				Intended to land in the plain.
1515	3100	Monte Pau	10	270	30				Good speed.
1530	2900	To the south of Asiago	10	280	20				Mist. Poor visibility.
1550	2300	5 km before Bassano	9	100	9				Decided to start the descent.
1600	1800	10 km before Bassano	8	110	10				Change of course. Opposite direction. Went back towards the mountains.
1615	640	Conco Sta Catarina di Lusiana	5½	110	5				Preparation for rapid descent. - 1, - 2½, - 3, - 3½m/sec. 1 bag of ballast. Splendid landing in green field.

Other remarks:

2½ bags of ballast used in landing. We are in an enclosed valley, known as "La piccola Svizzera". It is situated between Asiago and Marstica, and is bordered by the rivers Astico and Brenta, and contains 7 communes. Perfect landing. The ground is not damaging. No tears in the balloon. Still inflated, we had it transported on to flat ground, and there I pulled the rip cord (for safety reasons). M. Nater had the balloon packed up in an hour. Grand and very friendly reception. The locals considered our landing the event of the century. The civil and ecclesiastical authorities, and all the population of Sta Catarina saw that we lacked nothing. Although it is a very poor region, they invited us to spend a week with them. Alas, we had to leave the next day. The carabinieri will confirm by letter the arrival of the post, which we sent off the next day from Chiasso postoffice. We saw the Alps from 300m. All looked new under a covering of snow. This balloon flight was truly marvellous and without any untoward incident. It was a pity that neither Magadino nor Samedan passed on our radio calls. We traced them with some trouble and re-obtained the messages. We had to wait between 4 - 8 hours for urgent telephone calls. We have taken the balloon back to Schlieren with the help of our two trailers. No difficulties with the customs. End of report.

Aids for enlarging the flight report

Abbreviations for cloud formations:

Ci Cirrus	Ns Nimbostratus
Cc Cirrocumulus	Sc Stratocumulus
Cs Cirrostratus	St Stratus
Ac Altocumulus	Cu Cumulus
As Altostratus	Cb Cumulonimbus

Clouds : 3/8 Cu 1800 = 3/8 cover of Cumulus at 1800 m alt.
Winds : 280/15 = wind from 280° at speed of 15 km/hr
Warning : weather forecasts give speeds in knots (1853 m)

Status indications pupil pilot - ,*.

I let the balloon descend after we have passed the last mountains, most probably the Pau and the Mazze. We then recognize, 1 ½ to 5 miles in front of us, on the banks of the wide bed of the Brenta which is sprinkled with pebbles, the town of Bassano, and we go down silently to meet it at a speed of 3 ft per second. In the car we pack up the equipment and prepare everything for landing. We have 9 bags of ballast weighing 18 kilos each in reserve. Our height is 7,545 ft, the time 15.50 h (Swiss time).

16.00 h. Height 5,905 ft. An opposing wind is carrying us towards the mountains. We have to act quickly. A long way below us white bell-towers are signalling to us; they stand up above attractive villages surrounded by green meadows and hills. We must get down there somehow! We pull on the valve rope for a long time. We are going down at a speed of 6 then 7, 9, 10 ft per second. We empty a bag of ballast to break our descent. Silence reigns in the car. The only voice is that of the co-pilot giving our speed every two seconds, while the tense pilot watches the course of the balloon and the nature of the terrain below. An electricity wire is blocking our path! We empty another bag of ballast overboard. Then we let go the rope! A few seconds after brushing the ground, we land with no bumping at all, like princes; here we are, gently put down on the sloping meadow overhanging the church of Santa Catarina di Lusiana. 16.15 h. And here comes a small band of out-of-breath and excited people, clambering up the slope! The first ones to come to our aid are incapable of speech; they must first get their breath. Hundreds of people, adults and children are running up; they hug us and carry the balloon, which is still upright, down to the bottom of the slope, where, behind the cemetery wall, a path leads into the meadow; later on, it was by this path that the balloon was transported without difficulty.

There is quite an element of danger in slowly emptying a balloon filled with hydrogen by pulling the valve cord, when one is surrounded by a deliriously excited crowd. This was why I pulled the rip cord. After 30 seconds all is safe, the empty, flat envelope is lying on the ground. A magnificent journey through the sky had been brought to a happy conclusion. We had travelled 193 miles in eight hours and twenty minutes.

And here is the postscript! The welcome which we had received from the sky could not have been warmer than that from the authorities and inhabitants of Santa Catarina di Lusiana! We were smothered in invitations, presents, souvenirs, tokens of friendship. The vicar, whose parish included the communes of Conco and Lusiana, told me later that he was deeply sorry that in the general excitement he had forgotten to ring the church bells! Five minutes after our landing, the distinguished gentleman who represented the hamlet at the Council of the commune had already come up to us and said that he would be deeply honoured if we could stay for a week at the expense of the commune. A member of the Aeroclub of Bassano d.G. also invited us to stay. The representative of the Council wanted us to stay in the headquarters of the commune of Lusiana, 360 ft higher up, but the Padre decided that, since we had come down at Santa Catarina, the honour of offering us hospitality was entirely his. It was true that there was no hotel there, but we could stay with him and take our meals in a very good *osteria*. Meanwhile, a contractor came upon the scene with two lorries, and offered us the use of his garage to shelter our balloon. We could keep the key of the garage until our departure to make sure that no accidents befell our balloon.

Twenty men did not spare themselves in loading the envelope and the net under the orders of the co-pilot. The crew were asked to step into a limousine, and behind were the two lorries carrying the 'Zurich' HB-BIX (the largest free balloon in Europe) which seemed very small now. To the accompaniment of tooting horns and endless cheers, the convoy moved off on a tour of honour: they went as far as the end of the village and returned to the Piazza where the 'entry of the gladiators' took place. At nine in the evening there was an official banquet: two syndics, one from Conco and one from Lusiana; Don Gian-Franco, the Padre of the two communes, the commanders of the carabinieri and all the Councillors of the commune who could be gathered together. Those people certainly knew how to improvise! Every face shone with pleasure. Mixed with this joy was the satisfaction that we had not come down in a neighbouring commune or in the town of Bassano. We felt completely at home! *N.B.* We had come down in the territory of the commune of Conco, 30 ft away from the border of the commune of Lusiana, on whose land was the meadow into which the balloon was carried (the electrified fences which barred our way were promptly removed). The church and the cemetery of Santa Catarina were on the frontier of the two communes. At the head of the parish was the Padre Don Gian-Franco, an open natured man, full of initiative, very close to his flock, and who looked after us like a brother.

To leave is to die a little... When, the next day at noon, after the official reception in the new offices of the commune (which were fitted out in a very modern style), my two friends in the car, followed by a trailer, had at last found me, we were really upset at the thought of leaving our kind hosts. But we had to return to Switzerland with all possible speed, to post the letters, 9,000 of them for the benefit of the "Pestalozzi Foundation for the upbringing of the young people of the Swiss mountains", which all bore Swiss stamps.

The departure was as splendid as the arrival. All the village, adults, children and even the *bambini* in the care of the nun, the keeper of the kindergarten, had assembled on the Piazza. We left amid cheers, toots of horns and general jubilation. Torrential rain fell as we reached the Swiss border; it was at that moment that we realized our good fortune in having had such wonderful weather for our unforgettable flight to "Piccola Svizzera" in Venezia.　(Taken from "Aero-Revue", Zurich.)

ALL ABOUT BALLOONS

The sensations felt during a balloon flight are hard to describe and hard to share with people. It takes us up and carries us at the mercy of the winds: no effort, no fear, calmness and silence found at last! Around us, Nature is immense and beautiful. Such an exciting adventure is worth more than distance and time records, it transcends figures to give man the experience of his true measure within the bosom of Creation.

This peaceable and almost poetic use of balloon erases 200 years of errors. In the past, man has demanded from the balloon services for which it was not suitable: its use by armies proved limited and deceptive; distance trials were a complete contradiction of the nature of the balloon itself; and public demonstrations could not take into account unforeseeable meteorological phenomena. Today, a balloon ascent is undertaken just for the love of it, and free from any strictly utilitarian application.

The following pages refer to balloons, free balloon navigation and certain technical aspects. Here we would like to warn the reader against a widely-held belief: a balloon ascent is not only the simple result of a physics theorem or a mathematical formula. It is much more complex than is usually imagined because there exists an immense gulf between book learning and practice. It is almost impossible to predict the course of a free balloon, for it is continually influenced by atmospherical conditions which do not always turn out like the weather forecast of even the best meteorologist. This explains why theorists are often mediocre balloonists.

In the preface of his book entitled *Basis of Balloon Navigation*, published in 1910, a great ballooning specialist, Robert Embden, wrote: "Balloon navigation is a science of which knowledge should be acquired first of all by practice. Of course it requires a deep theoretical knowledge, but the balloonist should never confine himself to the strict application of laws or principles... A quick decision, which might be imperative, should never be modified by theoretical reasons. A careful, brave and common-sense sportsman will always be worth more than a savant lost in his intellectual speculations. For a captain, the knowledge of his ship alone is not enough, he must also know the seas on which he sails. It is the same with the aeronaut, he must have more than a good smattering of meteorology".

In spite of these relevant remarks, the official schools of aeronautics have, for years, neglected all teaching of meteorology in favour of a mass of mathematical formulae. Let us make it clear: we do not deny the utility of theorems and rules, but we are conscious of the conditions of their application. Changes in atmospherical conditions, air currents, variable influence of sun rays or clouds, demand from the pilot a constant attention, a great patience and the capability of taking quick decisions. These are the qualities which are absolutely necessary to a balloonist worthy of the name.

FRED DOLDER

This picture, which has been taken by a camera tied to the appendix of the balloon shows two aeronauts flying over a glacier. The suspension hoop, fastened to the suspension ropes of the net, is in the foreground.

THE ANATOMY OF A BALLOON

The free balloon is made up of an envelope, a net, a car and a certain number of accessories.

The *envelope* is a gas-tight cloth sphere, inflated with a lighter-than-air gas, opened at the top by a valve which exhausts gas—which starts the descent when operated—and opened on its lower part by the inflating pipe which is used for the

The ballon below is preparing to land : the guiderope is uncoiled. Note the net, the suspension hoop, the ballast suspended from the car, the appendix, the valve and rip-panel ropes.

admission of the gas in the envelope and acts as a safety valve for the free emission of an excess of expanded gas during flight. The envelope also carries a rip-panel, which is a rectangular cloth frame with a flap to which is fixed a rope which when pulled helps to deflate the balloon rapidly, thus avoiding the car being dragged on the ground when landing.

The *net* is the main suspension component of the car, which covers the envelope and contains suspension ropes which are tied to the suspension hoop of the car. The net spreads the load evenly over the surface of the envelope.

The *suspension hoop of the car* is either made of wood or metal. To it are attached the suspension ropes of the net and those of the car, forming the junction between the lifting force (envelope) and the load (car).

The *car* is a rectangular basket, generally made of willow, in which the balloonists are contained ; it is fastened to the suspension hoop by suspension ropes.

The *guiderope* is a cable from 111 to 222 yds long. One of its extremities is tied to the suspension hoop and the rest of it is coiled up and fastened on one side of the car. When uncoiled and touching the ground, its weight and its friction force make it a good ballast, a partial brake and a means of directing the balloon before landing.

The *anchor* was in the past a necessary brake for landing but it has today completely disappeared with the use of the rip-panel.

The *ballast* is a heavy body, generally sand bags, which the balloonist carries in the car and which he jettisons to control the ascent of the balloon.

The *altimeter* is a barometer graduated for measuring altitude. The pilot's other instruments are an ordinary barometer, an anemometer, a thermometer and a watch and compass.

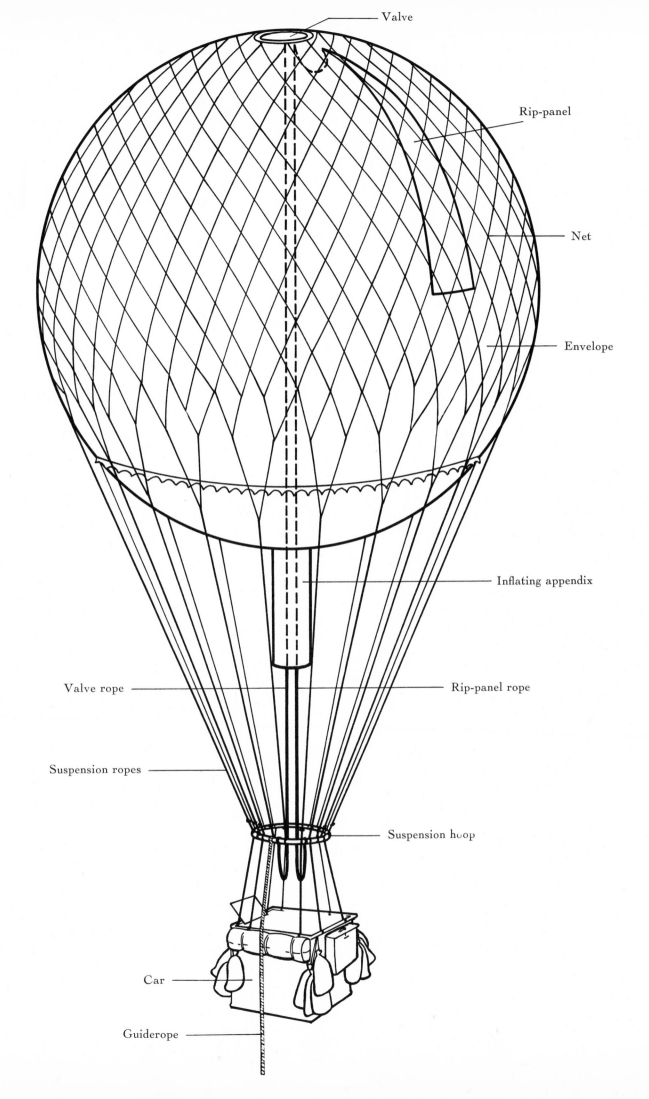

Valve

Rip-panel

Net

Envelope

Inflating appendix

Valve rope

Rip-panel rope

Suspension ropes

Suspension hoop

Car

Guiderope

The Envelope

The capacity of a balloon is always given in m³, and balloons are rated according to their capacity. In the manufacture of spherical or pear-shaped passenger balloons, cotton fabrics, linen, silk or, very infrequently, gold-beater's skin are used. The fabric can be of one thickness or two, rubberized or varnished. The material should have a close weave and a relatively high resistance to tearing, proportional to the capacity of the balloon. The joins of the different gores must be gummed with a rubber solution and sewn together (as should the reinforcing parts of the envelope). To make them airtight, a strip of material must be stuck over the seams. The openings for the valve and inflating appendix must either have a fabric lining with a diameter twice that of the opening, or be protected by circular bands.

The edge of the rip-panel opening should either be reinforced by a circular ribbon or by a lining at least 2·7 ins wide. The tongue of the rip-panel must invariably be made of a double thickness of bias material, must overhang the opening point of the rip-panel by at least 0·4 in, and should also be lined at this point.

The Valve

There exist many kinds of valves among which the two principal types are the French, with a double clack and the German, with a single clack. Those constructions are authorized where the ventilator is lifted up by pulling on the valve cord and where a spring or rubber band exerts pressure on the base of the valve thus ensuring the automatic airtight closure when the cord is released. There must be some guarantee of safety when the cord is released abruptly. The interior diameter should be the same for inflation with lighting gas or with hydrogen, and must be at least 1/30th of the maximum diameter of the envelope. The length of the valve must correspond at least to one quarter of the diameter of the valve, or otherwise the basis of the outflow volume must be at least: 0.125 m²

for balloons with a capacity of up to 1,000 m³ and 0.195 m² for balloons with a capacity of up to 2,500 m³. In the case of both new and used valves the strength of pull needed to operate them should be between 33 and 44 lbs. This should be checked regularly by the use of weights.

The inflating pipe is used first for the admission of the gas in the envelope and it must stay opened during the flight to act as a safety-valve to exhaust a possible excess of expanded gas which could cause the balloon to explode. The opening of a balloon's inflating pipe must have a diameter no smaller than 1/30th of that of the balloon and must be connected to the suspension hoop or to the rope network by at least two ropes. The length of the appendix must be at least twice its diameter.

The Net

Balloon nets must be made only of tightly woven Italian hemp with long fibres whose resistance to tearing when new should be from 198 lbs for a rope of ·112 in diameter to 2,420 lbs for a rope of ·433 in diameter. There exist thicker ropes for balloon nets.

Note: — The safety factor of a rope is a ratio where the numerator represents the breaking point of a rope, i.e. the maximum load, and where the denominator represents the effective load that is to be applied to the rope. For example, if a rope of ·112 in diameter reaches its breaking point at 198 lbs, and if for safety reasons there should be applied a safety factor of 15, we find the effective load that can be applied to it as follows:

$$\frac{\text{breaking point load}}{\text{effective load}} \quad \text{or} \quad \frac{198 \text{ lbs}}{x} = 15 \text{ (safety factor)}$$

i.e. $\dfrac{198 \text{ lbs}}{15} = X$ or 13.2 lbs.

When calculating the resistance of ropes in new nets, the resistance of unknotted ropes must be multiplied by 20.

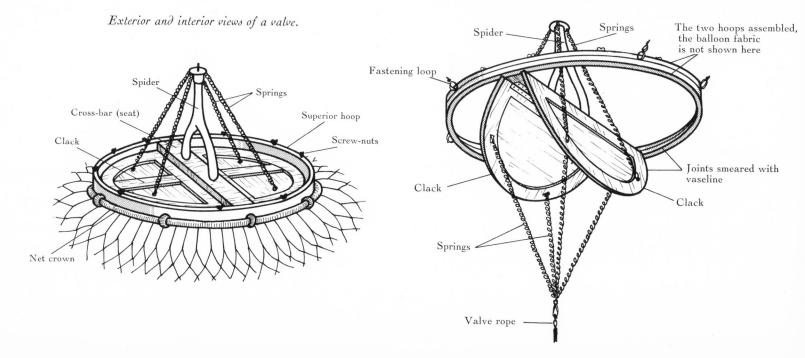

Exterior and interior views of a valve.

Spider · Springs · Cross-bar (seat) · Superior hoop · Clack · Screw-nuts · Net crown

Spider · Springs · The two hoops assembled, the balloon fabric is not shown here · Fastening loop · Joints smeared with vaseline · Clack · Clack · Springs · Valve rope

Above, close-up of a suspension hoop. On the left, a barometer is suspended. In the centre, the valve and rip-panel ropes hang down conveniently.

This high degree of security is necessary because the mesh of the nets is subjected to particular wear and tear from the suspension of weights or bags of ballast from it during the inflation of the balloon. The proportion between height and width of the mesh below the equatorial line must not be less than 2 :1. The width of the mesh should be no greater than 26 ins in any part of the net.

As with the mesh ropes, the resistance specifications of the suspension ropes of the nets of free balloons are as for new suspension ropes, a security coefficient of 15 and for used suspension ropes, after overhauling, a security coefficient of 10.

The number of suspension ropes must not be less than :

    10 for balloons with a capacity of up to   600 m³
    20 for balloons with a capacity of up to 2,500 m³
    24 for balloons with a capacity exceeding 2,500 m³

Concerning splices and knots in the mesh of the net and in the suspending ropes, each splice must be intertwined at least four times. The only knot used must be a netting knot. To avoid any friction of one rope upon another and the ensuing excessive deterioration in the rope network, all the joins in the net must be covered with moveable eyelets or metal rings. These eyelets and

rings, as with any metallic element used in the construction of a balloon net, must not have any projecting or rough surfaces at the points where they come into contact with the ropes. The metallic parts must be made of a rust-proof substance or protected from rust by the appropriate treatment.

The use of worn nets is only authorized if the resistance to tearing of the most worn cords represents in relation to the calculated maximum load a safety coefficient of 7 in the case of knotted ropes and 15 for unknotted ropes.

Suspension Hoop of the Car

The suspension hoop can be made of unwelded metal tubing, or a wooden circle. The metal parts must be protected against rust.

The Car

Balloon cars are made out of willow, bamboo, rattan or Spanish reed. The material used must not be dry or easily breakable, but must be sufficiently pliable.

As a general rule, the size of the basket depends on the size of the balloon and the number of people to be carried

179

therein. A car for four people must measure at least 4.6 ft by 4 ft and be 3.5 ft high (interior measurements). However, exceptions can be authorized for balloons having a smaller capacity than 1,000 m³ or special balloons. In principle, cars should be made rectangular not square. When a car has not been made considerably larger for a special reason, care must be taken that the shorter side of the car can fit into the back of an average goods van.

The construction of the car is governed by certain conditions :

— The edge of the car must be reinforced to a minimum height of 2 ins with an appropriate substance which has an adequate resistance.

— The floor of the car must be reinforced with 3 or 4 wooden crosspieces. The joints between the floor and the sides must be made with care so as to be particularly strong and reliable.

The basket is hung to the suspension hoop by suspension ropes. Each side of the car must have at least two or preferably three suspension ropes; as a general rule the short sides have two ropes and the long sides three. The ropes must be passed under the floor of the car through the wickerwork, care being taken that they cannot be damaged by sharp bars or by metal parts. The resistance of the suspension ropes of the car must be calculated according to the criteria of security of the other suspension ropes. The minimum resistance of car ropes must exceed 3,100 lbs.

The Accessories

The guiderope, mooring, valve control and rip-panel ropes.

In the making of guideropes, hemp ropes or coir-fibre can be used. With hemp ropes the minimum resistance must not be less than 1 in, and 1.2 in with coir-fibre. Their weight must not be less than 3.8 oz per foot in the lower half of the rope. The breaking strain in new guideropes must not be less than 6,160 lbs and 4,840 lbs in used ropes. The minimum effective length of a guiderope is 100 ft. The maximum length depends on the size of the balloon, and, taking the danger of high tension electric wires into account, must be as follows :

197 ft for balloons with a capacity of less than 1,200 m³
220 ft for balloons with a capacity of less than 1,680 m³
263 ft for balloons with a capacity of less than 2,310 m³
296 ft for balloons with a capacity exceeding 2,310 m³

To stop a balloon two quite basic mooring ropes are used, attached separately to the hoop on the right and on the left, each having a minimum resistance of ·58 in. Each rope must be at least 33 ft long.

The valve control rope must have a diameter of at least 0·4 in; so that it can be distinguished from the other ropes, it must be blue or bicoloured (red/white).

The ripcord can sometimes be replaced by a strap at least 0·98 in wide and ·156 in thick. In both cases it has to be red. The resistance of these two ropes must not be less than 880 lbs when in use.

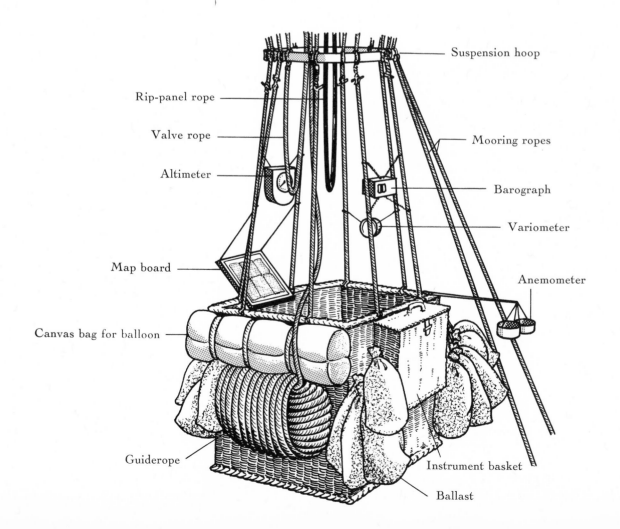

Suspension hoop

Rip-panel rope

Valve rope

Altimeter

Mooring ropes

Barograph

Variometer

Map board

Anemometer

Canvas bag for balloon

180

Guiderope

Instrument basket

Ballast

PRIMER OF BALLOONING

Unlike birds and aeroplanes, the free balloon is not self-governing. Its course cannot be directed, for it floats driven on by atmospheric currents. A ballon trip offers — beside the fascinating and ever changing spectacle — the feeling of an inspiring adventure full of unforeseen events, which makes it even more exciting.

A balloon flight brings the aeronaut in touch with realities often unknown by the layman, it makes him abandon some traditional ideas and put in their place scientific definitions.

For example, air is a gas in which we swim, like a fish in the sea. Wind is an atmospheric "disturbance", caused partly by the rotation of the Earth, by the effect of the solar rays and by thermal and hygrometric influences. This movement obeys laws similar to those governing tides, in so far as it is not affected by such phenomena as fronts, cyclones, anticyclones, solar eruptions, etc., phenomena which one can rarely forecast with any degree of accuracy.

Local weather conditions — for example in mountains, in valleys, in falls of rain or snow, when in lifting or descending air currents, etc., — often affect balloon flights. In opposition to lay opinion, the pilot's duty is not only to jettison ballast in order to reach a higher altitude and to operate the valve in order to go down. A balloonist should have an excellent theoretical knowledge of the behaviour of a free balloon in the atmosphere, moreover he should also be intuitive and have good self-control. One cannot extemporize the profession of aeronaut, which needs the wisdom to use the forces of Nature, and the ability not to become their toy or sometimes their victim.

A balloon ascent consists of three stages: departure, flight, landing.

At the departure time, the pilot controls the inflation of the balloon, manages the "weighing" in order to evaluate its lifting force, and decides on the moment of departure by saying: "hands off". The ascent phase remains critical until the ground obstacle level is cleared. Then the real flight starts. This is the part of the ascent when we can enjoy best the beauty of the scenery flown over, in the most complete silence and calmness. The pilot's duty consists of watching the course of the balloon and the atmospheric conditions in order to use or to counter the influences encountered by the balloon. The flight is practically finished when the pilot judges that the stores of ballast are reduced to the quantity necessary for a normal landing.

The landing is the most delicate phase of a balloon trip. It demands from the pilot a solid experience and cool judgement of the conditions close to the ground (hilly topography, winds, obstacles, etc.) which often prevent a soft landing; the pilot attempts then to re-establish his balloon's equilibrium at the ground level by the combined actions of guiderope, valve and ballast.

Balloons and the Principles of Physics

1. When the balloon is inflated and fully equipped, the first operation consists of "weighing" the balloon. Having, as a preliminary, ballasted the car with bags of sand, the pilot and the passenger climb in and jettison the ballast until the balloon reaches its height of equilibrium. "Equilibrium" means that the total weight (envelope, net, car, gear, the mass of the gas which lifts it, passengers, provisions, radio, navigational instruments, personal effects, etc.) corresponds exactly to the weight of the air displaced by the envelope of the balloon, by virtue of Archimedes' principle.

Archimedes' principle : (Greek mathematician and physicist, 285-212 BC).

"A body wholly or partially imersed in a fluid experiences an upthrust equal to the weight of fluid displaced."

As the weight of the air varies with the temperature, the height and relative humidity, the rising force of the balloon and consequently its lifting force, varies with the atmospheric conditions.

2. With height, the atmospheric pressure, and therefore the weight of the air, diminishes and the expanding pressure of the gas, which is becoming lighter, increases, according to Boyle's law.

Boyle's law : Robert Boyle, English chemist and philosopher 1627 - 1691.

"At a constant temperature, the volume of a given gaseous mass varies in inverse ratio to its pressure. The product of the volume and pressure is constant."

For example : every aerostat has an inflating tube (or appendix) through which the gas is introduced. If a completely inflated balloon i.e. a "rigid balloon" were to lift off with the appendix closed, it would explode after rising about 900 ft.

3. The lifting force of a balloon is equal to the difference between the weight of the air displaced by the balloon and the weight of the balloon itself.

Thus, we state that the lifting force of a balloon varies continually during a flight.

Rigid and Flaccid Balloons

When a balloon is not completely filled, it is termed a "flaccid balloon". If by diminishing its weight (jettisoning ballast) one gives it a rising force, it rises at a constant speed, in normal atmospheric conditions, until the envelope is completely filled out ("maximum inflation") and it then becomes a "rigid balloon" which continues rising until it reaches the point of equilibrium with the weight lifted at departure.

Thus we can state that any balloon, unless hampered rises to its equilibrium point.

A completely inflated balloon is called a "rigid balloon" Departure in a rigid balloon presents several problems and the fact of being able to carry up more ballast in a rigid balloon than in a flaccid balloon is only an illusory advantage because once it reaches the height of maximum inflation of a flaccid balloon of same capacity, a rigid balloon is not more stable than a flaccid balloon. It has exhausted gas and the ballast has to be jettisoned during the ascent, requiring all the attention and activity of the pilot.

On the contrary, departure in a flaccid balloon presents several advantages. The flaccid balloon rises above its height of maximum inflation without needing any intervention from the pilot except in the event of an inversion in temperature or an error in his appreciation of the lifting power. As its lifting power remains constant up to the height of maximum inflation, it reaches this height twice as quickly as the rigid balloon. It consequently passes twice as quickly the level of dangerous obstacles for the balloon or the guiderope, such as buildings, telephone wires or high tension electric cables. For this reason it is better protected from unforeseeable contingencies than a balloon whose lifting power diminishes progressively. To this overwhelming advantage, it is fitting to add that there is an important saving in gas.

In order that maximum inflation is acquired at a relative height of 1,500 ft and that the balloon reaches its first state of equilibrium between 1,650 and 2,000 ft, it need only be 94% full. The quantity of gas needed for the inflation depends on the conditions under which the inflation is made.

Behavioural Differences between Rigid and Flaccid Balloons

Any balloon which, having already reached its maximum altitude, descends or moves about below this height, maintains a constant mass of air in its envelope. The weight of the air is constant but its volume is variable. The gas expands inside the folded envelope (ascent) or contracts (descent) and the volume of gas increases or diminishes, but its total weight remains unaltered. Until the moment when it again reaches its maximum height, it loses no more gas.

If the balloon becomes rigid again, that is to say if it is filled once more with gas, which happens automatically as soon as the maximum altitude is reached, the superfluous gas escapes through the appendix. The volume of gas remains constant because the envelope is always full, but the total weight of gas changes inside the balloon.

Rigid Balloon or Balloon with a Constant Volume of Gas	Flaccid Balloon or Balloon with a Constant Weight of Gas
Departure : unfavourable 1. Needs more gas, incurs more expense. Excess gas escapes during ascent until the first static ceiling. This gas is therefore useless.	Departure : *more favourable* 1. *Needs less gas, incurs less expenditure.*
2. In general, slow ascent requiring close attention in avoiding obstacles and jettisoning ballast as there is a risk of reaching the static ceiling too quickly.	2. *Generally more rapid ascent. Does not require great attention in jettisoning ballast and avoiding obstacles.*
3. One must only lift off in a rigid balloon if : a) one wants the static ceiling to be as low as possible. b) violent or gusty winds hinder stopping, attaining equilibrium and the departure.	3. *In principle, one should always lift off in a flaccid balloon, but this has its disadvantages under conditions of violent or gusty winds because the wind has more effect on the folds of the balloon.*
Beginning of the Ascent : Slow ascent, about twice as slow as with the flaccid balloon. Slow rise above the obstacle level. Great care needed. Constant attention to ballast.	Beginning of the Ascent : *More rapid ascent, about twice as fast as with the rigid balloon. Rapid rise above the obstacle level. Less care needed. No point in jettisoning ballast.*
Flight : Stable equilibrium.	Flight : *No stability. The least lifting or depressing force makes the balloon rise or descend without letting out gas.*
On Descent : Becomes a flaccid balloon.	On Descent : *The descending force remains constant down to the ground.*
On Ascent : Unstable, each ascent caused by rising currents of air is followed, when the flow stops, by an immediate descent to the ground.	On Ascent : *Stable, climbs to the height of maximum inflation.*

Departure Operations

Before departure, certain operations have to be made methodically :

a) careful scrutiny of the local meteorological conditions (prospective storm forecast, wind speed) conditioning the departure ;

b) control of the balloon (inflation, equipment) and search for optimum lifting power.

At departure time, the pilot proceeds with the weighing of the balloon, i.e. an operation which permits him to find the equilibrium of the balloon at ground level, and the disposal of a weight of ballast corresponding to the lifting force wanted. In favourable conditions, the minimum quantity of ballast jettisoned during this operation is 33 lbs. After this, the pilot opens the inflating pipe in order to let out the excess gas during the ascent. The command "hands off" frees the balloon, which begins its ascent. As long as the balloon has not risen above the obstacle level, the pilot pays attention to the course of the balloon, and is ready to intervene if any disturbance or obstacle occurs. The pilot should take into account the fact that his balloon does not obey as quickly and as handily as a ground vehicle.

Primer of Ballooning

Every balloon descends to the ground from the moment when it has reached its equilibrium of weight (i.e. the height of maximum inflation) if it is not kept in the air by jettisoning ballast. Its speed of descent varies between 1.6 and 4.9 feet per second.

The height of maximum equilibrium can be calculated in advance, which enables one to limit the inflation of a balloon to a particular extent if one wants to send it up to a specific height. This height of equilibrium depends, given the size of a balloon and the degree of its inflation, on the amount of ballast which can be jettisoned before a decision to land, as also on the temperature conditions. However, it is not always possible to reach the precise maximum height. A fall of rain or snow, insufficient reserves of ballast, prolonged cloud cover or a night ascent can reduce the length of the flight. The balloonist's art consists of effecting as slow an ascent as possible in order to reach maximum height over the longest possible period of time. However, to judge the *quality* of an ascent, one does not use as a basis the curve of the flight in ascent: but instead, *the average consumption of ballast per unit of time*. The smaller this is, the slower the balloon rises to its maximum height.

The nature of the gas used has no bearing on the amount of ballast necessary to halt the balloon's progress; the amount of excess ballast jettisoned increases and decreases in proportion to the total amount of ballast thrown overboard and represents a percentage which varies according to the skill of the pilot.

One can only keep a balloon at the same height by alternatively throwing out ballast (the balloon rises) and letting out gas (it descends). The pilot's skill consists of lessening these contrary actions to the point where they are imperceptible. The better the atmospheric conditions, the easier it is to steer the balloon smoothly. The further the balloon is from the ground, the more stable are the atmospheric conditions, for near ground level, and above all in warm weather, changes in temperature and terrain can cause violent disturbances. In this situation, piloting becomes more complicated because the balloon responds to orders almost against its will, that is to say with a delay of 6 to 10 seconds due to its inherent inertia. This situation severely tries the pilot's nerve but at the same time allows him to prove his ability, especially in an obstructed or confined air space.

The classic formula for flight under favourable meteorological conditions is as follows: a slow ascent to the height where the stores of ballast are reduced to the quantity necessary for a normal landing; descent and braking at about 600 ft above the ground in order to be able to land rapidly on an open stretch of land. The more ballast one has, the longer the flight. Ballast is the "motor-fuel" of free balloons.

Use of Ballast

The pilot decides the minimum amount of ballast he takes up depending on the weather, the wind speed and the size of the obstacles over which he must pass (towns, industrial areas, etc.) bearing in mind all the time the following minimum quantities: (1 normal bag of ballast = 33 lbs net).

Balloons of 1st category	(600 m³)
	4 bags = 66 lbs
Balloons of 2nd and 3rd category	(up to 1,200 m³)
	8 bags = 132 lbs
Balloons of 4th category	(up to 1,600 m³)
	12 bags = 198 lbs
Balloons of 5th category	(up to 2,600 m³)
	15 bags = 235 lbs

A discharge of ballast which only slows down the descent of the balloon without stopping it definitely, is just a waste of ballast, even if the descending force is totally or partly voided by a cold air zone on which the balloon floats. In order to stop completely the descent of the balloon, the pilot must jettison more ballast than is needed to annul the descending force. If after such a loss of ballast, the motion downward has completely stopped, the balloon, which has been excessively lightened, rises again to reach a new equilibrium point, situated at higher altitude than the first.

Any discharge of ballast which does not make the balloon reach a new zone of temperature, can slow down the descent or cause an ascent, but can never stop the balloon completely.

Utilisation of the Valve

The utilisation of the valve is sometimes necessary to comply with the air circulation laws (air space controlled or forbidden).

One must think twice before pulling the valve rope for each pull shortens the flight time. However, operating the valve can be necessary when the balloon needs to descend under the clouds to give the pilot an idea of the territory beneath. The use of the valve becomes necessary when a flight must come to an end quickly and when the pilot cannot wait for a regular loss of altitude leading to a normal end, or when the pilot must use the guiderope; however, the above cases are relatively rare. There exists only one case when operating it becomes obligatory and it is when the effect of an excessive discharge has to be annulled. Except for the landing phase, a great many flights are performed without operating the valve.

A law, at first glance paradoxical, states that each pull on the valve, during the flight, increases the height; another law, equally paradoxical, can be added to this first one: any overweight carried by the balloon (like dew, rain or snow) increases the point of equilibrium height by demanding an excessive loss of ballast. Any overweight causes the balloon to sink and in order to avoid landing, the pilot must discharge ballast. If this operation stops the descent, it means that too much ballast has been jettisoned and the flight curve increases. If the ballast jettisoned is not sufficient to counterbalance the overweight supported by the balloon, the flight come to an end quickly. For example, rainfall uniformly spread over the top half of a balloon forms a coat ·019 in thick and corresponds to an overweight of 187 lbs for a 600 m³ balloon and to an overweight of 330 lbs for a 1,440 m³ balloon.

Influence of Atmospherical Conditions

The absorption of rain water by the envelope, the net and the accessories varies from 132 lbs for a 600 m³ balloon to 297 lbs for a 2,200 m³ balloon.

The impermeability of the fabrics depends on the treatment they have undergone; varnished fabrics absorb only 1/8 of the water absorbed by the rubberized fabrics. Furthermore, worn fabrics absorb more than the new ones.

When the balloon becomes dry again, all the ballast jettisoned before is then a superfluous loss, and the flight curve increases steeply. Any decrease in the solar rays, any persistent clouds, necessitates a discharge of ballast and finally causes the balloon to rise again.

Humidity, snow or rain falls, or lack of solar rays depress the temperature. Any decrease in the temperature of a gas causes a diminution in its volume and consequently a descending force equal to 4% of the weight of air displaced.

In order to make clear the importance of this force, let us say that, at an altitude of 6,400 ft, one meter cube of air weighs approximately 2.2 lbs. Then a 1,000 m³ balloon is submitted to a descending force of approximately 8.8 lbs for a decrease of 10° C in the temperature of the gas, independently of the type of gas used. If the presence of clouds provokes a decrease of the gas temperature of 10° C, the state of descent which immediately follows cannot be stopped except by discharging 88 lbs of ballast. In this case, the excessive but necessary discharge of ballast will cause an increase of the flight curve. If the sun shines again, the total of ballast discharged appears to be a superfluous loss; the height of the equilibrium point is increased and the flight time is reduced. So, any cloud for which the pilot cannot predict the dispersion finally causes the balloon to rise. All pilots have cause to remember the important sacrifices of ballast due to clouds.

What happens with clouds happens also to a greater or lesser degree by passing from day to night; and then the ballast which needed to be discharged at twilight appears in the morning as a regrettable loss.

Any disturbance of equilibrium, directed either upwards or downwards, finally causes the balloon to rise, to the detriment of the ballast and the flight time.

There exist peculiar cases, for example: a balloonist, who is also a good meteorologist, and who takes off on a relatively clear winter day or on a summer day before dew or after twilight, knows that he is going to meet at a height of 9,600 ft or less a reversal zone of temperature. Therefore he will carefully prepare enough ballast to cross this invisible ceiling. This is a case where the flaccid balloon presents great advantages. In warm air, the temperature of the gas increases and the difference between its own temperature and the temperature of the ambient air returns it to its preceding point. The balloon can then cross this zone without any loss of ballast.

Lifting and descending currents operate seriously on the balloon even if they are slow. The balloon pushed upwards without loss of ballast reaches a new equilibrium point when its descending force is equal to the pressure of the lifting current. And even a weak descending current operates immediately on a flaccid balloon.

It is impossible to give rules for every case when air currents interfere to disturb the equilibrium of the balloon, so, in such circumstances, we must trust the pilot's skill and instinct.

In the presence of fast air currents, the pilot would be wise not to intervene at all, either with the valve, or with ballast, for the descending or lifting force which he will give the balloon will be weak compared to the forces then operating on the balloon.

Too weak a pull on the valve rope is of no importance, for the gas exhausts simultaneously through the appendix as well as through the valve without the balloon descending. An excessive use of the valve can easily increase the loss of gas. Each time an air current causes the balloon to rise, if its stores of ballast are poor, the pilot can expect serious difficulty. In most cases, it is wise to lighten the balloon again by a carefully calculated discharge of ballast. On the contrary, when the balloon is pushed downwards by a strong pressure, it is better to delay as much as possible the discharge of ballast in order to avoid an excessive loss in the case of the balloon changing direction after having left the descending current. In a case when the rest of the ballast proves to be insufficient to brake the descent in the last 6,500 - 9,500 ft, the pilot is unable to control the situation.

When the vertical motions (lifting or descending) operating on a balloon are weak, the pilot is better to wait for their dispersion; for each cubic meter of gas expelling by the valve, each pound of ballast discharged can become a waste which is sometimes dangerous. When the balloon floats at the borderline of two different belts of temperature, it is better to let it follow the wave-motion of these layers of air.

When the pilot notices that the altitude of his balloon has changed, his first task is to know whether it is due to a disturbance in the equilibrium of his balloon or to the influence of a thermal current. By the way, the instruments which indicate the changes of altitude (barometer, variometer) do not give an answer to this question. A vertical anemometer, like the dropping of small pieces of paper, indicates only the relative motion of the balloon with regard to the mass of the surrounding air.

The pilot's experience and judgement will stop him from intervening without knowing what causes his balloon to rise or to sink. A skilled pilot will never correct immediately the course of his balloon at the simple reading of the barometric instruments.

Behaviour of Balloons compared with the Type of Gas Used

Free balloons are generally inflated with lighting gas, hydrogen or, rarely, helium. These gases have different weights: the lighting gas weighs 1.1 lbs per m^3 and the hydrogen weighs 2 lb per m^3 at a temperature of 0° C, sea level. The lifting force of a hydrogen balloon is 70 % greater than that of the lighting gas balloon; and its quantity of ballast has to be greater than that of the lighting gas balloon. Consequently the flight time of a hydrogen balloon is longer. For the same sun fade-out a 600 m^3 hydrogen balloon is submitted approximately to the same descending force as a 1,200 m^3 lighting gas balloon; for these two types of balloons the quantities of ballast needed for braking are in proportion 1 : 2 and so are the quantities of ballast discharged superfluously. As far as hydrogen balloons are smaller than lighting gas balloons, the consumption of ballast per hour diminishes, the flight time lasts longer and the flight curve increases steeply (in proportion of 70 % for a same size of balloon).

Landing Techniques

For the pilot landing is the most important thing. Statements on flight durations, on heights reached or on distances covered have little importance compared to a good landing, performed without any person being injured and without damage. A balloon flight is practically finished when the pilot has only that quantity of ballast left necessary to a proper landing. Such an estimation is hard to make, and cannot be precise unless the pilot knows exactly the temperature of the different atmospheric layers during the state of descent. In many cases the skill and the intuition of the pilot counterbalance the information given by the instruments or by the observation of the ambient meteorological phenomena. By experience the pilot is aware of the fact that he has to keep a bigger quantity of ballast if he has to land on a hot summer afternoon than if he has to land on a cool day.

When the pilot is preparing for landing, all heavy or loose items are safely stowed away, the guiderope is uncoiled, the mooring ropes are near at hand and ready to be released, and the ballast is placed so that it can be discharged easily. Then the pilot waits for the proper moment to finish the descent, which depends on the thermal conditions of the different layers of air through which the balloon descends. There exist no laws or precise rules for performing a landing. Each time the pilot improvises the landing, which plays a great part in the aeronaut's art.

Let us look at a landing performed without any mishap. After having reached its equilibrium point, the balloon starts to go down by itself, unless the atmospherical conditions suddenly change or unless the pilot decides to interfere. This state of descent is slow. In a situation where the ambient air becomes colder than the gas inside the balloon, the pilot has to pull the valve rope in order to proceed with the descent. This he will also do if he wishes to quicken the motion downwards. When will the pilot need to brake the descending force of his balloon with a discharge of ballast? Theoretically, it is immaterial if the ballast is partly discharged during the descent or totally discharged all at once at the end. Since the descending force should never exceed the weight of the guiderope, a successful landing is supposed to be performed without any shock or bump. What matters really is that the balloon finds its new and last state of equilibrium with the help of the guiderope, just before touching the ground.

In practice, the pilot is guided by his estimation of the situation. However, if his balloon goes down with a speed of/or exceeding 480 ft per second, he will be sure to have to discharge ballast, and will have to recreate a situation for a safe landing. Depending on the kind of ground (rocky, sandy) and on the meteorological conditions (winds, rain, etc.) the operation of landing can prove difficult and put the pilot through a hard test of good reflexes and judgement.

If the pilot wishes to land rapidly he discharges his ballast all at once at the end of the descent. In extreme necessity, the pilot can forget about the search for the state of equilibrium which usually precedes the landing, and use the valve, or even more radically, the rip-panel.

In the event that the balloon, having been excessively lightened, bounces and starts to rise again, the pilot should pull the valve rope strongly to avoid the balloon rising above its previous equilibrium point and reaching a new state of equilibrium with insufficient ballast.

Just before the landing proper, the flight can be carried on by navigating with the guiderope. The pilot manages in such a way the balloon finds its equilibrium point at about thirty feet above the ground; this operation is done by throwing down part of the guiderope, which is made to drag on the ground. If the balloon is driven on by a favourable wind, it can carry on in its course until the pilot finds a good place to land. However, navigating with the guiderope down has now become dangerous due to so many artificial obstacles, especially electric cables and telegraph wires. Thus, favourable conditions for navigating with the guiderope are becoming rare.

Landings are always difficult. If some are beautiful examples of flexibility and smoothness, others are full of bump and incident. It may happen that the car of the balloon ceases to move only after having bounced or having been dragged for a certain distance on the ground. The history of ballooning is full of examples of all the possible kinds of landings. Some aeronauts have experienced dangerous and sometimes fatal situations, others have had uncomfortable ones and even some funny ones (funny for everybody but themselves).

During the past years, many balloons have caught fire spontaneously after a good landing. Researches on the causes of these accidents have led to the following conclusions : during the descent the air entering the envelope (by the Pöschel circle which keeps the extremity of the appendix open) mixes with the gas inside the balloon (hydrogen) and forms an explosive gas which may catch fire and explode spontaneously.

Since this discovery, the largest firm in balloon manufacturing makes only balloons which do not have the Pöschel circle. Moreover, most of the Aeronauts' clubs have ordered their members to close the appendix during the descent in order to avoid the admission of ambient air.

Before the last war, the physicist Auguste Piccard showed that it is preferable during the descent to handle a balloon in which the appendix is shut. It is, then, most important to close the appendix before using the valve during the descent.

THE PRACTICE OF BALLOONING

As early as 1932, Auguste Piccard drew attention to the fact that a balloon *is a means and only a means* to rise above the ground. It is not power-driven, it literally floats at the mercy of the winds; its speed can be neither accelerated nor slowed down. This fundamental statement is the basis of the aeronaut's sport; and this is why distance or duration trials are incompatible with the definition of a balloon itself. When freed from any utilitarian application, ballooning is the "most noble sport". The first "Bazenheid Free Balloon International Meeting" in 1970 proved—if ever it was necessary—that the lack of competitions, trials and prizes did not affect the general enthusiasm of balloonists or that of the public. Spectators were fascinated by the beautiful sight of these gaily-coloured globes rising in the clear blue sky like enormous toys floating in space.

In order to reach perfection within the sport, the balloonist should approach ballooning without any longing for victory or for records. He should only keep in mind the legitimate desire to make successful flights and good landings. This explains why the pilot is a unique type of man: he is calm and thoughtful, sure when taking decisions, and quick in action. He is a skilful and intuitive man who never stops learning and discovering.

The practice of such a sport becomes possible only under certain conditions which involve the pilot, the balloon and the development of the flight. Only persons in possession of a pilot's licence and having an officially qualified balloon at their disposal can legally make an ascent.

The pilot carries the whole responsibility for persons and materials during the whole duration of the flight until such time as all the material is back in store. He is also responsible for the respect of legal provisions and rules concerning the authorisation for the flight itself and for the flight over the locale, etc. The pilot also has to decide on the number of passengers he will take with him. He is obliged to take out insurances: injury insurance, civil liability insurance and passenger insurance.

The apprentice-pilot applies to a balloonists' club, which will undertake his theoretical education as well as his practical one. It would be wrong to think that once he has acquired his pilot's licence his education stops. On the contrary, he will keep on learning, for a pilot is only considered to be really experienced after having made at least 250 ascents.

Preparations for Flight

While the balloon is being inflated, the pilot has to make sure that the balloon is in good condition (envelope, valve, net, etc.), he has also to watch the development of operations and take care that nobody smokes. He has to be informed of the meteorological conditions, both locally and at a distance from the point of departure, and he has to be aware of the probable changes in the weather during the next 24 hours.

No ascent can be undertaken without the formal authorization of the Air observation and security control organisations. The pilot should make sure that all the necessary items are carried in the car of the balloon:

a) official papers: pilot's licence, permit of balloon navigation, insurance certificates, passports, etc.

b) instruments: altimeter, variometer, barometer, barograph, anemometer, thermometer, compass, watch. It is also obligatory to take on board a transmitting-receiving radio with special channels for air traffic.

c) miscellaneous items: a diversified collection of maps: geographical ones and air route ones; a telescope, a knife, a corkscrew, a flashlight, some twine, etc.

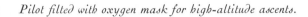
Pilot fitted with oxygen mask for high-altitude ascents.

The inflation has started. In the foreground, the inflating appendix and the inflating pipe ; the envelope is kept on the ground by the net, to which are tied sand bags.

First stage in the flight preparations : the aeronaut and his helpers spread out the envelope on the ground and unfold the net

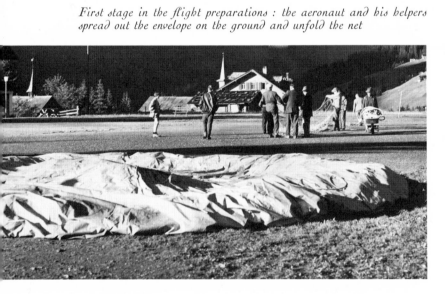

The different stages of inflation

Far left : as the inflation proceeds, the helpers re-adjust the net (which keeps the envelope on the ground) by hooking or taking off sand bags. This operation continues (left and below left) until there is nothing touching the ground but the appendix. Below : the inflation is finished and they fasten the car to the suspension hoop. The balloon, which is kept on the ground by the mooring ropes and by an excess of ballast, is now ready for departure (right).

191

d) some food, easy to prepare and to eat, like sandwiches, cold chicken, ham, chocolate, fruits, wine, a flask of rum or brandy and a Thermos of coffee. It is advisable to bring foods like those which alpinists take with them. Since the air at an altitude does not generally predispose to heavy meals, it would not be wise to bring large quantities of food.

The aeronaut's equipment is dictated more by experience than by fashion: he has to wear a good cap to protect his head from sun, a jacket or any coat with big pockets, a pull-over, a comfortable and stout pair of trousers, a light, strong raincoat, a scarf and a good pair of walking shoes, for the landing can sometimes be followed by a long walk on rough ground. The pilot has to wear a distinguishing sign (jacket or cap of a special colour) so that anybody can recognize him easily and help him in his work (especially people on the ground helping a landing).

The Preparation of the Balloon

Nowadays, most of the balloons are inflated with hydrogen, for the domestic gas supplied by gas-works has too high a specific weight. This preference for hydrogen is easy to understand when an increase of the specific weight from 0.3 to 0.55 corresponds to an excess weight of 660 lbs for a 1,000 m³ balloon.

During inflation, the inflating appendix, the inflating pipe and the feed-cylinder have to be watched carefully. The inflating appendix has to be placed in such a way that the gas can enter freely. There should be nobody under the envelope during inflation. Until the end of this operation, the envelope is kept on the ground, and all the precautions have to be taken in order to avoid an unwanted departure. If the wind blows hard during the inflation, during the suspension of the car or during the releasing of the envelope, a man facing the wind must keep the rip-panel rope in his hand and be ready to tear the balloon in case of emergency.

When inflation is finished, the car is fixed to the suspension hoop. For this operation, the balloon is turned in such a position that the rip-panel is placed above the guiderope. The suspension ropes are then tied one by one to the suspension hoop. The pilot takes care that the valve rope and the rip-panel rope are clearly separated and checks the working of the valve.

When the car is fixed, the envelope, covered by the net, is free and rises slowly in the air. This operation is done by shifting the sand bags which hold it down and by removing them gradually so that the ropes of the net do not chafe the balloon.

When the envelope is free and floats above the ground, the pilot checks carefully the position of the net, the steadiness of the car and the respective places of the valve and the rip-panel ropes. He also checks the

guiderope, the amount of ballast and the instruments. He should so arrange it that the side of the car which carries the guiderope faces the wind and he adjusts the altimeter.

The Weighing

The weighing is an essential operation, which consists of determining the lifting power of the balloon. This operation involves the help of a team to hold it down. They should be detailed in such a way that half of them hold down the car while the others hang on to the mooring ropes. For this operation, the envelope has to be exactly vertical to the car, or it would be impossible to properly evaluate the lifting power.

The method of procedure is as follows: the pilot and his passenger (or passengers) take their places in the car, and everything is in readiness for departure. The superfluous ballast is discharged from the car. The helpers put their hands on the edge of the car and hold it down. When the pilot shouts "Attention everybody", everyone should be at his post and listening carefully. The pilot shouts "hands off" and all the helpers take their hands off at the same time, but they should be ready to seize it again at the command "hold on". During the interval between these last orders, the pilot has estimated the motion of the balloon; he now adds or discharges ballast. He repeats this operation until he has obtained the lifting power he wishes; this lifting power is rarely below 33 lbs.

The pilot makes sure that the appendix is open and that everything is ready and he then shouts the famous command "Hands off". The ascent starts.

The Ascent

During the ascent, the pilot is the only responsible person aboard. He informs his passengers about the flight, he assigns them their place and gives them instructions concerning their behaviour. He keeps the ship's log as the flight proceeds; he notes the altitude, the ballast left, the shape and place of clouds and changes in meteorological conditions. He also observes what happens below the balloon; he compares the territory he has flown over with his map in order to find out the direction of the flight and to take the balloon's bearings. The observation of smoke and flags indicates to him the direction of the wind and its approximate speed at ground level. The practice of sports like sailing, gliding and parachuting have given rise to a thorough study of thermal currents, clouds and effects of solar ray reflection, and aeronauts now pay great attention to those phenomena which have a direct influence on their ascents.

The important development of commercial and sports aviation imposes on aeronauts certain restrictions. The pilot must keep his balloon outside clouds or maintain it at a height of 960 ft above cloud formations. He must

The twentieth century Montgolfier: Don Piccard lands in Washington with a synthetic fabric hot-air balloon. This experiment has been made for the "Smithsonian Institution's Transportation Day" and was used to show the methods employed by the aeronautical pioneers.

193

also take care to keep a good horizontal visual look-out within a radius of 5 miles approximately. For general air traffic safety reasons, he will sometimes be limited in manoeuvring his balloon. In compensation, all the commercial aviation safety and guidance network is available to balloonists, who can use the control stations and information services.

The pilot's great concern is to determine the course of his balloon; this is difficult, especially as the movement takes place in perfect calmness, and as the balloon moves at the same speed as the mass of air on which it floats.

In order to gain a proper picture of the variations in the winds at various altitudes, the pilot marks on the map at regular intervals the trajectory of the balloon (compass) and indicates for each separate point the corresponding height (barograph). However, this method proves to be inadequate when immediate information is needed, for example when the balloon draws near to coasts, mountain masses, etc.; for then it is too slow. To obviate the deficiencies of this method, little balloons heavier than air are used; they are dropped and while descending, they indicate the direction of the currents. Another method consists of suspending a small balloon to a thread about 128 ft long and observing its behaviour; this is called the "suspended pilot" method.

The Landing

When the pilot has decided to put an end to the ascent, he packs up or puts away all unnecessary items and ensures that the ballast, the valve and rip-panel ropes are near at hand.

Concerning ballast, it is well to remember that an excess of braking ballast is never harmful, while an insufficient quantity of it can be fatal. When the flight involves passengers, the landing must be executed when the ballast left corresponds to:

— 2 bags, or 66 lbs, for a 600 m³ balloon (cat. 1)

— 3 bags, or 99 lbs, for 900 to 1200 m³ balloon (cat. 2 & 3)

— 4 bags, or 132 lbs, for a 1600 m³ balloon (cat. 4)

— 5 bags, or 165 to 198 lbs for a 2200 m³ balloon (cat. 5)

The pilot should never forget that, during hot and calm summer days, the air warms quickly in the last 320 ft above ground, which can necessitate a discharge of ballast and cause an important loss. On the contrary, on a cold and clear day, just opening the valve can ensure a good landing.

During the descent, the speed should never exceed 8 ft per second in order to permit the guiderope to brake the landing. The guiderope is uncoiled when the place for landing is clearly in sight and when its use is obviously safe. The pilot has to throw out the mooring ropes early enough to avoid the balloon being brought to a standstill

by the action of the guiderope. The pilot has also to take precautions to prevent an accidental ascent which would put the balloon and its passengers in a critical situation. In the case of a hydrogen balloon, as soon as the balloon comes to rest, the pilot has to pull the rip-panel rope to avoid having an mixture of explosive gas inside the envelope. When on the ground, nobody can leave the car without the pilot's consent and passengers have to wait for the envelope to be sufficiently deflated.

After the Landing

The landing is followed by the taking down, the folding and the wrapping of the balloon. These operations are carefully executed under the pilot's supervision. He makes sure that the material goes back where it belongs (to its home port) in good condition.

The pilot should also know what to do in case of a landing on foreign territory. He has to give a flight report within the required time. Of course, the pilot's task becomes complicated when some accident or damage happens to ground installations. However, if we can judge by the ascents made within the "International Week of Free Ballooning over the High Alps", accidents are rare. From 1962 to 1972, 90 ascents have been made over the Alpine mass and no accident has yet been recorded.

Note Concerning the Twentieth-Century Montgolfier Balloons

Recently, the Montgolfier balloons or hot-air balloons have been brought back in fashion. The first have appeared in the United States and in England. These balloons have the following characteristics:

— a synthetic fabric envelope, of which lower part is wide open and has no appendix;

— under the opening, at the level of the suspension hoop, is suspended a Bunsen burner which heats the air inside the envelope. This burner replaces the straw which was used by the first aeronauts.

Mongolfier balloons can be used as spare balloons when it is impossible to find hydrogen or domestic gas. A comparison between hot-air balloons and gas balloons shows the following differences:

1. In a hot-air balloon, the ballast is replaced by fuel for the burner. A gas balloon flight must end with the last bag of ballast while a hot-air balloon flight ends either when there is no more fuel left or when there is a burner failure.

2. When the gas balloon has no ballast left, it goes down with a speed between 1.6 and 4.8 ft per second; this speed is slowed down by the guiderope when it is

close to land. In the case of a Montgolfier balloon, when there is no more fuel left, the balloon descends with an increasing speed which cannot be slowed down by jettisoning anything.

3. When landing in a forest, the gas balloon is stopped by the trees, when falling into water, it floats. In the same circumstances, the hot-air balloon behaves very differently : in the first case, it falls to the ground for it has no lifting force, and in the second case, it sinks because of its weight.

4. When landing in strong winds, it seldom happens that the passengers of a gas balloon are seriously injured ; however, the landing of a Montgolfier balloon in the same conditions presents certain dangers :

a) the tanks can explode and injure passengers.

b) the burners and other metallic apparatus can fall and cause serious injuries to people.

5. If an involuntary landing in an unsuitable place (town, railway station, moor, etc.) arises, the pilot of a gas balloon can always lighten his balloon by throwing overboard food or personal effects, but the fall of a Montgolfier balloon is uncontrollable.

6. The pilot of a gas balloon knows precisely how much ballast is left at a given time. The pilot of a hot-air balloon cannot know exactly what is the precise quantity of gas per unit of time his burners consume and furthermore, he is at the mercy of a failure in the feeding system (a dust squall can imperil the whole flight).

7. One of the most wonderful advantages of the gas balloon is silence ; in the car of a Montgolfier balloon, passengers have to shout every time they want to speak because the burners are so noisy. During the operation of the radio, the burners have to be turned off.

8. An ascent of a Montgolfier balloon is not cheaper than that of a gas balloon. Furthermore, the Montgolfier balloon is dangerous, as has been proved by several recent accidents.

The existence of these modern Montgolfier balloons will be of short duration, as were those of the eighteenth century, for the advantages of the gas balloon are overwhelming.

QUESTIONS AND ANSWERS

How Does One become an Aeronaut ?

Except for small national divergences, one becomes pilot by the following steps :

a) The candidate has to be at least 20 years old, be in good health (medical certificate) and to have no police record.

b) The would-be aeronaut should apply to an official flying-school. These schools are generally supervised by Aero-Clubs. During his education period, he is taught theoretical knowledge (gas physics, meteorology, navigation) and practice (knowledge of the material, flight preparations, a number of ascents supervised by a qualified instructor). When the candidate is ready for the piloting examinations, he has himself registered for them. They include :

— a 4 hours approx. theoretical examination ;

— a first practical examination, which is an ascent supervised by an official expert. The flight has to last two hours and reach a height of 6,400 ft. The apprentice-pilot has to first inflate the balloon and, after the landing, to fold and wrap the material ;

— a second practical examination which consists of an ascent lasting at least one hour executed by the apprentice-pilot alone with no altitude limit. Experts supervise the flight from the ground ;

— a radio operator examination, supervised by air traffic sponsors.

The licence is generally valid for a period of two years. To renew it, the pilot has to show a medical certificate and the proof that he has made in the meantime three ascents of two hours at least. When the pilot reaches his fortieth year, the permit has to be renewed every year.

How and where is a Balloon obtained ?

Clubs generally give addresses of balloonmakers. The price of a balloon depends on its size and varies from $ 6,250 to $ 12,500 (£ 2,500 - £ 5,000). Aeronauts' Clubs also hire out balloons. There exist such clubs in France, Belgium, Germany, Netherlands, England, Austria, Poland, Czechoslovakia and in Switzerland. A few clubs are now being formed in Italy, Sweden and Spain. Clubs are members of national Aero-Clubs which are united in an "International Aeronautic Federation".

Here are some addresses which we recommend to our readers interested in aeronaut's activities :

FRANCE

CLUB AÉROSTATIQUE DE FRANCE
82, Rue Ranélagh
Paris XVIᵉ.

BELGIUM

ASSOCIATION AÉROSTATIQUE DU NORD
DE LA FRANCE
60, Rue de Ratisbonne
Lille 59.

SECTION CENTRALE D'AÉROSTATION
DE L'AÉRO-CLUB ROYAL DE
BELGIQUE
53, Avenue des Arts
Bruxelles 4

GERMANY

There exist aeronauts' clubs in the
following cities:
Augsburg, Allgäu, Düsseldorf, Essen, Halberg-Brebach, Bremsen, Hamburg, Köln, Munich, Münster/ Westfalen, Neunkirchen, in the valleys of the Moselle and the Saar, in Salzach (Inn), Schweinfurt, Stuttgart, Wahlwies, Wuppertal.

NETHERLANDS

HAAGSE BALLON CLUB
Statenlaan 2A
Den Haag

ENGLAND

THE BRITISH BALLOON AND AIRSHIP
CLUB,
73, Victoria Street,
London S.W.1.

AUSTRIA

BALLON CLUB WIEN
Spitalgasse 9/21
Vienna IX

CANADA

CANADA BALLOON CLUB
6A, Beaumont Road,
Toronto 8, Ontario

U.S.A.

NATIONAL AERONAUTIC ASSOCIATION,
Suite 610,
Shoreham Building 806,
15th Street N.W.
Washington, D.C. 20005

BALLOON FEDERATION OF AMERICAN,
200, Snell Building,
Fort Dodge, Iowa 50501

BALLOON CLUB OF AMERICA,
Box 114,
Swarthmore, Pa.

AEROSTAT SOCIETY OF MINNESOTA,
310, Codar St,
St. Paul, Minnesota 55101

WINGFORT LIGHTER-THAN-AIR
SOCIETY,
1210, Massillon Road,
Akron, Ohio 44306

FREE BALLOON PILOT'S SOCIETY,
333, Southgate Drive,
Northbrook, Illinois 60002

NATIONAL ASSOCIATION OF BALLOON
CORPS VETERANS,
634, Wagner Road,
Lafayette Hill, Pennsylvania 19444

HOT AIR BALLOON PILOT'S
ASSOCIATION,
3300, Orchard,
Concord, California 94520

JAPAN

JAPAN BALLOON CLUB,
18-2-506 4-chome,
Minamiaoyama, Minato-ku,
Tokyo

SWITZERLAND

AÉRO-CLUB SUISSE
Hirschgraben 22
CH-8001 Zürich

How Does One attend or participate in free Balloon Flight?

At the end of the last war, there existed in the whole of Europe only three or four balloons; there are now, in 1972, more than a hundred.

Balloonists of all countries meet occasionally at international meetings. The most famous among these are:

— The International Precision Landing competition for free balloons which takes place every year the first weekend of September in the small town of Sint Niklaas-Wals, in Belgium;

— The "Haagse Ballon Club" short distance competition which takes place in the Netherlands;

— The Free Balloon Week in the High Alps (Dolder Ballooning Week) in Mürren, Switzerland. This week, which is organized by the "Internationale Spelterini Gesellschaft", takes place in the second half of June. This demonstration celebrated its tenth anniversary in 1972. During these ten years, pilots from all over Europe and overseas have made, without any accident, ninety ascents over the highest summits of the Alps and have landed in Italy, Germany, Austria and in France. All these balloonists are amateurs only, for ballooning is just a hobby for them.

Other meetings are held less regularly in Germany and in other countries. All these meetings and competitions are organized by aeronauts fully conscious of the limits of their sport. So are the balloonists when preparing a public attraction for a celebration. Since there remains always a doubt concerning the weather conditions, the pilot has to have, when such a thing happens, more courage to give up the ascent than is needed to yield to organisers and public pressure. The pilot must take this decision knowing well that the people greeting him with cheers when everything goes well would have no pity in case of accident. A true pilot is first interested in safety and secondly in the wishes of sponsors.

SOURCES, ACKNOWLEDGEMENTS
AND BIBLIOGRAPHY

SOURCES

THE ASTONISHING YEAR

THE MONTGOLFIER BROTHERS' FIRST EXPERIMENT, in: "*Journal de Paris*" No. 208, 27 July, 1783.

NARRATIVE OF JOSEPH MONTGOLFIER (Statement read to Lyons Academy, January 1784), cit. in: Faujas de Saint-Fond, "*Première suite de la description des expériences aérostatiques...*", Paris 1784.

LETTER FROM ETIENNE MONTGOLFIER, cit. in: Faujas de Saint-Fond, "*Description des expériences de la machine aérostatique...*", Paris, 1783.

EXTRACT FROM THE REPORT MADE BY THE ACADÉMIE DES SCIENCES on 23 December 1783, Paris.

THE ROBERT BROTHERS' EXPERIMENT, in: "*Journal de Paris*" No. 240, 28 August 1783.

CONSTERNATION IN GONESSE, in: "*Le Mercure de France*" (Paris) No. 37, 13 Septembre 1783.

EXCERPT FROM A REPORT SUBMITTED TO THE ACADÉMIE DES SCIENCES, in: "*Rapport de l'Académie des sciences*" of 23 December 1783, Paris.

THE CONQUEST OF THE SKIES, in: "*Journal de Paris*" No. 326, 22 November 1783.

THE PHILOSOPHER'S VIEW, in: Grimm, Frédéric-Melchior, "*Correspondance littéraire*", Paris, August 1783.

THE FIRST LONDON TRIALS (Zambeccari's letter of 28 November 1783), cit. in: Savini, Savino, "*Notizie biografiche del conte Francesco Zambeccari Bolognese*", Torino, 1847.

CHARLES AND ROBERT'S FLIGHT, in: "*Journal de Paris*" No. 336, 2 December 1783.

JACQUES ALEXANDRE CHARLES' NARRATIVE, in: "*Relation du voyage aérostatique de Charles*", Paris, 1783.

THE RESULT OF A YEAR'S EXPERIENCE, in: "*Rapport fait à l'Académie des sciences*" on 23 December 1783, Paris.

DELIRIOUS ENTHUSIASM

BALLOON MANIA, in: "*Le Mercure de France*" (Paris) No. 3, 17 January 1784.

THE FLIGHT OF THE "LA FLESSELLES", in: Faujas de Saint-Fond, "*Première suite de la description des expériences aérostatiques...*", Paris, 1784.

THE FIRST ITALIAN ASCENT, in Gerli, Carlo & Agostino, "*Opuscoli*", Parma, 1785.

EXTRACT FROM A LETTER WRITTEN BY THE BROTHERS GERLI, in: "*Journal de Paris*", No. 92, 1 April 1784.

AN UNFORTUNATE EXPERIENCE, extract from the Memoirs of the Baroness of Oberkirch, cit. in: Heitz, Ferdinand, "*1784 — les débuts de l'aéronautique en Alsace*", Colmar, 1961.

THE DIJON ACADEMY'S REPORT OF ITS EXPERIMENTS; EXTRACT FROM A LETTER WRITTEN AT DIJON, in: "*Journal de Paris*" No. 123, 2 May 1784.

M. FLEURANT'S ACCOUNT, in: Lecornu, J., "*La navigation aérienne*", Paris, 1903.

THE ASCENT OF THE "MARIE-ANTOINETTE", in: Pilâtre de Rozier, "*Première expérience de la montgolfière construite par ordre du Roi...*", Paris, 1784.

THE FIRST AMERICAN ASCENT, in: "*Maryland Journal and Baltimore Advertiser*", 25 June 1784.

A FIRST ATTEMPT AT SCIENTIFIC OBSERVATIONS, in: "*Journal de Paris*" No. 178, 26 June 1784.

VINCENT LUNARDI'S FLIGHT, in: Lunardi, Vincent, "*An Account of the First Aerial Voyage in England*", London, 1784.

AN UNHAPPY EXPERIENCE — THE REWARD OF FAILURE, extract from a contemporary print, Bibliothèque Nationale, Paris.

EXTRACT from "*Journal de Paris*" No. 194, 12 July 1784.

EXTRACT FROM DR JEFFRIES' LETTER, dated Calais, January 1785, British Museum, London.

THE DEATH OF PILÂTRE DE ROZIER, in: Grimm, Frédéric Melchior, "*Correspondance littéraire*", Paris, 1785.

THE EXTENSIVE FLIGHT MADE BY BLANCHARD AND THE CHEVALIER DE L'EPINARD, in: "*Journal de Paris*" No. 242, 30 August 1785 and "*Journal de Paris*", 7 September 1785.

SATIRES AND FANTASIES

LETTER TO M. DE SAINT-JUST, in: "*Lettre à M. de Saint-Just sur le globe aérostatique de MM. Montgolfier*", Paris, 1784.

POEM, cit. in: Lecornu, J., "*La navigation aérienne*", Paris, 1903.

NOTES & NEWS, Villiers' account, Bibliot. Nationale, Paris.

THE AEROSTATIC GRAPE-PICKER, in: "*Journal de Paris*", 30 January 1785.

ROBERTSON'S FANTASTIC MINERVA, in: Robertson, Etienne Gaspard, "'*La Minerve', vaisseau aérien, destiné aux découvertes et proposé à toutes les Académies de l'Europe*", Paris, 1820.

BLANCHARD'S FLYING SHIP, in: Michaud, Joseph François, "*Biographie universelle ancienne et moderne*", Paris, 1843-1865.

PRACTICAL MILITARY BALLOONS ... AND OTHERS, in: Selle de Beauchamp, Baron, "*Extrait des Mémoires d'un officier des aérostiers aux armées de 1793 à 1799*", Paris, 1853.

A HALF CENTURY OF FREE BALLOONS

EXTRACT in: *Wöchentliche Nachrichten aus dem Berichthaus zu Basel*", 8 May 1788.

BLANCHARD'S ACCOUNT, cit. in: Sircos, A., and Pallier, T. "*Histoire des ballons...*", Paris, 1876.

PHILADELPHIA, 9 JANUARY 1793, in: Blanchard, Jean-Pierre, "*Journal of my Forty-fifth Ascension, being the First performed in America*", Philadelphia, 1793.

CITIZEN TESTU-BRISSY'S AMAZING ASCENT, in: "*Le Moniteur Universel*" (Paris), 27 vendémiaire An VII (16 October 1798).

A VERY INTERESTING REPORT BY A LOFTY PATRIOT, in: Sainte-Croix, B. L. de, "*Procès-verbal très intéressant du voyage aérien qui a eu lieu aux Champs-Elysées le 18 juillet 1791, jour de la proclamation de la Constitution*", Paris, 1791.

EXTRACT from: "*Journal des Débats*" (Paris), 17 thermidor An VIII (3 August 1800).

THE POLICE REPORT OF ZAMBECCARI'S ASCENT, cit. in: Guasti, T. C., and Bertarelli, A., "*Francesco Zambeccari, aeronauta*", Milano, 1932.

DESCENT INTO THE ADRIATIC, cit. in: Lecornu, J., "*La navigation aérienne*", Paris, 1903.

THE CORONATION BALLOONS, in: "*Le Moniteur Universel*" (Paris), 19 frimaire An XII (4 December 1804).

WILHELMINE REICHARDT'S ASCENT, Munich, in: "*Münchener politische Zeitung*" No. 233, 2 October 1820.

MADAME BLANCHARD'S ACCIDENT, in: "*Le Moniteur Universel*" (Paris), 8 July 1819.

JAMES SADLER'S ACCOUNT, in: Forster, T., "*Annals of some remarkable Aerial and Alpine Voyages*", London, 1832.

ROBERT COCKING'S UNHAPPY END, in: "*The Times*" (London), 25 July 1837.

THE AMAZING FLIGHT OF CHARLES GREEN, cit. in: Sircos, A., and Pallier, T., "*Histoire des ballons...*", Paris, 1876.

THE ASCENT OF M. KIRSCH'S BALLOON CARRYING WITH IT A CHILD, in: "*L'Illustration*" (Paris), 1843, vol. 1, p. 352.

NOTABLE EXPLOITS

WILLIAM HYDE'S ACCOUNT OF THE AMAZING FLIGHT OF THE "ATLANTIC", in: The "*New York Times*", 11 July 1859.

COXWELL AND GLAISHER'S DANGEROUS ASCENT, in: Glaisher, J., Flammarion, C., Fonvielle, W., de Tissandier, G., "*Voyages aériens*", Paris, 1870.

THE DRAMA OF NADAR'S "GÉANT", in: Nadar, "*A terre et en l'air... Mémoires du 'Géant'*", Paris, 1864.

OVER THE PRUSSIAN LINES, in: Tissandier, Gaston, "*Histoire de mes ascensions*", Paris, 1888.

GAMBETTA'S ESCAPE FROM PARIS, in: "*Le Moniteur Universel*" (Tours), cit. in: Sircos, A., and Pallier, T., "*Histoire des ballons...*", Paris, 1876.

REPORT OF THE ARRIVAL OF GAMBETTA, in: "*Journal officiel*" (Paris), 11 October 1870.

THE TRAGEDY OF THE "ZENITH", in: Tissandier, Gaston, "*Histoire de mes ascensions*", Paris, 1888.

A FLIGHT OVER AFRICA—FICTION, in: Verne, Jules, "*Cinq semaines en ballon*", Paris, 1863.

SCIENTIFIC ASCENTS

GAY-LUSSAC'S SCIENTIFIC ASCENT, in: "*Relation d'un voyage aérostatique fait par M. Gay-Lussac*", Annales de chimie, LII, Paris, An XIII (1805).

FRANÇOIS ARAGO'S ACCOUNT OF THE ASCENT OF BIXIO AND BARRAL, in: Institut de France, Académie des sciences, Paris, "*Comptes rendus des séances*", t. XXXI, meeting of 1 July 1850.

THE ANDRÉE EXPEDITION, in: Andrée, Salomon August, "*Dem Pol entgegen*", Leipzig, 1930.

AUGUSTE PICCARD CONQUERS THE STRATOSPHERE, in: Piccard, Auguste, "*Au-dessus des nuages*", Ed. Grasset, Paris, 1933.

THE DRAMATIC END OF THE "EXPLORER", in: Stevens, Capt Albert W., "*Exploring the Stratosphere*" in: "*The National Geographic Magazine*", Stratospheric series No. 1, Washington, 1935.

THE GORDON BENNETT AERONAUTIC CUP

SEVENTY-THREE HOURS IN A BALLOON, in: "*L'Illustration*" (Paris) No. 3427, 31 October 1908, 1945-1971.

1945-1971

STOWAWAY IN THE SKY, in: Lamorisse, Albert, "*Le voyage en ballon*", Ed. Gallimard, Paris, 1960.

FLIGHT OVER AFRICA—FACT, in: Smith, Anthony, "*Throw Out Two Hands*", George Allen and Unwin, London, 1963. "*Jambo: African Balloon Safari*", E. P. Dutton & Co., Inc., New York, 1964.

FRED DOLDER FLIES THE ALPS, in: Dolder, Fred: "*Piccola Svizzera*" in: "*Aero-Revue*" (Zürich) No. 9, 1970.

PHOTOGRAPHIC SOURCES

Archives photographiques, Paris: 101.

Biblioteca Nazionale Braidense, Milano: 33, 34.

Douglas Botting, London: 153, 155-158.

Comet-Photo, AG Zürich: 6-7.

Edita, Lausanne: 21, 70, 91, 94, 105 bottom left, 109-110, 113 below, 169-170, 177, 178, 180.

Edita/Bibliothèque Cantonale et Universitaire, Lausanne: 12, 28, 79, 93, 102 left, 103 above, 104, 105 top left, 105 bottom right, 106, 107, 121, 138, 140.

Edita/Bibliothèque Nationale, Paris: 14-17, 18 left, 19, 20, 23, 24 above, 26, 30, 35, 36, 40, 42, 44 below, 45, 46 above, 47, 48, 49 above, 49 bottom left, 50, 51, 55-65, 67 above, 68, 69 above, 72 above, 73, 75, 76, 78, 82-84, 85 below, 87, 88, 90, 92, 102 right, 113 above, 120.

Edita/Bibliothèque des PTT, Berne: 22, 24 below, 38, 39, 41, 46 below, 67 below, 69 below, 77, 85 above, 99, 100, 103 below, 105 top right, 114, 115, 118, 122.

Edita/Musée Carnavalet, Paris: 18 right, 25, 27.

Fotoservizi Bozzetto, Cartigliano, Italy: 172 right.

John Freeman/Norman Collection, London: 44 above, 49 below right, 54.

Gränna Hembyssförening, Gränna, Sweden: 123-126.

Bryan Holme, New York: 52.

Kunstbibliothek der Staatlichen Museen, Berlin: 81

Albert Lamorisse, Films Montsouris Hélivision, Paris: 144, 146-152, 196.

Maison suisse des transports et communications, Lucerne: 127 left, 130 right, 141-143, 160, 161.

New York State Historical Ass., Cooperstown: 96-98.

Collection Jacques Piccard, Lausanne: 127 right, 128, 130 left, 131.

Dölf Reist, Interlaken: 179, 189 top left.

Editions Rencontre, Lausanne: 116, 117.

Carl Reuther, Mannheim: 165, 172 left.

Erwin A. Sautter, Zumikon: 159, 163, 164, 166, 176, 189 bottom left.

Staatsarchiv Basel Stadt: 72 below

Stern, Hamburg: 5, 8, 174.

The Historical Society of Pennsylvania, Philadelphia: 74.

USIS, Berne: 132-137, 193.

Verkehrsverein, Mürren/Fritz Lauener, Wengen: 189 bottom right, 190, 191.

ACKNOWLEDGEMENTS

The Publishers wish to extend their grateful thanks to all the curators of museums, librarians, the directors and staff of official organisations and private societies who have helped them to assemble the text and the illustrations contained in this book. They would like to thank particularly Madame Albert Lamorisse, Fred Dolder, Jacques Piccard, Karl Zumstein, director of the Library, section générale des PTT, Berne, and Jost Brunner, director of the station of Mürren, who have all given invaluable help and advice from their own knowledge and experience.

BIBLIOGRAPHY

GENERAL WORKS, HISTORY OF BALLOONING

ALEXANDER, JOHN, *The Conquest of the Air. The Romance of Aerial Navigation*, London, 1902.

L'Art aérostatique. Histoire des ballons, aérostats, globes aérostatiques, montgolfières, etc., Paris, 1852.

BRUEL, FRANÇOIS-LOUIS, *Histoire Aéronautique par les Monuments Peints, Sculptés, Dessinés et Gravés des Origines à 1830*, Paris, 1909.

DOLLFUS, CHARLES; BOUCHÉ, CHARLES, *Histoire de l'Aéronautique*, Paris, 1932.

DOLLFUS, CHARLES, *Les Ballons*, Paris, 1960.

DUPUIS-DELCOURT, *Mémoire sur l'Aérostation et la direction aérostatique*, Paris, 1824.

FONVIELLE, W. DE, *Aventures aériennes et expériences mémorables des grands aéronautes*, Paris, 1876; *Les grandes ascensions maritimes. Traversée de la Manche*, Paris, 1882.

FORSTER, T., *Annals of some remarkable aerial and alpine voyages*, London, 1832.

GRAND-CARTERET, JOHN; DELTEIL, LEO, *La conquête de l'air, vue par l'image 1495-1909*, Paris, 1910.

HILDEBRANDT, A., *Die Luftschiffahrt nach ihrer geschichtlichen und gegenwärtigen Entwicklung*, München, 1907.

HODGSON, J.E., *The History of Aeronautics in Great Britain*, Oxford, 1924.

LA VAULX, Cte H. DE, *L'Aéronautique des origines à 1922*, Paris, 1922.

LECORNU, J., *La navigation aérienne*, Paris, 1903.

MAREY-MONGE, EDMOND, *Etudes sur l'aérostation*, Paris, 1847.

MARION, F., *Les Ballons et les Voyages aériens*, Paris, 1867.

MARSH, W.L., *Aeronautical Prints and Drawings*, London, 1924.

ROLT, L.T.C., *The Aeronauts. A History of Balloons 1783-1903*, New York, 1966.

SIRCOS, ALFRED; PALLIER, T., *Histoire des ballons et des ascensions célèbres*, Paris, 1876.

SUPF, PETER, *Das Buch der deutschen Fluggeschichte*, Berlin, 1935.

TISSANDIER, GASTON, *Histoire des ballons et des aéronautes célèbres*, Paris, 1887; *Les naufrages aériens*, Paris, 1875.

TURNOR, HATTON, *Astra Castra*, London, 1865.

BALLOONS IN THE EIGHTEENTH CENTURY

ANDREANI, DON PAOLO, *L'Aerostato Montgolfier in Francia ed Andreani in Italia*, Milano, 1784; *L'Art de voyager dans les airs et de s'y diriger*, Lunéville, 1784.

BABINET, LÉON, *Notice sur Pilastre de Rozier*, Metz, 1865.

BALDWIN, THOMAS, *Airopaïda*, Chester, 1786.

BEAUCHAMP, baron SELLE DE, *Extrait des Mémoires d'un officier des aérostiers aux armées de 1793 à 1799*, Paris, 1853.

BLANCHARD, JEAN-PIERRE, *Relation de la quatorzième ascension de Blanchard*, Lille, 1789; *Journal of my Forty-Fifth Ascension being the first performed in America on the Ninth of January 1793*, Philadelphia, 1793; *Journal et procès-verbaux du quatrième voyage aérien*, Londres, 1784.

CASTELLI, CARLO, *Il viaggio aereo dell' illustre cavaliere Milanese don Paolo Andreani*, Milano e Bologna, 1784.

CAVALLO, TIBERIUS, *The History and Practice of Aerostation*, London, 1785.

CHARLES, JACQUES ALEXANDRE, *Relation du voyage aérostatique de Charles*, Paris, 1783.

DARBLET; DESGRANGES; CHALFOUR, *Relation de deux voyages aériens faits à Bordeaux*, Bordeaux, 1784.

Discours sur les découvertes en général et particulièrement sur deux des principales découvertes de ce siècle, Paris, 1784.

EHRMANN, F.L., *Montgolfières ou machines aérostatiques*, Strasbourg, 1784.

Die ersten Versuche der Aeronautik in Wien, Wiener Zeitung Nr. 1-2, 1.-2.1., Wien, 1909.

FAUJAS DE SAINT-FOND, *Description des expériences de la machine aérostatique de MM. de Montgolfier et de celles auxquelles cette découverte a donné lieu*, Paris, 1783; *Première suite de la description des expériences aérostatiques de MM. de Montgolfier*, Paris, 1784.

GAUGLER, DE, *Les Compagnies d'Aérostiers militaires sous la République, de l'an II à l'an X*, Paris, 1857.

GERLI, CARLO E AGOSTINO, *Opuscoli*, Parma, 1785.

HEITZ, FERNAND, *1784, les débuts de l'aéronautique en Alsace*, Colmar, 1961.

Idées sur la Navigation Aérienne et sur la Construction d'une Pirogue Aérostatique, Paris, 1784.

JEFFRIES, Dr JOHN, *A narrative of the two aerial voyages of Dr. Jeffries with Monsieur Blanchard*, London, 1786.

LA VAULX, Cte DE; TISSANDIER, PAUL, *Joseph et Etienne de Montgolfier*, Annonay, 1926.

LEFEBVRE, ALPHONSE, *Exposition des souvenirs et reliques relatifs à F. Pilâtre de Rozier et P.-A. Romain, aéronaute*, Boulogne-sur-Mer, 1885.

LENOIR, *Eloge funèbre de Pilâtre de Rozier*, Londres et Paris, 1785.

Lettre à un ami sur l'utilité des globes volants de M. de Montgolfier et sur la possibilité de la prise de Gibraltar, Amsterdam et Paris, 1783.

Lettre à MM. de Saint-Just sur le globe aérostatique de MM. Montgolfier, Amsterdam, 1784.

LUNARDI, VINCENT, *An account of the first aerial voyage in England*, London, 1784; *An account of five aerial voyages in Scottland*, London, 1786.

MARAT, *Lettre de l'observateur Bonsens à M. de... sur la fatale catastrophe des infortunés Pilâtre de Rozier et Romain, les aéronautes et l'aérostation*, Paris, 1785.

MILBANK, JEREMIAH, *The First Century of Flight in America*, Princeton, 1943.

MONTGOLFIER, JOSEPH DE, *Discours prononcé à l'Académie des sciences de Lyon*, Paris, 1784.

MORAZZONI, G., *Un Pioniere dell' Aeronautica. Vincenzo Lunardi*, Milano, 1931.

MORVEAU; BERTRAND, *Procès-verbal de l'expérience aérostatique de 'L'Académie de Dijon'*, Dijon, 1784.

PILATRE DE ROZIER, F., *Première expérience de la Montgolfière construite par ordre du Roi*, Paris, 1784; *La Vie et les Mémoires de Pilâtre de Rozier*, Paris, 1786.

Rapport fait à l'Académie des sciences sur la machine aérostatique inventée par MM. de Montgolfier, Paris, 1783.

REBAIL, S., *La colonne Blanchard ou la première traversée du détroit du Pas-de-Calais en ballon*, Calais, 1885.

RIVAROL, *Lettre à M. le Président de... sur le globe aérostatique*, Paris et Londres, 1783.

ROBERT, JEAN et NICOLAS, *Mémoires sur les expériences aérostatiques*, Paris, 1784.

SAGE, Mrs. L.A., *A letter adressed to a female friend*, London, 1785.

SAINTE-CROIX, B.L. DE, *Procès-verbal très intéressant du voyage aérien qui a eu lieu aux Champs-Elysées le 18 septembre 1791, jour de la proclamation de la Constitution*, Paris, 1791.

BALLOONS IN THE NINETEENTH CENTURY

ANDREE, SALOMON AUGUST, *Dem Pol entgegen*, Leipzig, 1930.

ARAGO, FRANÇOIS, *Oeuvres complètes*, Paris, 1854.

ARNOULT, EUGÈNE D', *Voyage du 'Géant', de Paris à Hanovre*, Paris, 1863.

BARRAL, GEORGES, *Impressions aériennes d'un compagnon de Nadar*, Paris, 1864.

BERNHARDT, SARAH, *Dans les nuages. Impressions d'une chaise*, Paris, 1879.

BIXIO et BARRAL, *Voyages aéronautique*, Institut de France, Académie des sciences, comptes rendus des séances, t. XXXI, Paris, 1850.

BUNELLE, Cap., *Ascension de Jules Favre à Odessa*, Odessa, 1874.

CARTHAILHAC, EMILE, *Voyage en ballon de Paris en Norvège du capitaine Rolier, le 112e jour du siège de Paris*, Toulouse, 1871.

CASPARI, E., *Rapport sur le ballon 'Le Jacquard'*, Paris, 1872.

CÉZANNE, *Relation d'un voyage aérostatique*, Paris, 1872.

CHEVALIER, EMILE, *Eugène Godard*, Montréal, 1856.

CLERVAL, G. DE, *Les ballons pendant le siège de Paris*, Paris, 1871.

COXWELL, HENRY, *My Life and Balloon Experiences*, London, 1887-89.

DAGRON, *La poste par pigeons voyageurs. Souvenir du siège de Paris*, Bordeaux, 1870-71.

DEGEN, JAKOB, *Beschreibung einer neuen Flugmaschine*, Wien, 1808.

DUPUIS-DELCOURT, *Relation du voyage aérien fait à Paris, le 29 juillet 1831*, Paris, 1832; *Des ballons dans les fêtes publiques*, in: *L'Epoque*, 8 juin 1846, Paris.

DURUOF, *Les soixante ascensions de M. Duruof*, Paris, 1875.

FALIGAN, ERNEST, *Les ballons pendant le siège de Metz*, Paris, 1872.

FANTASIO, *Nadar et le ballon 'Géant'*, Bruxelles, 1864.

FLAMMARION, CAMILLE, *Voyages aériens. Impressions et études*, Paris, 1881; *Voyages en ballon*, Paris s.d.

FLAMMARION, CAMILLE et BOISSAY, CHARLES, *De Paris à Vaucouleurs à vol d'oiseau. Relation d'un voyage scientifique en ballon*, Paris, 1873.

FONVIELLE, W. DE, *L'espion aérien. Episode du siège de Paris*, Paris, 1884; *Les ballons pendant le siège de Paris*, Paris, 1871; *La Science en ballon*, Paris, 1869.

GARNERIN, JACQUES, *Air balloon and Parachute*, London, 1802; *Voyage et captivité du citoyen Garnerin*, Paris, 1797.

GARNERIN, ELISA, *Ascensione aerostatica de Madamigella Garnerin*, Milano, 1824.

GAY-LUSSAC, JOSEPH-LOUIS, *Relation d'un voyage aérostatique fait le 29 fructidor an XII*, Journal de physique, t. LIX, Paris, 1804.

GLAISHER, JAMES; FLAMMARION, CAMILLE; FONVIELLE, W. DE; TISSANDIER, GASTON, *Voyages aériens*, Paris, 1870.

GODARD, EUGÈNE, *Aventures aériennes*, Vienne, 1881.

GODARD, PHILIPPE, *Vingt-cinq ascensions en Orient*, Paris, 1893.

GUASTI, TIMINA CAPRONI; BERTARELLI, ACHILLE, *Francesco Zambeccari, aeronauta*, Milano, 1932.

HAYDON, F. STANSBURY, *Aeronautics in the Union and Confederate Armies*, Baltimore, 1941.

LACHAMBRE, HENRI; MACHURON, ALEXIS, *Andree and his Balloon*, London, 1898.

MAINCENT, P., *Textes et documents pour servir à l'histoire vraie des ballons du siège de Paris*, Paris, 1952.

MALLET, F., *Les aéronautes et les colombophiles au siège de Paris*, Paris, 1909.

MONCK, THOMAS MASON, *Account of the late Aeronautical expedition from London to Weilburg*, London, 1836; *Aeronautica*, London, 1838.

NADAR, *A terre et en l'air... Mémoires du Géant*, Paris, 1864; *Les ballons en 1870. Ce qu'on aurait pu faire; ce qu'on à fait*, Paris, 1870.

POTERLET, *Notice sur Mme Blanchard*, Paris, 1819.

ROBERTSON, ETIENNE GASPARD, *Relation d'un voyage aérien fait à New York*, Nouvelle-Orléans, 1827; *Mémoires récréatifs, scientifiques et anecdotiques*, Paris, 1831-32; *La Minerve*, Vienne, 1804, Paris, 1820; *Manifesto sobre los peligros de las Mongolfieras o Globos de fuego*, Madrid, 1822.

ROCH, EUGÈNE, *Essais sur les voyages aériens d'E. Robertson*, Paris, 1831.

SADLER, JAMES, *An authentic narrative of the aerial voyage of Mr. Sadler across the Irish Channel*, Dublin, 1812.

SAVINI, SAVINO, *Notizie biografiche del conte Francesco Zambeccari Bolognese*, Torino, 1847.

TISSANDIER, GASTON, *Histoire de mes ascensions*, Paris, 1888.

VERNE, JULES, *Cinq semaines en ballon*, Paris, 1863.

WISE, JOHN, *Through the Air*, Philadelphia, 1873; *A System of Aeronautics*, Philadelphia, 1850.

WOODCROFT, B., *Abridgements of Specifications Relating to Aeronautics 1815-1866*, London, 1869.

ZAMBECCARI, FRANCESCO, *Descrizione della macchina aerostatica del cittadino Francesco Zambeccari*, Bologna, 1803; *Relazione dell' esperienza aerostatica eseguita in Bologna il 22 agosto 1804*, Bologna, 1804.

BALLOONS IN THE TWENTIETH CENTURY

BACON, GERTRUDE, *The Record of an Aeronaut: John Bacon*, London, 1907.

BEAUCLAIR, VICTOR DE, *Im Ballon über die Alpen*, Winterthur, 1935.

BUTLER, FRANK HEDGES, *5,000 Miles in a Balloon*, London, 1907.

FRIEDLI, WERNER, *Alpenflug*, Bern, 1969.

GUYER, GEBHARD A., *Im Ballon über die Jungfrau nach Italien*, Berlin, 1908.

The National Geographic Society - U.S. Army Air Corps Stratosphere Flight of 1934 in the Balloon 'Explorer', Washington, 1935; *The National Geographic Society - U.S. Army Air Corps Stratosphere Flight of 1935 in the Balloon ,Explorer II'*, Washington, 1936.

PICCARD, AUGUSTE, *Au-dessus des nuages*, Paris, 1933.

SMITH, ANTHONY, *Throw Out Two Hands*, London, 1963 (USA: *Jambo: African Balloon Safari*, New York, 1964).

SPELTERINI, EDUARD, *Uber den Wolken*, Zürich, 1928.

TECHNIQUES AND NAVIGATION

L'Art aérostatique. Construction et technique, Paris, 1852.

BERNIS, J.-M., *Mémoire sur la science et l'art de la navigation aérienne*, Bayonne, 1867.

BREWER, GRIFFITH, *Ballooning and its Application to Kite Balloons*, London, 1940.

Des ballons aérostatiques, de la manière de les construire, de les faire élever, avec quelques vues pour les rendre utiles, Lausanne, 1874.

DOLLFUS, CHARLES, *En Ballon*, Paris, 1962.

EMDEN, Dr ROBERT, *Grundlagen der Ballonführung*, Leipzig, 1910.

Der Freiballon in Theorie und Praxis, hgb. von Adolf Mehl, Stuttgart, 1912.

MARCHIS, M.L., *Leçons sur la navigation aérienne*, Paris, 1904.

TILGENKAMP, ERICH, *Das Buch vom Ballonflug*, Zürich, 1947.

WALKER, FREDERICK, *Aerial Navigation. A practical Handbook*, London, 1902.

BIBLIOGRAPHICAL WORKS

BOFFITO, GUISEPPE, *Biblioteca aeronautica italiana*, Firenze 1929.

BROCKETT, PAUL, *Bibliography of Aeronautics*, Washington, 1910.

DARMON, J.E., *Dictionnaire des Estampes et Livres Illustrés sur les ballons et machines volantes des débuts jusque vers 1880*, Montpellier, 1929.

DIAZ ARQUER, G.; VINDEL, PEDRO, *Historia bibliografica e iconografica de la Aeronautica en España, Portugal, paises Hispanos-Americanos y Filipinas desde los origines hasta 1900*, Madrid, 1930.

The History of Flight. A descriptive catalogue of books, engravings and airmail stamps illustrating the evolution of the Airship and the Aeroplane, London, 1936.

TISSANDIER, GASTON, *Bibliographie aéronautique*, Paris, 1887.

This book was printed by
Imprimeries Réunies S.A., Lausanne,
and bound by Maurice Busenhart, Lausanne

Printed in Switzerland